French-Speaking
Women Film Directors

French-Speaking Women Film Directors

A Guide

Janis L. Pallister

Madison ● Teaneck
Fairleigh Dickinson University Press
London: Associated University Presses

© 1997 by Associated University Presses, Inc.

All rights reserved. Authorization to photocopy items for internal or personal use, or the internal or personal use of specific clients, is granted by the copyright owner, provided that a base fee of $10.00, plus eight cents per page, per copy is paid directly to the Copyright Clearance Center, 222 Rosewood Drive, Danvers, Massachusetts 01923. [0-8386-3736-1/97 $10.00 + 8¢ pp, pc.]

Associated University Presses
440 Forsgate Drive
Cranbury, NJ 08512

Associated University Presses
16 Barter Street
London WC1A 2AH, England

Associated University Presses
P.O. Box 338, Port Credit
Mississauga, Ontario
Canada L5G 4L8

The paper used in this publication meets the requirements
of the American National Standard for Permanence of Paper
for Printed Library Materials Z39.48–1984.

Library of Congress Cataloging-in-Publication Data

Pallister, Janis L.
  French-speaking women film directors : a guide / Janis L.
Pallister.
     p.   cm.
  Includes bibliographical references and index.
  ISBN 0-8386-3736-1 (alk. paper)
  1. Women motion picture producers and directors—French-speaking
countries—Credits.   2. Women motion picture producers and
directors—French-speaking countries—Biography—Dictionaries.
I. Title.
PN1998.2.P28   1997
791.43'0233'0820917541—dc21   97-8224
                                                        CIP

Contents

Introduction

THE PAST

The idea of preparing a manual on francophone women filmmakers was inspired by Annabelle Rea's encounter with *Frauen/Film: New Approaches to Teaching Film.*[1] Professor Rea, then chair of Women in French (WIF), found it to be an excellent and useful resource, so it occurred to her that a guide ought to be available to members of WIF. She, therefore, entered an inquiry in the WIF newsletter about whether anyone would be interested in working on such a plan. Since I possess an uncommon desire to look at and to speak about movies and have taught courses on film and have written several articles and a book on the subject, I enthusiastically offered my services. She proposed my name at the December 1993 annual meeting of WIF, and I was assigned the task—a pleasant one, to be sure.

THE PRESENT

As the project evolved, it became evident that this directory, while originally intended for French professors teaching women's studies and film courses, could be of use to others too. For that reason, most of the French citations have been translated or paraphrased, and the English titles of films, when available, are provided. Similarly, a glossary of elementary cinematographic terms (many derived with his kind permission from Henry Garrity's *Film in the French Classroom*) has been provided, so those who have never taught film or read about it may have a ready reference and teaching tool.

It has become clear to me while preparing this work that women filmmakers of considerable talent and even renown fail to be mentioned in histories of film, be it video, the seventh art, or the eighth—unless of course, the reference book is dealing directly with women in film and filmmaking. For example, a special edition of *France-Amérique*[2] at the end of 1995 contained an insert on French film, in celebration of cinema's one hundredth birthday. I observed that there was no mention whatsoever of Alice Guy-Blaché or Germaine Dulac.

7

In fact, only two or three times was a woman filmmaker mentioned—and I mean by that mentioned en passant: these were Christine Pascal, Coline Serreau, and Claire Denis. Though articles are devoted to the *patrimony* of French cinema, the word in its structure and in its meanings seems to preclude the authors' recapitulation of women's contribution to the art of directing, despite the fact that some women directors are bona fide auteures and extremely famous by now. Although Sinyard gives us a chapter on European masters of the silent movie, he mentions none of the women directors we have cited in this guide, except for Germaine Dulac, whose *Seashell and the Clergyman* is cited as an example of the meaningless obscurity characterizing surrealist film.[3]

In the same vein, Charles Solomon's *History of Animation,*[4] for example, mentions none of the women I have cited in this manual as important animation artists: It passes over Denise Charevin, Clorinda Warny, Suzanne Gervais-L'Heureux, Lise Gagnon, Francine Desbiens, Cilia Sawadago, Yona Friedman, Claire Parker, Irene Starevich (and her father), Viviane Elnécavé, to mention but a few. Of course, Solomon is almost exclusively interested in the American "history," though he does speak about early European contributions to the genre and also manages to mention the great Canadian animation artist Norm McLaren. Moreover, he devotes some time to explaining how women were regarded in this industry (while excluding important European women from his account). Similarly, Sadoul's famous *Dictionnaire des films* and his *Dictionnaire des cinéastes*[5] give us very few titles by women directors in the one, and very few of their names in the other. I do not think I need to explain the reasons for this. Or why, if we are to teach this as an academic subject, we need reference materials, and indeed, in view of the importance of the subject, dictionaries or handbooks devoted exclusively to the subject of French-speaking women film directors. It is ironic, however, to note that the title of Gwendolyn Foster's recent book—*Women Film Directors: An International Bio-critical Dictionary*[6]—suggests we would not fail to find the names of Elsie Haas, Yannick Bellon, Claire Devers, Pomme Meffre, Paule Baillargeon, Mireille Dansereau, Luce Guilbeault, Anne Claire Poirier; yet they are not even mentioned en passant. (Others of considerable note are mentioned only en passant, e.g., Nadine Trintignant, whose name is misspelled.)

Of course, as my bibliography will show, information on a number of French women directors or on Québec women directors is quite available in certain specific books: But putting these together along with women from other areas of the globe has not been done before. Moreover, I have concluded that if our guide book, though specifically prepared for Women in French, is to have maximum use both for the general reader and for the (beginning or anglophone) teacher of film, the basic information must be presented in English and in an accessible format. For similar reasons, the general glossary mentioned earlier provides cinematographic terms both in French and in English.

The chief problem I have encountered in preparing this guide has been simply to identify the names of francophone women filmmakers and their films. I have gleaned these through many lists, catalogs, books, dictionaries, newspapers, cinema journals, and so forth. And often I have not found anything beyond a name or a title; not even a date! Nevertheless, I have included these references for completeness' sake, and assume others may do still deeper research that will bring out additional information. Ironically, even specialists of certain areas, such as Belgian or African film, do not have good and complete documentation of women filmmakers of those regions. Once again, I have found scattered mention of names of persons and films that I have included under the appropriate geographical rubric, even though material concerning them was more than a little scarce.

The matter of just getting information is one thing; the problem anyone will have in viewing many of these films is yet another. I have suggested in a special section some possible sources for many of the best-known films, and on occasion I have mentioned in the body of the text where a less well-known film might be available. In the preparation of the African section I leaned heavily on Schmidt's listings (see bibliography) and am grateful to Professor Françoise Pfaff for leading me to two bibliographic sources that were of considerable interest while also yielding some fruit. And of course, I am especially thankful that Professor Ruth Hottell of the University of Toledo, Professor Georgiana Colvile of the University of Colorado at Boulder, and Professor Josette Déléas of Mount Saint Vincent University in Halifax responded to my requests for syllabi by providing us with course plans that show how francophone women directors' films can be incorporated into film courses or women's studies/literature courses. In particular, Professor Colvile's syllabus demonstrates that the day has come when a modern American university will allow an entire course to be devoted exclusively to French women directors (though, through her own choice, of course, her study plan does not include the extrahexagonal francophone directors, not even Akerman). Professor Colvile may well be the subject of our envy in this seeming luxury. The existence of her course may also be a trump playing card in the effort others will make to mount similar courses at their own universities.

THE FUTURE

In this presentation, I have sought to list every woman whose name has been important enough to have been mentioned in some context or other. Though, as I have indicated earlier, I have not always been able to get much information on certain of them, their very presence may prove that they had a role to play, and may shed some light on history or stimulate further research on them in particular, and, in a more general way, on this fascinating and important though under-studied manner of addressing women's issues—not to mention the applicability of film analysis to the whole area of francophone studies, language, and culture alike. (The chapter "Core Concepts and Themes" is also presented for use of film in women's studies courses and is not restricted to films in French or by women.)

Obviously, as further studies and new films and filmmakers come forth, this guide book will become out of date. When this happens, I hope that some other scholar will undertake to revise and to update the outline I have set forth here.

A NOTE ON METHODOLOGY

Finding and, therefore, giving the correct dates of films has been one of the most problematic tasks involved in this project. I have given, as a rule, what seemed the date most agreed on by various sources and often have indicated an alternate date and its source in parentheses.

About my methodology, I have used boldface to separate one entry from another, and sometimes to highlight what I consider an especially important name or title. Similarly, I have set in boldface the names of important scholars I am citing.

The bibliography includes many useful references for general information as well as works specifically on women's film and more particularly on francophone women. All references to scholars throughout the main body of this book will be found in this bibiliography; and complete information regarding any quotes will be given only the one time, in the bibliography. Exceptionally, any bibliographies pertaining to the syllabi are attached to that material; they provide important complements to the master bibliography preceding the syllabi.

I have in no way attempted to show all possibilities in my "Core Concepts" chapter, and I do not necessarily regard the women directors' filmographies as complete. The index is meant to help in the use of the guide, and it references all important names and all films listed.

There is no attempt to index concepts or geographical names. Definite articles have been excluded from titles in the index; indefinite articles are placed at the end of the title, which is alphabetized under the lead noun, adjective, or adverb.

As I stated earlier, on occasion I have mentioned a possible source for a film in the body of the text, because I thought that particular film especially rare and difficult to locate. Many of the films are easily located in subtitled video form (see film sources section); some are difficult or impossible to obtain. It will be obvious that there has been no intention on my part to attempt to cite a source for every film.

I follow the prescription of editors of *The French Review* in the capitalization of French titles. Additionally, the word *québécois(e)* becomes capitalized when it refers to a person. I adopt the style of most modern Québécois in writing *auteure, professeure, écrivaine*, and so forth.

ACKNOWLEDGMENTS

I want to thank Professors Françoise Pfaff (Howard University) and Eloïse Brière (SUNY-Albany) for their kind assistance on the African directors section of this guide, and Professors Renée Linkhorn (Youngstown University) and Philip Mosley (Penn State University-Worthington) for their extraordinary help in the establishment of the Belgian directors guide. Professor Mosley's name appears opposite names of Belgian directors and titles he contributed. Nor do I overlook all the help I have received from Professors Ramona Cormier, Annabelle Rea, and Colette Hall, who have proofread and done many other time-consuming tasks for me.

NOTES

1. *Frauen/Film: New Approaches to Teaching Film*, ed. Linda Kraus Wroley (University of Kentucky, place of pub. and pub. unspecified, 1989). Under sponsorship of Women in German.

2. "Le Cinéma a 100 ans," *France-Amérique*, Supplément spécial, 1229 (30 December–5 January 1995–96): pp. A–P.

3. Neil Sinyard, *Silent Movies* (New York: Gallery Books), 1990.

4. Charles Solomon, *Enchanted Drawings: The History of Animation* (New York: Knopf, 1989).

5. Georges Sadoul, and Emile Breton, *Dictionnaire (microcosme) des cinéastes,* 4e ed. mise à jour, octobre 1989 (Paris: Collection de Poche, 1989); *Dictionnaire (microcosme) des films,* 4e ed. mise à jour, mai 1989 (Paris: Collection de Poche, 1989).

6. Gwendolyn Audrey Foster, *Women Film Directors: An International Bio-Critical Dictionary* (Westport Conn.: Greenwood Press, 1995).

French-Speaking
Women Film Directors

1

Directors and Their Films

African (incl. Madagascan, Réunionaises, and North African)

Sanni Assouma Adjike (Togo)
L'Eau sacrée (1995)
Femmes Moba (1995)

Rosalie Mbelé Atangana (Cameroon)
La Production d'Africa Jin (1994)

Selma Bakkar (Tunisia)
L'Eveil (1972)

Michèle Badarou (or **Akan Badarou**) (Benin)
Les Tresseuses de natte de Gbangnito (1985)
Bénin le temps au féminin (1985)

Mina Bataba (Togo)
Agbassa (1990; video)
Circuit commercial APP (1990; video)

Madeline Beauséjour (Réunion)
Oman I le la Sours (1988). Concerns a young mother whose house is a popular hangout for the neighborhood children.

Rose Bekale (Gabon)
Le Tison enchanteur (1988)

Thérèse Sita Bella (Cameroon)
Tam-tam à Paris (1963; 30 mins.). A well-known documentary on the Cameroon national dance troupe.

Farida Benlyazid (Morocco)

Marie Roger Biloa (Cameroon)
Requiem pour un président assassiné (1989)

Nadia Cherabi (Algeria) b. 1954 in Algiers.
Fatima et la mer Documentary on Algerian women.

15

Fatima el Amaria (1994; 22 mins.; with Malek Laggoune) Portrait of a young black Muslim girl who loves to sing.

Lancine (Lancina) Diabi (Ivory Coast)
L'Africaine à Paris (1993)
La Jumelle (1994)

Adrienne Diop (Senegal)
Le Riz dans la vallée du fleuve (1990; video)
La Pêche artisanale au Sénégal (1991; video)
Le Sida au Sénégal (1992; video)

Maguette Diop (Senegal)
Les Fauves en liberté (1975)
Le Fils de qui (1981)
Code électoral (1982)
Ndiguel et Touba (1984)

Assia Djebar (Algeria) b. 1936, she is a novelist [*La Soif*, 1957; *Les Impatients*, 1958; *Les Alouettes naïves*, 1967; *Femmes d'Alger dans leur appartement*, 1982; *Ombre sultane*, 1987; *Loin de Médine*, 1991; and more recently *Vaste est la prison*; Albin Michel, 1995; Prix Maeter-linck] as well as a filmmaker. She wrote and directed
La Nouba des femmes du mont Chenoua (1979) Pseudo-documentary technique is used to show lives of elderly and young women in post-Independence Algeria. Parallels between colonialist oppression and silencing of women.
La Zerda ou les chants de l'oubli (1982) Uses archival footage of French-colonial Africa subversively to present yet another study of woman in postcolonial Algeria.
See **Foster** 112–14; 357.
There exists a documentary by Kamal Dehane entitled *Assia Djebar, entre ombre et soleil* (1992; 52 mins.). It is sometimes considered a Belgian film. (Contact the Belgian Embassy about it.)

Adèle Djédjé (Ivory Coast)
La Culture de la banane plantain de contre-saison (1991)

Valerie Djira (Ivory Coast)
Afrique, étoiles: Kanda Bongoman (198-)

Marie-Claire Elizabeth (Seychelles)
Magazin ekonomik: pti metye (1989)

Fanta See Nacro

Safi Faye (Senegal) b. Dakar, 1943. Considered by some as the domi-nant female figure in African film production, Faye is of Serer origin.

As actress and assistant, she worked with Jean Rouch, from whom she acquired her interest in ethnocinematography and in cinéma vérité, a technique she has been much influenced by. She has a doctorate in ethnology from the University of Paris VII (1979) and has made films in several countries. She lives in Paris, but only some of her films are in French. Many of her films are severely critical of the government, and they are banned from public showing in Senegal. They also often touch on gender issues as well.

Petit à petit ou les lettres persanes 1968 (1969). A young man from Niger goes to France to learn about contemporary French life.

La Passante (1972) Locus is France. Faye herself plays an African woman who arouses the interest of both a Frenchman and an African man.

Revanche (co-directed in 1973) A madman wants to climb the Pont-Neuf in Paris.

Kaddu beykat (or *The Voice of the Peasant;* or *News from My Village;* or *Lettre paysanne;* 1975; a docudrama in Wolof) Considered the first feature by an African woman, it is the telling of the daily life of the peasant and of the peasants' refusal of colonialism, in voice-over and in letter form. The film won many international prizes.

Fad'jal (or *Un Certain Regard;* 1979) Faye portrays her parents' native village and Serer culture. She also taught in Fad'jal after receiving her teaching certificates.

3 ans, 5 mois (1979; edited in 1983) Faye seeks to show through her daughter how children can readily adapt to a foreign culture.

Goob na nu (*The Harvest Is In*) (*La Récolte est finie*) (1979)

Man sa yay (*I, Your Mother*) (1980)

Woman (1980)

Les Ames au soleil (1981) Documentary focusing on problems of drought, health, and development and the effect of these problems on women and children.

Selbé et tant d'autres (or *Selbe: One Among Many;* 30 mins.; 1983) See N. Frank **Ukadike,** for a complete discussion of this film. Faye works here to delineate the sociopolitical and economic problems of Senegal and to lend support to the oppressed Serer peasantry. The men, however, are depicted as village parasites. Stylistically, the film presents a realistic portrayal of the situation while juxtaposing fictional and documentary elements. Overpopulation, family planning, malnutrition, and lack of education for women are all touched on if often obliquely. **Pfaff** says the film is concerned with the problems of village women, left behind when their men go to urban centers to find work. Available—Women Make Movies Catalog 1996, p. 32 and 38.

Ambassades nourricières (or *Culinary Embassies;* 1984) A documentary about ethnic restaurants in Paris (Armenian, African, Asian, Hungarian, Italian, Latin American). The idea is to penetrate specific cultures through their culinary rites.

Negu Jaargon (*Cobweb; La Toile d'araignée*) (1988) Intended as Faye's first fiction film.

Mossane (made in 1990; finally shown at Cannes festival, 1996) The pure and beautiful girl Mossane, who is fourteen years old, prefers suicide to giving in to her mother's pressure that she marry a rich husband rather than the young man from a modest family whom she loves. (The love her brother bears her figures as a view of incest, rare in African cinema.)

See **Foster** 130–32.

Sofia Ferchiou (Tunisia) Began her career in 1966 with a documentary on the making of chéchias (red wool head covering usually worn by African men).

La Zarda

Le Mariage de Sabria Customs of traditional Moslem marriage.

Michèle Fieloux (Burkina Faso)

Les Mémoires de Binduté Da (1988; with Jacques Lombard)

Anne-Laure Foll(e)y (Togo) Although two works by this director are available in the United States in English, she is not even mentioned by **Foster** in her 1995 *Women Film Directors*

Le Gardien des Forces (1991)

Les Femmes africaines face à la démocratie (1993)

Femmes du Niger (*Women of Niger*)(1992; video 26 mins.) Problems of polygamy in an Islamic nation. Though Niger is called a democracy, men vote by proxy for their wives and daughters. Women who speak out are often physically harmed. Meanwhile, the women work together to gain equal rights. Available in subtitled version, Women Make Movies 1996 Catalog, p. 36.

Femmes aux yeux ouverts (1993–94; video, 52 mins.) A panorama of African women. One of the women has fled to a convent to take cover from a forced marriage; one is a community health worker who is demonstrating the use of a condom; one is an activist who claims it is more important to attack female clitoridectomy than women's rights. There are entrepreneurs, too. We learn that women are organizing to participate in Africa's move toward democracy. [Compare with Désiré Ecaré's *Visages de femmes* (1985), though by a man.] This film is available from California Newsreel.

Margaret Fombe Fube (Cameroon) Films in native language with French subtitles: see **Schmidt**, *ALA Bulliten*. 21, no. 1 (winter 1995): 21.

Anne-Laure Folly. *Femme aux yeux ouverts.* California Newsreel Catalog.

Portraits de femmes (1989)
Les Femmes pompistes (1989)
Les Femmes avocates (1989; video)

[Izza Genina (?)—see World of Film: Africa (Bono Film and Video Services, Arlington, VA)]

Mariama Hima (Niger)
Baabu Banza (Rien ne se jette) (1984)
Falaw (1985)
Toukou (1986)
Katako (Les Planches) (1987)
Hadiza et Kalia (1994)

Martine Condé Ilboudo (Burkina Faso)
S.I.A.O. (1992; video)

Artisinat 1993 (1993; video)
Jazz à Ouaga (1993; video)
Un Cri dans le Sahel (1994; video)
Féminin pluriel (1994; video)

Callixte Kalisa (Rwanda)
Rwanda les collines de l'effort (1991)

Yasmine Kassari See Belgian directors

Rachida Krim (Algeria) b. 1955 in Alès of Algerian parents.
El Fatha (France/Algeria; 1992; 18 mins.) A film about a return to sources, to tradition, and to the country of one's origins. Part of this film was shot in the region of Krim's paternal family, in Marnia (in Oranais). It celebrates the beauty of tradition (ritual ceremonies, splendor of costumes and jewelry, songs and music), but it also shows the heavy side of life: the extreme violence done to women . . . and to men.

Wèrèwèrè Liking (Ivory Coast)
Dieu-chose (Regards de fous) (1987)

Najet Mabaouj (Tunisian)

Sarah [Ducados] Maldoror (Angola, France) b. in 1939 in France (Condom, in le Gers) of parents from Guadeloupe. Wife of the celebrated leader of the Angolan resistance to Portuguese, Mario de Andrade. Has lived and worked in Moscow, Morocco; Guinea-Bissau; France; Republic of Congo; Cape Verde; Angola, and so on. Maldoror does not always film in French. She is a neorealist who is committed to political agency and postcolonial consciousness (Foster).
Collaborated with Pontecorvo on *The Battle of Algiers* (1986)
Monangambee or *Le Portefaix* (1969; Foster and Lejeune give 1970) Adaptation of *Le Complot de Mateus* by Luandino Vieira. The film took a number of prizes. Mixture of real and fictionalized (staged) material characteristic of Maldoror's neorealistic style.
Des Fusils pour Banta (1971) First full-length feature film. Made in Algeria and Guinea-Bissau.
Louise Michel, la commune et nous (Pfaff: La Commune, Louise Michel, et nous) A 13 min. short shot in France in 1971.
Et les chiens se taisaient (1971; shot in France) Filmed version of play by Aimé Césaire.
Viva la Muerte (A short)
The Poor and the Proud (A short)
Saint-Denis-sur-Avenir A short film shot in France in 1972.
Sambizanga (1972) Financed by the French Centre National du

Cinéma and by the French Ministry of Cooperation, and shot in the People's Republic of the Congo with a crew made up predominantly of French technicians. Languages used are Portuguese, Lingala, and Lari. One professional actor only—Jacques Poitrenaud. Based on a story by the Angolan writer Luandino Vieira (*A Vida verdadeira de Domingos Xavier,* or *La Vraie Vie de Domingos Xavier*), adapted for the screen by Mario de Andrade (husband of the director) and Maurice Pons. Though white, Vieira was a nationalist. He spent ten years as a political prisoner of the Portuguese, because of his political views.

The story concerns a tractor driver (a nationalist) arrested by Portuguese police and tortured to death for underground activities. His wife, who had not known of his involvement, undergoes a political awakening and takes up the cause for the independence of Angola. "The film reinscribes the role of women in revolutionary politics" (Foster 236). (Sambizanga is the name of the village in Angola that is the locus of the main action of the film.)

This was the first full-length feature Maldoror completed; it is the first one in the history of film to be devoted to Angola's revolution against Portuguese colonialism. **Larouche** (*Films d'Afrique*) studies the dual structure of this film contained in the search of the heroine for her husband and his experiences in the resistance movement; the political and the poetic, and so on. **Vieyra** (42) finds some faults (overdone aestheticism of color and *cadrage* [framings]; weakness of the (nonprofessional) acting on the part of Elisa Andrade who plays the role of Domingo's wife.

La Basilique de Saint-Denis (1976) (Lejeune says 1978)

Velada (*Solitude*) Shot in Panama, and dealing with Panamanian nationalism.

Un Homme, une terre: Aimé Césaire (1977)

Paris, le cimetière du Père Lachaise (1977)

Un Masque à Paris: Louis Aragon (1978)

Miro (1979)

Wilfredo Lam (1978–79)

Fogo, l'île de feu (1979) Shot for the Cape Verde government.

Un Carnaval dans le Sahel (1979) Shot for the Cape Verde government.

Un Dessert pour Constance (1980) Based on Maurice Pons's adaptation of a short story by French writer Daniel Boulanger. Two African workers in racist Paris.

L'Hôpital de Leningrad (1982) Based on a novella by Victor Serge.

Vladimir Kibalchich (1982)

Le Passager de Tassili (1986) Based on the novel of Akli Tadjer, "Les A.M.I. du Tassili."

Portrait de Madame Diop (1986) About Christiane Diop, head of Présence Africaine.

Tragédie du roi Christophe An adaptation of the play by Césaire.

Aimé Césaire, le masque des mots (1987)

Damas (France, 1994; documentary, 30 mins.) Played in New York at Gramercy Theater 5 December 1995.

See **Diawara** 90–91; **Malkmus** 43; 57. See esp. chapter on Maldoror in **Pfaff** (*25 Black African* . . . : 205 ff.; here there is discussion of Maldoror's philosophy of film and of criticism of her work.) See also **Foster,** *Women Film Directors:* 235–38 and "Le Temps que l'on met à marcher: *Sambizanga* de Sarah Maldoror" by Michel **Larouche** in *Films d'Afrique,* Larouche, ed.: 22–39, as well as Lejeune 173–74.

Colson-Maleville Work done in Algeria: see under France

Marie-Constance Melome (Benin)
Pudeur de femme (1991; video)
Un Groupement pas comme les autres (1994; video)

Karim Miske and Brigitte Delpech (Mauritania)
Derrière le voile (1993; video)
Economie de la débrouille à Nouakchott (1988; video)
USSR-Afrique, voyages d'amour (1991; video)

Patricia Moraz b. in Kartoum of Egyptian-Swiss parents. See Swiss directors.

Camille Mouyeke (Ivory Coast)
L'Eprouvé du feu (1993)

Denise Mugugu (Burundi)
Des anges en enfer (1991)

Monique Muntcho Made films on Madagascar. See under France.

Regina Fanta Nacro (or Fanta Regina NACRO or Regina FANTA) (Burkina Faso) (Mostly in Mori; but may sometimes be in French.) Lives in Paris.
Un Certain Matin (1992) Winner of the 1992 Carthage film festival gold medal award for short films.
Une Si Longue Lettre The director is reportedly working on a film version of this novel by the late Mariama Ba (Senegal).

Barbara Nkono (?)
Etre veuve et réussir (1995)

Franceline Oubda (Burkina Faso)
Accès des femmes à la terre (1992)
Sadjo la Sahélienne (1994; video)

Femme de Boussé: survivre à tout prix (1994; with Benjamin Nama; video)
Hommage aux femmes de la Sissili (1995)

Aminata Ouédraogo (Burkina Faso)
L'Impasse (1988)
A qui le tour? (1991)
Alcoolisme (1992)

Lacina [or Lancine] Ouédraogo (Burkina Faso)
Approche participative et foresteerie [sic] villageoise (1994; video)

Marie-Clémence Paes (Madagascar) and Cesar Paes (Brazil) Some participation in the making of Madagascar film *Agano . . . Agano* in the collection from California Newsreel.

Monique Phoba (Benin) (Zaire)
Rentrer (1993; video)
In situ (1993; video)
Rêves en Afrique (1993; video)

Djamila Sahraoui (Algeria/France) b. in Algeria but presently lives in France. She believes Algerian woman is always a stranger wherever she may be, even in Algeria.
Houria
Avoir 2000 ans dans les Aurès
Prénom Marianne
La Moitié du ciel d'Allah (1995; 53 mins.) Without veils, Algerian women speak of their problems and struggles: their participation in the war of independence, the instituionalization of violence against women, the obligatory tradition of "hidjab," the Family Code of 1984.

Kadida Sanogo (Burkina Faso)
Le Joueur de kora (1989; super 8)
Un Siao des femmes (1992; video)
Une Semaine au féminin (1994; video)

Cilia Sawadogo (Burkina Faso)
Naissance (1994; 16 mm; 2 mins.) Animation. "A man is on his own until he meets nature. Freedom results from their union." Directed by Sawadogo; scénario by Charles Mangat; photography by Raymond Domas; editing by Sawadogo; sound by L. Bélanger and Denise Boucher; music by Denise Boucher. [Production: Planète Films at

401 Bourget Vaudreuil, Québec, Canada, J7V 7E5. Tel.: 1-514-455-2399.]
L'Arrêt d'autobus (1994; video)

Fatma Scandrani (Tunisia) Makes films for children.

Mariam Kane Selly (Senegal)
Cars rapides (1990; video)
Xessal (1991; video)
Femmes rurales (1993; video)

Sarah Taouss (Algeria) See France

Moufida Tlatli (Tunisia) Born near Tunis of an unknown father, Tlatli earned her diploma from the school of cinema (Idhec) in Paris in 1968. After having worked as scriptwriter and director for French TV, she returned to Tunisia in 1972. In 1994 she made a film regarding memories of her childhood: a time when one called woman "the colonized of the colonized."
Les Silences du palais (Tunisia, 1994–95) An important first film; takes place in times of French protectorate, in the muted atmosphere of the bey's palace. It deals with taboo themes revolving around the condition of women. Alia, recalling her childhood, spent among the servant women (sometimes mistresses) of the sovereign, finally seeks to impose herself in a society where woman is relegated to the role of servant, living within the walls of the palace and without any contact with the outside world. In this film, Alia and her mother, Khedija, are "walled" into the imposing silence of the palace.
Alia is played by Ghalia Lacroix and her mother by Amel Hedhili. With Kamel Fazaa and Hend Sabri. See coverage in *Journal Français d'Amérique* (4–11 August 1995): 11.j] Also **Decock**, *French Review* (March 1994): 764: "elegiac, slow and heavy film about mother 'colonized by the colonized' and her daughter who says 'no' to servitude." And Josée Lapointe, "La Mémoire du silence, *Le Soleil* (Saturday, 3 August 1996): D 3.

Nadine Wanono (Niger)
Demain, au bout du fleuve (1987)

Zara Mahmoud Yacoub (Tchad)
Dommemo Féminin (19–) Film dealing with "female circumcision." Yacoub and the actors who worked on this film have received death threats. (Kenneth Harrow, interviewed by Lee Nichols, in *ALA Bulletin* 22; no. 2 (Spring 1996): 14.

Florentine Yameogo (Burkina Faso)
  Harmattan (1995; in process)

Salifou Yaye (Niger)
  L'Excision (1994; video)
  Funérailles Gulmance (1994; video)

Dominique T. Zeida (Burkina Faso)
  Une Chanson à deux voix (1992)

Mme Abdou Zoulaha (Niger)
  Santé pour tous en l'an 2000 (1993) video

Léonie Yangba Zowe (or **Zoé**) (Central African Republic)
  Yangba bolo (1985)
  Lengue (1985)
  N'Zale (1986)
  Paroles de sages (1987)

Argentine

Nelly Kaplan See under French directors.

Tilda Thamar See under French directors.

Belgian

(Belgian video is, according to Philippe Dubois [*Encyclopédie des ciné-mas de Belgique:* 250–61] "the margin that holds the whole page together.")

Yasmina Abdellaoui
  Gigi et Monica (1994–95; 52 mins.; with Benoît Dervaux)

Chantal Akerman b., Belgium, 1950. Daughter of Polish Jewish par-ents, survivors of concentration camp who settled in Belgium. Some-times makes films in France and the United States. (Came to United States to study at twenty-one.) For her, Belgium is a "country that has little respect for culture" (Head 45). "Enfant terrible of cinema" (Acker 317). Seeks to arouse angers, desires, and expectations through her cinema. Her films usually have an auteure signature, and signature long-takes, and invariably present complex feminist discourse. (See Foster.)

Chantal Akerman. *J'ai faim, j'ai froid.* Coutesy Belgian Embassy.

[Akermania, v. I] "Shorter Works" (1992 video) contains
J'ai faim, j'ai froid (1984) starring Maria de Medeiros
Saute ma ville (1968; made in Belgium when A. was 18.)
  Hotel Monterey (made in United States—1972) A. claims she
stole the money to make this film. Its theme: transient nature of
urban life (often encountered in her films).
L'Enfant aimé (or *Je joue à être une femme mariée*) (1971)
La Chambre (1972)
[*La Chambre 2* (1972)]
Hanging Out [in]Yonkers (1973)
Le 15/8 (codirected with Samy Szlingerbaum; 1973)
Je tu il elle (1974; 86 mins.) Akerman herself stars as the protago-
nist of this film in which a young woman eats raw sugar and rearranges
furniture, after which she goes on the road, accepting a ride with a
truck driver (whom she masturbates, off screen) and winding up in
the home of her woman lover. They make love; the lengthy "uneroticized" scene is photographed from a distance. Stars, in addition, Niels
Arestrup and Claire Wauthion. Themes of estrangement, alienation,
lesbianism.

Jeanne Dielman 23 Quai du Commerce 1080 Bruxelles (1975; 225 mins.) Constructed around a woman's chores. Three and one half hours of film present a detailed account of three days in the life of a Belgian housewife [a discreet prostitute, who, after servicing Thurs-day's caller stabs him to death with a pair of scissors]. She cares for her teenage son, Sylvain, and she scrubs a tub until it is spotless . . . and does so in "real time." Audience is drawn to the experience of preparing a dish or making a bed. Angered the audience at first show-ing. Written by Akerman, photographed by Babette Mangolte, music by Beethoven. Acted by Delphine Seyrig, Jan Decorte, Henri Storck, Jacques Doniol-Valcroze, Yves Bical. Bergan (292): "The focus of the feminist argument is clouded by Akerman's failure to reveal the root cause of Jeanne's final action, but this still, bleak film remains original and intriguing for those with the patience to engage with it."

This film is widely studied and commented upon; it appears to be a pivotal film for many critics of women's cinema.

News from Home (90 mins.; 1976; 1977 according to *Encyclopédie des cinémas de Belgique*) Portrait of Manhattan in a succession of geometrically framed streetscapes. "It's a spare and ravishing city sym-phony that takes its cues from Manhattan's own relentless grid" (J. Hoberman in *The Village Voice*). I find this film somewhat oppressive.

Les Rendez-vous d'Anna (1978; 122 mins.) (*The Meetings of Anna*) A Belgian filmmaker named Anna Silver travels about Europe in an effort to publicize her latest film. She sleeps with a German journalist in Essen, visits her mother, and goes out with a former lover in Paris, and so on, but ultimately returns to the solitude of her apartment. Bergan (174): "For those who are willing to enter Aker-man's world—static camera, medium long shots, mournful mono-logues and solemn silences—it does bring some rewards. The cryptic style and dislocated characters . . . get close to the heart of a modern malaise in cool and understated images." Written by Chantal Aker-man; photography Jean Penzer. Stars Aurore Clément, Helmut Griem, Magali Noël, Hans Zieschler, Lea Massari, and Jean-Pierre Cassel.

Aujourd'hui, dis-moi (1980)

Toute une nuit (1982; 89 mins.) On a hot summer night, when sleep will not come, many wander. A woman leaves her husband for a rendez-vous with her lover; a voyeur watches a woman through her window, and so forth. Stars Angelo Abazoglou, Natalia Ackerman, and Véronique Alain. See Païni's discussion of this film in *Une Ency-clopédie des cinémas de Belgique*, 243–44. He finds this an exceptional "documentary" on Brussels and a film in which Akerman shows the specific effects of documentary feeling in Belgian fiction film. (Yet at the same time it has a fantastic, almost surreal, quality.—Mosley.)

Les Années 80/The Eighties (1983) Montage of auditions for parts in a musical comedy; combined with a musical extravaganza, and set in a shopping mall. This is a documentary of Akerman's auditions for a film that subsequently became the fiction film *Golden Eighties* (Mosley).

L'Homme à la valise (1983–84)

Pina Bausch Un Jour Pina m'a demandé (Foster gives 1983)

J'ai faim, j'ai froid. (1984)

Family Business (1984)

New York, New York bis (1984)

Lettre d'un cinéaste (1984) Video

The Golden Eighties (1986; 93–96 mins.) (aka *La Galerie*) [The 1983 and 1986 are similar titles for different films.] (**Window Shopping** is alternate English title). (Romance in a shopping mall.) Cast: Delphine Seyrig; M. Boyer; F. Cottencon.

Letters Home (1987)

"Sloth." Segment in the film *Seven Women, Seven Sins* (1987; 101 mins.) A film on the seven deadly sins made by seven women filmmakers. Available Women Make Movies 1996 catalog p. 76. (*Le Journal d'une paresseuse* [1986] [Mosley].)

Rue Mallet-Stevens (1986) Short video (Mosley)

Les Trois Dernières Sonates de Franz Schubert (1988) Video (Mosley)

Jean-Luc Vilmouth (1988) (aka *Le Marteau*) Video

[*De l'autre côté de l'océan* (1987–8?)]

Histoires d'Amérique: Food, Family and Philosophy (1989; 97 mins.) (This film is almost certainly the same film as the one above; this title is the correct one.—Mosley)

Trois Strophes sur le nom de Sacher (1989) Short

Le Déménagement (1992) (Mosley)

Nuit et Jour (*Night and Day*) (1991) Protagonist explores her sexuality but always leaves the men without remorse. With Thomas Langmann, Guilaine Londez, and François Négret.

D'est (From the East) (1993; 110 mins.)

Contre l'oubli (1991)

Portrait of a Young Girl at the End of the 1960s in Brussels (1993)

Bordering on Fiction (video that includes *D'est*)

Un Divan à New York (1996) with William Hurt and Juliette Binoche (Mosley)

See **Foster,** *Women Film Directors:* 4–7; 48; 55; 109; 154; 194; 239; 240; 307; 357. Akerman is the only Belgian mentioned by **Foster.**

Excellent short and very sensitive appreciation of Akerman by Anne-Marie **Faux** in the *Encyclopédie des cinémas de Belgique* , 15–17. Also see Annette **Kuhn** and Susannah **Radstone**, 8–10. (Mosley)

Complete information regarding Akerman and her films found in *Hommage à Chantal Akerman.* (See bibliography.)

Marie André b. 1951 in Brussels. An important video artist.
Galérie de portraits (1982)
Come ti amo (1983)
Répétitions (1984) About Anne Teresa De Keersmaeker.
Un Ange passe (1985)
Evento (1986)
Hus Walter Compositie (1985) (Mosley)
On l'appelait président (1989)
Premier Amour (1991)
Le Fil des jours (1993–94)
Hombre alado (1994–95) Dance and music loosely based on the myth of Prometheus.

Emanuelle Bada
Hindou, une parole libre (1995–96; 26 mins.; with Pierre-Yves Vandeweerd, Marie-Soleil Frère and Benoît Mariage) Hindou is a twenty-eight-year-old woman from Mauritania who has engaged in a certain amount of political activity.

Olga Baillif b. 1969 in Geneva.
L'Atelier (1990)
Une Petite Histoire (1991)
La Vie courante (1992–93)
L'Après-midi (1993–94)

Catherine Bauchet b. 1968 in Paris.
Au-delà de l'eau (1994–95)

Liria Bégéja
Paris-Paparazzi (1986) Short
Avril brisé (1987)
Rendez-vous à Tirana (1993)
Loin des barbares (1994?)

Corinne Behin
Papilio Blumei (1992–93)
Technicien de surface (1993–94)

Marta Bergman b. 1962 in Bucharest.
Luna (1988)

Loredana Bianconi. *Avec de l'Italie qui descendrait l'Escaut.* Courtesy Belgian Embassy.

Une Femme comprise (1989)
La Ballade du serpent: une histoire Tzigane (1990)
Bucarest visages anonymes (1993–94 with Frédéric Fichefet)

Loredana Bianconi (Mosley-Pallister) b. 1954 in Haine-St. Paul. Both of the following are full-length films drawing on the director's experience of immigrant Italian coal-mining families (cf. *Déjà s'envole la fleur maigre*, directed by Paul Meyer, 1960; see also Anne-Marie Etienne, infra).
La Mina (1989–90)
Avec de l'Italie qui descendrait l'Escaut (1993; 90 mins.) Video documentary
Comme un air de retour (1994; 105 mins.) 16 mm.; fiction
Café de l'Europe

Eva Birinyi
Mutants (1994; with Christian Van Cutsem)

Yaël Bitton b. 1971 in Geneva.
J'attends de vos nouvelles (1994–95) Portrays three patients in a

Loredana Bianconi. *Comme un air de retour.* Courtesy Belgian Embassy.

psychiatric hospital. (Nonfiction; filmed in a psychiatric clinic over six months.)

Pazam (1995–96; 31 mins.) Two young Israelis attempt to find their identity as citizens as they finish their two years of military service.

Milena Bochet b. 1965 in Madrid.
Paris-Brazza (1991)
Rêve entre deux (1992–93)
Gejza (1993–94)
Les Coulisses du réveil (1994–95; 23 mins.; with Stéphane Olivier)
About making films.

Eve Bonfanti b. in Uccle 1949; of Corsican descent.
Madame P . . . (1984). A profoundly moving film about aging and old age. Elise Peeters is a seventy-three-year-old "dame des toilettes" (dame-pipi) in the basement of a Brussels brasserie. Shots from the basement looking up; the demeaning ring of the coins on the plate set out to receive tips; all makes for a very disturbing film.

Bonfanti wrote the *scénario* in 1978 and had a great deal of difficulty getting support for the script, then for the film itself. Title role played by Hélène Van Herck.

Un film, une enquête, neuf minutes (A la recherche d'un cinéma perdu) (1989) Video; short

Marie Borrelli. *Nature morte avec femme.* **Courtesy Belgian Embassy.**

L'Astronome (1990) Video
See *Une Encyclopédie des cinémas de Belgique*, 181–84 on Bonfanti.

Nicole Borgeat
  Acquitte, faute de preuves (1988)
  Approche pour un portrait vidéo (1988)]
  Emile, Emile (1989–90)

Marie Borrelli b. 1971 in Paris (Chatenay Malabry).
  Nature morte avec femme (1993–94)
  Leda, la Rose rose et le scarabée (1994–95)

Litsa Boudalika b. 1962 in Greece. Since 1983 she has made
  L'Escrime
  La Pince à ongles
  Un Sogno di Angelo
  Friteries Athènes
  Huizingen
  Monogramme
  Photo de classes (1992–93)

Lissette de Broyer Films on the Andes.

Lydia Chagoll
  Au Nom du Führer (1977)
See **Lejeune** 102.

Isabelle Claudé and Sabine Houtman
Derrière le rideau (1990)

Christelle Coopman b. 1960 in La Hestre.
Noces de lard (1995–96; 4 mins. 11 secs.) Animation. A very fat woman decides to slim down to find a husband.

Elisabeth Coronel
Françoise Dolto (1994–95; with Arnaud de Mezamat; three parts 53 mins; 56 mins.; 53 mins.) About the teaching methods of Dolto.

Fabienne Couvreur
Une Vie de petit château (1992 with Gilles Bechet)

Martine Crucifix
La Revanche de l'instinct (1989–90)

Claudine Delvaux b. 1946.
Lettre à Jean-Luc Godard (1987–88)

Françoise Demey b. 1970 in Brussels.
Vertiges (1994)

Greta Deses
Dada

Michèle Dimitri
Tour de chance

Martine Doyen b. 1961.
Herman et le gangster (1994–95; 12 mins.) Based on Hugo Claus's "Een gezonde gangster."
L'Insoupçonnable univers de Josiane (1995–96; 26 mins.)

Bénédicte Emsens
Le Plongeoir (1991)
Le Musée (1992–93)

Anne-Marie Etienne b. Brussels, 1956.
Impasse de la Vignette (1990; 107 mins.) Annie Cordy plays the colorful heroine of this film that evokes a specific *quartier* of the big city. Set in a mining community. Cf. Loredana Bianconi, supra. (*Encyclopédie des cinémas de Belgique*, 149; *Longs Métrages* [Communauté Française de Belgique brochure 12 (1989–90): 18–19]).

Beatriz Flores b. 1956 in Montevideo, Uraguay.
Ecoutez, mortels

39 Marches (remake of Hitchcock)
Les Lézards (1989–90)

Anne François
Le Geste indélicat (1987–88) Film on the photographer Marie-Françoise Plissart in preparation.

Marie-Soleil Frère. See Bada supra.

Juliette Frey b. in Switzerland in 1964.
Le Froid du matin (1987)
Un Jour comme un autre (1990)
L'Autre (1990)
Le Jardin d'Eden (1992–93)

Nathalie Fritz
Back to the Roots (1995–96; 52 mins.) Documentary. Belgian miners who moved to Chicago in the 60s drown the anguish of exile in the blues clubs of the black ghetto and become successful as musician and musician's manager.

Nicole Gilbert
Sans parole

Geneviève Grand'Ry
Mardi Gras

Marie-Eve de Grave b. 1965 in Furnes.
Les Acharnés (1993–94)

Pauline de Grunne
La Femme Michel w/ Claude Schwarz (1982)
Ils (1989–90)

Marion **Haensel** [Hänsel] See under French directors

Nadia Hamzaoui See Yacoubi infra

Florence Henrard b. 1971 in Etterbeek.
Sortie de bain (1994; 4 mins. 16 secs.) Animation
Noces de lait (1995–96; 4 mins. 11 secs.) Animation

Françoise Honorez b. in Uccie in 1965
Bois des Ombres (1992–93)

Mary Jimenez A native of Lima, Peru (b. 1948), she went to Belgium at twenty-four. She returned to Peru in 1984 to film *Du verbe aimer*.
A propos de vous (1976)
La Version d'Anne (1977)

Miserere (1978)

La Distance sensible (1981)

Piano Bar (1981–82) also known as *21h12 Piano Bar*. First full-length picture, shocked some. About female homosexuality, masochism, mutilation, and suicide.

Le Stylo stylet (1982)

La Moitié de l'amour (Love's Half) (1984)

Du verbe aimer (About the Verb to Love) (1984) Jimenez shows herself to be an auteure in the creation of this film: She conceived, wrote, directed, and starred in it (with a nonprofessional Peruvian cast). It is autobiography in the new mode; confessional; first-person singular cinema. The plot concerns a daughter's unrequited desire for the mother and unfulfilled desire that she become the object of her mother's desire. **Louis** finds it to have a strong emphasis on language, to be drunk on words, to be a kind of *poésie éclatée*. It sometimes becomes chant or incantation. The movie has moved some immensely, for example, Wim Wenders. (See the article by Théodore **Louis** in *Encyclopédie des cinémas de Belgique*, 98–101.)

Différences Video. five portraits

Fiestas (1988)

L'Air de rien (1989) Feature length

Isabelle Jooris b. 1966 in Ixelles.

Parmi tous ses travaux (1992)

Vice Versa (1992)

Tête à claques (1992)

Sabrina Joris b. 1975 in Monaco.

Zoom (1 min. 3 secs.) Animation. Closeups of animal furs and then the revelation of the animals these furs belong to.

Yasmine Kassari b. 1968 in Morocco.

Chiens errants (1994–95) In certain cities of Northern Morocco the city authorities regularly destroy stray dogs. On the days when this occurs, people carefully keep their dogs at home.

Le Feutre noir (1994–95)

Editha Kiel Born in Germany, she was companion and assistant to Jan Vanderheyden, who was one of the first to realize that Belgians not only preferred Flemish subtitles on imported French films, but would even support films made directly in the language. One of the most important of these early films was *De Witte* (1934)—a film based on a novel of the same name about peasant mores. They made nine more films in five years, all in Flemish.

But Kiel also directed and produced sixteen more films in ten years

(Vanderheyden took part in the making of these films, but his name did not appear on them because he had been condemned for collaboration with the enemy during the war). These were comedies in the local patois, whose success was such that they continued to be shown on television years later. (*Encylopédie des cinémas de Belgique*, 142–43; 146.)

Corinne Kuyl
Solide Penchant (1994)
Deux sinon rien (1995–96; 6 mins.) Two fetuses compete in their mother's womb.

Marie-Jo Lafontaine (Mosley) b. in Antwerp in 1950. Video artist.
La Marie-Salope (1980)
Round around the Ring (1982)
A las cinco de la tarde (1985)
L'Enterrement de Mozart (1986)
Victoria (1987–88)
Passio (1989–90)
We Are All Shadows (1991)
Feuer!!! (1991–92)

Carole Laganière b. 1959 in Montréal.
Le Tzigane (1985)
La Grande Vie (1986)
Le Mouchoir de poche (1987)
Charles Loos juste un rêve (1985)

Tamara Laï
Féla (1986)
Mouvement 2 (1987)
Mouvement 3 (1987)
Mouvement 2 et 3 action (1987)
Mouvement 4 (1988)
Cheval corps et âme (1989–90)
Un Temple lyrique (1994–95)

Annick Leroy
Berlin de l'aube à la nuit (1981)
Il fait si bon près de toi (1997–88)

Guionne Leroy b. 1967 in Liège
Délit de fuite (1986–70
Chiquéchoque (1987–88)
Humeurs (1987–88)
Jeux de mains (1989–90)

Tango (1989–90)
La Traviata—noi siamo zingarelle (1994)

Françoise Levie Writer, historian, and filmmaker. Makes documentaries in which fiction, historical fiction, and reporting are mixed.
Le Voyageur
Joseph Plateau, théoricien de l'animation (with Pierre Levie)(1978) (Mosley)
Pixel Tree (1987–88) Based on a story by her husband Pierre Levie, who writes children's books, and makes films.
Nylon blues (1991)
Le Chewing Gum cet inconnu (1992)
Le Mystère des tombes gelées en Sibérie (1993)
Les Grandes Dames du Strip-Tease (1994–95; 52 mins.)
Aérogyne et le cinématographe (1995?)

Catherine Libert b. 1971 in Liège.
L'Etranger (1994–95)

Bénédicte Liénard
Let's Play (1987)
Le Bruit de la ville est si proche (1988)
L'Ecole maternelle, c'est ma chance (1988)
En attendant Mireille (1990)
Les Petites Choses qui font la vie (1992–93)
L'Adoption, une autre vie (1993–94)

Dominique Loreau b. 1955.
Le Saut dans la vie (1984)
Zig-zags (1987)
Documentary on AIDS (in French: SIDA) in Senegal (1988)

Marie Mandy (Mosley) b. in Louvain in 1961.
Pardon Cupidon (1992) Full-length film
The Man Who Thought Too Much (1986) Short
The Trouble with Mary (1986) Short
Judith (1989) Short

Cecilia Marreiros-Marum
Dessin d'enfant (1993–94)
D'Amour et d'os frais (1994–95; 6 mins.30 secs.) A little old lady and her dog live out their lives seated on a park bench.

Marie-Hélène Massin b. 1956 in Waremme.
Et si on se passait des patrons? (1978 with Monique Quintart)
Grosso modo (1982)

Cécilia Marreiros-Marum. *Dessin d'enfant.* Courtesy Belgian Embassy.

Voyage (1987)
Rue de l'Abondance (1994–95)

Ursula Meier b. 1971 in Besançon.
Le Songe d'Isaac (1994)

Geneviève Mersch b. 1963 in Luxembourg.
Mama boit, papa boxe (1987)
Mégapolis (1988)
La Balade de Billie (1989)
Le Pont rouge (1991)
Le Courage (1992) Part of *Les Sept Péchés capitaux* [See Aker-man's *Greed.*]
Sentimental Journey (1994) Documentary
John (1994–95; 40 mins.) Juliette makes a video of herself and her life for John, who is in Boston.

Mathilde Mignon b. 1962 in Paris.
Matticara (1990 with Michel Cauléa)
Sept Alphabets pour une seule mer (1992–93)

Sylvia Minnaert b. in Anvers in 1964.
Pas d'histoire (1988)

Papillon (1989)
Animitis (1989–90)
Porgy and chess (1990)
Chessmess (1991)
Au pied de la lettre (1992–93)

Cathy Mlakar b. 1965.
Carnaval en Haïti (1992; with Jean-Paul Zaeytijd)
Quelque Chose (1994; with Jean-Paul Zaeytijd)
Si Bondié Vlé (1995; with Jean-Paul Zaeytijd)

Françoise de Mol

Claude Misonne An author as well, Misonne made puppet films in the 1940s:
Le Petit Poucet (aka *Kleine Duimpje*) Misonne's first film. (*Mosley*)
Le Petit Navire Misonne's second film. (Mosley)
Tintin et le crabe aux pinces d'or (1948; 1hr. 45 min.) Presented at the Festival de Venise, this film was said to be a financial disaster. Michel Roudevitch, in the *Encyclopédie des cinémas de Belgique*, 20; 26.
Formule X24 (13 mins.) 35 mm film
Car je suis empereur (13 mins.) 35 mm film
Il était un vieux savant (aka *Le Vieux Savant*) (13 mins.) 35 mm film; first Belgian animated film in color.
Dix petits nègres
Concerto
Documentaries:
Ici naît la fantaisie
La Huitième Merveille

Monique Moinet
Au bord de l'étang

Catherine Montondo b. in 1959.
Tyniec, au bout de la ligne 112 (1991)
Le Métro (1992)
Hésitations (1992–93)
Etrangetés du soir (1993–94)

Anne Lévy Morelle b. 1951 in Brussels.
Gare du Luxembourg (1986)
Tout va (très) bien (1987–88)

Chantal Myttenaere b. in 1952. Has a degree in psychology and has written four novels and a collection of novellas.
Le Moulin de Dodé (1987–88)

Aimée Navarra
Coeurs belges (shortly after WWI)

Danièle Nyst Since 1974 has worked with Jacques-Louis Nyst. Videos include
L'Objet (1974); *L'Ombrelle en papier* (1977); *J'ai la tête qui tourne* (1984); *Hyaloïde* (1985); *L'Image* (1987); *Saga sachets* (1989); *Comme s'il y avait des pyramides* (1990); *L'Apocalypse selon Thérésa* (199-).
Also:
Le Livre est au bout du banc (1992–93 with Jacques-Louis Nyst)

Coralie Pastor b. 1970.
Murmures (1995–96; 8 mins.)

Diane Perelsztejn b. 1959 in Brussels.
Escape to the Rising Sun (1987)
Rhodes Nostalgie (1995–96; 59 mins.) Documentary about the Jewish community of Rhodes, rebuilt after World War II, principally in Africa, especially Zaire (the Belgian Congo) and in Belgium.
Noctambulle (1996)

Annick Pippelart b. 1966
Reine d'un jour (1989–90)

Diane Pollet
Panseurs de secrets (1989–90 with Carol Sacré)

Monique Quintart b. Etterbeek in 1949.
Albert Trébla (1975)
Et si on se passait de patrons? (1979)
Hortensia, je t'aime signé Alexis (1982)
A l'ombre des buildings en fleurs (1983)
Pour quoi? (1987)
Terre Mère (1988)
La Souris peremptoire (199203) About the curator of the Museum of Ancient Art in Brussels.

Inès Rabadan b. in 1967 in Namur.
L'Autre Silence (1993–94)
En Belgique, terre d'Islam (1995)
Vacance (1995–96; 15 mins.)

Isabelle Raembonck b. 1964 in Brussels.
Dans la lune (1993–94)

Zlatina Rousseva b. in Bulgaria. She has directed more than twenty-four films, both documentary, and fiction.
La Nuit les poissons rouges (1991–92)
Portrait d'un homme du pouvoir (1991–92)
La Chasse aux loups (1993–94)

Carol Sacré b. 1966. Has worked on films in Africa and Hong Kong.
Le Monde magique de Sidi Marzouk (1988 with Roger Job)
Panseurs de secrets (1989–90 with Diane Pollet)
Melakou, Betty et Vladimir (1993–94 with Claude Briade)

Bernadette Saint-Remi b. 1956 in Liège
Duelle (1985)
No Woman's Land (1987)
Séparations (1989)
Destinées (1989–90)

Hélène Schirren (Mosley) She was the official filmmaker for Congo.
Sous l'étoile d'or (1939)
Tervuren musée du Congo belge (1939–40)
Guérir sous les tropiques (1946) with Guillaume Linephty
Sans Tam-Tam (1949) with Guillaume Linephty

Marie-Hélène Seller
Le Beau Rôle (1989)
Afrique, je t'aime . . . moi non plus (1989–90)

Marie-Paule Stokart b. 1962 in Namur.
Orfèvre de son métier (1989)
Paroles de danse (1990)
Le Lieu où je dois vivre (1991)
Géralde (1992–30)

Marie Storck
Calligraphe (1989–90)

Brigitte Thiriart
Margot et le Génie (1991)
Barbe-Blues (1992–93)

Marie Anne Thunissen b. 1955
Poussières (1989)
Femmes-Machines (1995–96; 52 mins.) Documentary about women who work in an arms factory.

Nina Toussaint b. 1964 in Cologne.
L'Histoire d'une disparue (1989)

Les Jumeaux (1992)

Le Crime quotidien (1994–95; 56 mins.) Nina has mistreated, humiliated, and raped his daughter every day for eight years. Today she is able to speak of it, but . . .

Varda See under French directors

Caroline Vatan b. 1966 in Avallon.

Je suis une égoïste (1993–94)

Lydia Vereecke

Sunrise sorcière

Lola, des fois (1995–96)

Rosa Verges Coma b. 1955 in Barcelona.

Boom Boom (1989–90) Sofia, a dentist, and Tristan, the manager of a shoe store, had both vowed never to love again, following unfortunate relationships in their past. However . . .

Séverine Vermersch b. 1966 in Lille.

Visite guidée (1982)

L'Histoire d'un autre (1983)

La Valise de Flora (1984)

Qui voit Quessant? (1989–90). About Marie and Jean Epstein. The sister talks of her brother.

Violaine de Villers b. 1947.

Pour les paus chauds (1983)

La Fadeur sublime . . . de Marguerite Duras (1983)

Place de Londres (1984)

L'Ombre des couleurs (1984)

Blanc d'Espagne (1987)

Madame V, Monsieur S. (1990)

Mizike Mama (1992)

La Tête à l'envers (1993–94)

Rwanda, paroles contre l'oubli (1995; 60 mins.) Three Tutsi women who have taken refuge in Brussels, speak of the massacres of their families during the uprise of 1994.

Revivre (1995–96; 60 mins.) Documentary about the civil war in Rwanda. Five Tutsi and Hutu women who survived the massacre of their whole family speak of their terrible experiences.

Eva Visneyi b. 1958

Chronique d'une menteuse

Deuxième conte pour enfant de moins de 3 ans d'Eugène Ionesco—animation

Troisième conte . . .
Cerise (1993)
Hans et Anna (1994–95)

Marilyn Watelet   Producer of many of Chantal Akerman's films and director of
Fin de siècle (Fin de siglo) (1994–95; 54 mins.; with Szymon Zaleski) How Havana's large department store, Fin de siglo, functions on a daily level since the collapse of the socialist camp.

Nicole Widart (Mosley) Video artist from Liège.
Ultima II (1983)
Paysage imaginaire (1983)
Images de grève (1984)
Fin de carrière (1985)

Anne Wilhelmi
Les Minimes aux Marolles (1989–90)

Sandrine Willems b. 1968 in Brussels
La Comédie qui pleure (1995–96; 12 mins.)

Nicole Widart (Mosley) Video artist from Liège.
Ultima II (1983)
Paysage imaginaire (1983)
Images de grève (1984)
Fin de carrière (1985)

Grace Winter   Filmmaker and ethnocinematographer. Director of Progrès Films, a distribution company in Brussels, specializing in quality art film (**Head** 118).

Kenza et Loubna Yacoubi
Kife Kife (1994–95; with Nadia Hamzaoui) Young women of mixed culture—part North African, part Belgian—try out dancing and acting.

Caribbean

Véronique Chénion (Cayenne, French Guyana) Present at Cannes, this young woman is a *pigiste* (writer paid by the page) at RFO-Guyane. She expects to become a director, after completing her studies. (See Demy.)

Gilda Gonfier (Abymes, Guadeloupe) Librarian, scriptwriter (*Saint-Michel Terrasson le démon*) and director of documentaries, as well as of
Grener, Grener Short produced for RFO-Guadeloupe.

Elsie Haas (Haitian; living now in Paris) Sometimes she films in Creole rather than in French. (See **Cham**, *Ex–iles*, 26 ff.; and interview between Haas and Claire Andrade-Watkins, 308–14.)

La Seconde Manche (1979) A letter arrives from Martinique at the home of a Martiniquan couple living in Paris; it inquires about whether the man wants to sell some property he owns in Martinique. An argument ensues because the man wants to sell the land and then to buy an automobile. The woman says no because she wants to return to Martinique in the future and to settle on this land. In the end the woman prevails.

Satrap (1980) (Creole word for *The Trap*) Identity of Martiniquans; a mother works as a servant for a bourgeois family; she passes on the responsibility for caring for her children to her oldest daughter, who in her turn dreams of leaving Martinique and going to France like her peers. Shows how some Martiniquans feel trapped between being themselves and being "French." (Readings from Frantz Fanon might accompany the viewing of this film.)

Des Saints et des anges (1984) Set in an African beauty shop in Paris, this film examines the condition of exile in Paris through the symbolism of hair and hairstyle. (European hair is "civilized.") A mother brings her daughter to the shop to have her hair done.

La Seconde Manche II (1985) Sequel to 1979 film in which the subject is the victory of the woman over the man.

La Ronde des Taps-Taps (1986) This and the following film were shot in Haiti following the fall of Duvalier. Deals with the problems of urban living and transportation, showing the swarms of minivans, jeeps, and trucks (called taps-taps like the "mammy wagons" of West Africa) used by Haitians to get around Haiti. (Taps-taps is variously spelled in Cham.)

La Ronde des Vodu (1987) Haas's most famous work; deals with religion—voodoo—in Haitian history, politics, economics, and culture. Intercuts interviews and scenes of everyday life with those of rituals and integrates music, poetry, dance, and art into the warp and woof of the narrative. (Compare Maya Deren.)

No Comment (1988) A TV piece in which a black woman agonizes over what to wear and how to do her hair for a date.

Boni (on or after 1992) First feature-length film; shot in Surinam; concerns the eighteenth-century war in Surinam between the Boni (maroons who were followers of the maroon named Boni) and the Dutch. Despite the collaboration of the Djukas (another group of maroons) with the Dutch, the Boni escaped the Dutch and settled in French Guyana where they are still to be found. (See **Cham** *Ex–iles*, 310–12.)

Exile II (on or after 1992) Work made for TV. Black intellectuals in exile in the West. (Title plays on the name for a Haitian musical group, Exile I.)

Haas has plans for a film on Blacks in Russia with emphasis on Alexander Pushkin.

Sarah Maldoror See African directors

Euzhan Palcy b. 1953 [Foster says 1957] in Martinique. Studied film arts in Paris. Filmmaker, poet, author.

La Messagère (1975; 52 mins. black and white; TV drama) Shot on location in Martinique.

L'Atelier du diable (1981) A short fiction based on a short story Palcy wrote. Produced by the Grain de Sable group.

Rue Cases-Nègres (or *Sugar Cane Alley*) (1983, 107 mins.) Set in Martinique. A young boy, José, lives in shantytown with his grandmother; she and the other blacks living there do heavy labor in the sugar plantation. The grandmother insists that the only way out for José is through education. He goes to the big city to be educated, and his adventures there are as interesting as those in shantytown.

Produced by Sumafa-Orca-Nef Diffusion. Stars Darling Legitimus (who gives a towering performance as the grandmother); Garry Cadenat (as José); Douta Seck. Based on the novel by Joseph Zobel. The film was made on an $800,000 budget. It took the Silver Lion at Venice Film Festival, and Legitimus took the prize for best female role. (See **Lejeune,** 181–82.)

Siméon (1992–93; 115 mins.) A town receives the gift of music from a little girl and a local man. Stars J.-Claude Duverger and J. Béroard. (Version Française catalog) Ghosts and a feu follet drive the action in this film that, though not without charm, lacks the power and nuance of *Rue Cases-Nègres.*

Aimé Césaire

[Palcy has also made *A Dry White Season* (United States, 1989) in English. This story revolves around the abuses inherent in the apartheid system. **Foster** discusses this film at length. See also **Acker** 118ff.]

See important writings on her (esp. Ménil, 155–75 and an interview with June Giovanni, 286–307) in **Cham**'s *Ex–Iles.*
See **Foster,** 98; 297–99

addendum

Christiane Succab-Goldman (nationality?)
Ernest Léardée ou le Roman de la Biguine (1988) A documentary

about a Martiniquan barber who immigrated to France and founded the Bal Nègre.

Chilean
Marilú Mallet See under Québec directors

Valeria Sarmiento b. Chile, 1948. Moved to France with her husband, the well-known filmmaker Raoul Ruiz, after the assassination of President Allende and the onset of the dictatorship of Pinochet (1973).

Made several documentaries on refugees (*Gens de toutes parts, gens de nulle part*); Chilean children uprooted and disrupted (*Le Mal du pays*). Then made a film on Latin American machismo (*Un Homme, un vrai*) broadcast on Antenna 2 in 1982: It dissatisfied just about everyone.

Notre Mariage (1984) A poor little girl is adopted by a rich couple. Exploration of the relationship between the foster father and this girl once she has grown into a beautiful young lady. Based on the novel *Mi boda contigo* by Corin Tellado.

[*In Patagonia*]
See **Lejeune** 194.

French

Jacqueline Audry b. Orange, France, in 1908; d. 1977. Began career as actress and then assistant to Pabst, Delannoy, Ophuls; then directed. She had a lasting affinity for the stories of Colette. Her chief *scénariste* was Pierre Laroche, her husband. Dates of films vary considerably from critic to critic.

Les Chevaux du Vercors (1943) Short documentary about the Resistance.

Les Malheurs de Sophie (1945) First feature

(Un)Sombre Dimanche (1948)

Gigi (1949) From Colette. A young woman is groomed by her mother and her grandmother to become a courtesan, but rebels and chooses marriage.

L'Ingénue libertine (aka *Minne*) (1950) Also from Colette, this story is about the love affairs of a young Parisian wife during the Gay Nineties. She ends up realizing that her husband is the best man of them all, but this did not prevent the censors from severely cutting the earlier scenes of "sexual exploration."

Olivia (*The Pit of Loneliness*) (1951) Implicit Lesbian love in a

fashionable French boarding school where young women are compet-
ing for the attention and affection of the headmistress.

La Caraque blonde (1953)

Huis clos (1954; 95 mins.) A screen adaptation of the play by Jean-
Paul Sartre. Stars Arletty and Frank Villard. (Available from Version
Française—see Film Sources.)

L'Ecole des cocottes (1957)

La Garçonne (1957) Adaptation of a story written by Colette in
the 1920s about a young woman who wants to live as a man.

C'est la faute d'Adam (1958) (Katz gives 1956; Lejeune 1956.)

Mitsou (1958; 98 mins.) Also from Colette. A cabaret girl convinces
her sugar daddy to teach her the manners necessary to capture the
heart of a young lieutenant. (Katz gives 1956; so does Sadoul.)

Le (Secret du) Chevalier d'Eon (1960) Deals with the famous
transvestite.

Cadavres en vacances (1961; Lejeune gives 1963)

Les Petits Matins (1961)

Soledad (1966)

(Les)Fruits amers (1967)

Le Lis de mer (1970)

Johanne **Larue** (*Séquences* (February 1994): 7–8) writes: "Audry's
style certainly doesn't shine for its originality or any finds in setting.
Like most French directors of her period, one can say of Audry that
she had the talent of a grind; that is, she directed correctly, but with
heaviness, taking cinematographic space for theatrical space. However
Jacqueline Audry's films astonish for the audacity of the subjects.
Almost all of them have featured heroines who assert their sexual
liberty and more than one of these films has an interest in lesbianism.
And this in the 50s! . . . At the time of their release, these films were
often banned through censorship, then judged too daring for TV, and
finally just too old to be shown. It is ironic that now that our mores
would find them acceptable, Audry's films cannot be shown on the
small screen because the majority of our channels show only products
made for television." (My trans.)

The films were shown in 1994 at the Cinémathèque québécoise,
which apparently has copies in their archives.

See Sharon **Smith** (118–19); **Foster** 26–28; Lejeune 59–62.

Anne-Marie Autissier b. 1950. Agrégation; former professor; widely
traveled. Early on, made a few documentaries.

Voyage en capitale (1977–78; with Ali Akika) Wrote scénario as
well as directed. Story of a young Algerian woman born in France
and an emigrant worker (*émigré*).

Larmes de sang (1979) Nonfiction. Interviews of Ali Akika and Autissier with Algerian women.

Merlin desenchanté (1980) A short filmed in the Brocéliande forest—a place in Brittany haunted by Arthurian legends. Actually, the film is about the difficult life of the people of the region, coal miners and blacksmiths.

Autissier now does another kind of work and appears to have abandoned filmmaking.

See **Lejeune** 76.

Josiane Balasko Actress of stage and film, film director, as well as script-writer. Balasko played the lead in *Les Hommes préfèrent les grosses,* directed by Jean-Marie Poiré (1981), and a role (Madame Musquin) in his *Le Père Noël est une ordure* (1982). She played Simone, the *aide-ménagère* in *La Smala* (Jean-Loup Hubert, 1984). In 1986 she played a role in *Nuit d'ivresse* (directed by Bernard Nauer and also starring Thierry Lhermitte). In 1989 she played in *Trop belle pour toi* (directed by Blier and also starring Gérard Depardieu).

Sac de noeuds (1985) b. directed this first film, which she also wrote and acted in. (*Sac de noeuds* also featured Isabelle Huppert.)

Les Keufs (1987; 96 mins.) A tough woman police officer, charged with being corrupt, is obliged to demonstrate that she is innocent. b. directed, acted in, wrote the *scénario,* and was co-producer. It stars Isaach de Bankolé, Jean-Pierre Léaud, while she herself plays the role of the lady-cop, Mireille Molyneux. (Version Française catalog.)

L'Ex-femme de ma vie (1989; 110 mins.) A man's life is interrupted by his ex-wife. Stars Jane Birkin and Thierry Lhermitte. (Version Française catalog.)

Ma vie est un enfer (1991; 90 mins.) b. directed and wrote this film. A woman sells her soul to the devil, and then has second thoughts. Stars Daniel Auteuil and Balasko herself. (Version Française catalog.)

Gazon Maudit [in English *French Twist*] Perhaps Balasko's most important work to date. (1994–95; 105 mins.). She directed, wrote, and starred in it; additional actors include Victoria Abril, Alain Chabat, Ticky Holgado, Michel Bosé, Catherine Hiegel, Catherine Samie. This film is about love, homosexual love in part, as it turns out here. A woman is betrayed by her husband, and (so some say) to get revenge, she has an affair with a woman. (*Gazon* refers to the female pubic region and *maudit* forbidden [to men].)

Elie **Castel,** in *Séquences* 178 (May–June 1995): 29, describes the film as follows: "In its affective context, the theme of female homosexuality is approached only as a pretext for a love story . . . different, it is true, but as authentic and credible as any love story." In this same

Josiane Balasko. *Gazon Maudit (French Twist)*. Victoria Abril, Alain Chabat, and Josiane Balasko. Internet.

place (28–32), Sylvie Gendron treats the work of Balasko as actress and as director in some detail. An important interview with Victoria **Abril** (who also starred in *L'Addition* and in Almodòvar's *Talons aiguilles*) is inserted in the article (30–31). Abril contends that people have not come to accept female homosexuality to the extent they have male: "les femmes homosexuelles . . . n'ont pas encore totalement été admises par la société. Avec ce film, on a tenté de secouer les men‑talités [. . . homosexual women . . . have not yet been totally accepted by society. With this film, "they" tried to shake up people's mental sets]." See *France‑Amérique* (20–26 January 1996): 13; *Time* (15 January 1996): 68; and **Lejeune** 78–79. Many reviews of this film are to be found on the Internet.

Laurence Ferreira Barbosa

Les Gens normaux n'ont rien d'exceptionnel or *Normal People Are Quite Ordinary* (1995; 95 mins.)

Geneviève Bastid b. in Paris in 1938. Was married to Jean‑Pierre Bastid for fourteen years; the couple separated in 1972. First was an editor but entered TV as a director in 1966. In 70s several of her films were broadcast in the United States. At this time she also became a part of the "Musidora group," and is a good friend of Nicole‑Lise

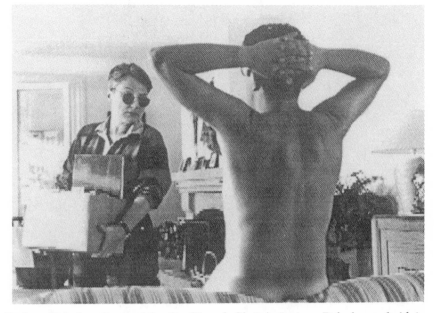

Josiane Balasko. *Gazon Maudit (French Twist)*. Josiane Balasko and Alain Chabat. Internet.

Bernheim (q.v.). Documentaries (1974–77) include *Objectif, Classe verte; Les Chiffoniers du merveilleux; Le Cirque; Le Château de Culan; Baba Guru*. Also has written many *scénarios* on the lives of women and recently two documentaries on drugs and on the creativity of women.

Si près, si loin, Place de la Réunion (1977–78) Depicts life in her quarter (district) of Paris.

Si près, si loin de Montbrison (1979) A portrait of her present with many childhood memories.

See Paule **Lejeune,** 80–81.

Liria Bégéja (or Bejega?). "D'origine albanaise."

Loin des Barbares, with Dominique Blanc and Timo Flloko. Mentioned in *France-Amérique* (16–22 July 1994): 10, as belonging to the "New Wave of French women filmmakers [La nouvelle vague des réalisatrices françaises]."

Yannick Bellon b. 1924. Edited with the great woman editor Myriam and worked with Nicole Védrès (q.v.) and with Denise Tual (q.v.). She also directed the following:

Goémons (1948) Sharon Smith says this is a realistic film about seaweed-gatherers on three small islands. It won the Grand Prix International du Documentaire at the Venice Biennial of 1948.

Colette (1950)

Le Tourisme (1951)

Varsovie quand même (1954)

Un Matin comme les autres (1956)

Les Hommes oubliés (1957)

Le Bureau des mariages (1958)

Le Second Souffle (1958)

Zoa le petit chameau blanc (1960) (Lejeune writes *Zaa* . . .)

Venise (1970)

La Femme de Jean (1971)

Jamais plus jamais (1976)

L'Amour violé (1978) (Maltin gives 1977 for *Rape of Love*.) Nurse Nell is raped by four drunks; but that's not the end of her troubles. Maltin finds film too preachy; says Bellon has tendency to depict all her male characters as insensitive chauvinists. (Aren't they?) Stars Nathalie Nell, Alain Foures, Michèle Simonnet, Pierre Arditi, Daniel Anteuil, Bernard Granger.

L'Amour nu (1981; 100 mins.) After discovering she has breast cancer, a woman renounces her lover. Stars Marlene Jobert and J.-M. Folon.

La Triche (1984; 103 mins.) Concerns an affair between a young homosexual musician and a married police inspector. Version Française catalog: "In this film a murderer tries to blackmail the officer investigating his case." Stars Victor Lanoux and Anny Duperey. (See **Colvile** 77.)

Les Enfants du désordre (1989–90; 97 mins.) An ex-prostitute forms a theater group after leaving prison.

L'Affut (1992; 103 mins.) Returning to country life with her son, a woman finds love. Stars Tcheky Karyo and Dominique Blanc.

Colette of the Goncourt Academy. Insightful portrait of Colette; includes filmed reading and dramatization of Colette's work.

Mentioned only en passant by **Foster** 26; 27; but see **Lejeune** 83–86.

Vera Belmont Belmont was the producer of *Quest for Fire*. She directed

Oeilllets rouges d'Avril (1974)

Prisonniers de Mao (1979)

Rouge Baiser or *Red Kiss* (1985–86; 112 mins.; Version Française gives 1991) Children of leftist parents in 1950s Paris. Fifteen-year-old Nadia (played by Valandrey) loves Apollinaire, cemeteries, Scarlett O'Hara, and is a committed Stalinist, as are her parents (Jewish immigrants from Poland), though she is also taken with American culture. She falls in love with Stéphane, a photographer (played by Wilson). Through him she discovers another world. With Charlotte Valandrey, Lambert Wilson, Marthe Keller, Gunter Lamprecht, and Laurent Terzieff.

Milena Destin (1991; 139 mins.) A young woman becomes a transla-tor for Franz Kafka. Set in the 1920s.

Anouk Bernard
Pourquoi (1976) This documentary seeks to understand the death of an adolescent coming through drug overdose.
See **Lejeune** 89.

Juliet Berto Born in Grenoble in 1947. Something of an auteure filmmaker. Began her movie career as an actress in the films of Jean-Luc Godard: *Deux ou trois choses que je sais d'elle; La Chinoise; Week-end.* Also had roles in *Les Camarades* (Marin Karmitz); *Défense de savoir* (Nadine Trintignant); *Out One* (Jacques Rivette) *Céline et Julie vont en bateau* (Rivette; 1974). She herself has directed the follow-ing films:

Babar Basses' Mother (1974;) (20 mins.; black and white) Short

Neige (1981) Berto not only directed but also wrote—or partici-pated in the writing of—the *scénario* and dialogues for the film, as well as acting in it. It is about the Pigaille district in Paris; took a prize in Cannes.

Cap-Canaille (1982–83) Berto not only directed but also wrote the *scénario* and dialogues for the film, as well as acting in it. About night life in Marseilles.

Havre (1986) Concerns violence and chaos in this port city, again seen in a nocturnal setting.
See Paule **Lejeune,** 89–91 Also see **Kuhn** 166 (views Berto as "postmodern").

Diane Bertrand
Un Samedi sur terre (1996; 95 mins.) Shown at Cannes film festival [Un Certain Regard] An orphan searches for her brother. Stars Elsa Zylberstein.

Raphaële Billetdoux b. Paris 1951. Began as a film editor and novel-ist—*Jeune Fille en silence* (1971); *L'Ouverture des bras de l'homme* (1978); *Prends garde à la douceur des choses* (1971). (This last was made into a film by Moshe Mishari.) She then wrote the *scénario* and directed

La Femme-enfant (1979–80).

After making this film she returned to writing: *Mes nuits sont plus belles que vos jours* (1985; Prix Renaudot).
See Paule **Lejeune** 92.

Catherine Binet b. in Tours, 1944. Chiefly an editor.
Le Printemps (1971) Codirected with Marcel Hanoun
Film sur Hans Bellmer (1972). Short about this German artist, admired by the surrealists.
Les Jeux de la Comtesse Dolingen de Gratz (1981)
See Paule **Lejeune**, *Cinéma des femmes*, 93.

Alice [Guy-]Blaché b. 1873; d. 1968. The first woman director in history, Guy-Blaché made three hundred films under name of Alice Guy (as director-producer) before coming to the United States (ca. 1912). In the beginning Gaumont's secretary, she was one of the inventors of the Gaumont style, filming on location; and she is also known as the pioneer of the first fiction film with her *La Fée aux choux*, dating from 1896, and predating Méliès's work [on fairies: see video, Pionniers du Cinéma Français, vol. 1)] by some months (*France-Amérique* [15–21 October 1994]: 11). She later (1906–7) directed some of the earliest *sound films* using Gaumont's "Chromophone," which recorded sounds while the camera recorded images. In 1906 Guy married the English cameraman Herbert Blaché, whom she met through her work with Gaumont; she had two American-born children, Reginald and Simone. The marriage ended in divorce. She returned to France in 1922, where she could not find employment, and she, therefore, never made another film. She was awarded the Legion of Honor medal in 1953 for lifetime achievements. When her daughter, Simone, retired from diplomatic service in 1964, Alice accompanied her to the United States, where she lived in Mahwah, New Jersey until her death, four years later at the age of ninety-five. A few of her early films have been found by the American Film Institute.

An abbreviated history of early French cinema, including references to Alice Guy is to be found in *Journal Français d'Amérique* 17 no. 3 (20 January–2 February 1995): 1; 10–11. Note: Dates in Sadoul differ considerably from mine, taken from other sources, including Katz.

See also Sharon Smith: 28; and see especially **Foster**, *Women Film Directors*: 160–66 under Guy; filmography; bibliography.
See **Marquise Lepage (Québec)**. See *Qui est Alice Guy?* 14 min. documentary video directed by Nicole-Lise Bernheim (Paris)—distributed by Vidéo Femmes (listed under Film Sources).

Some titles of Guy's early French films [See **Katz** and **Foster** for additional listings]:
La Fée aux choux (1896; ca. one minute) is the fictional story of

a fairy who made children in a cabbage patch. It is based on the French mythical tale about where children come from. (In the film, a young couple comes across the fairy in a cabbage patch; she wants to present them with a child.)

Les Dangers de l'alcoolisme (1899)
Hussards et Grisettes (1899)
Au Bal de Flore (1900) (Foster gives 1896)
La Danse des saisons (1900)
Sage-femme de première classe (1902)
Le Voleur sacrilège (1903)
La Première Cigarette (1904)
Paris la nuit (1904)
Le Crime de la rue du Temple (1904)
Une Noce au lac Saint-Fargeau (1905)
Triste Fin d'un vieux savant (1905)
Les Petits Voleurs du Bois-Vert *(The Little Thieves of Bois-Vert)* (1904) [alt. *Les Petits Coupeurs* . . .]
La Momie (The Mummy)
Le Courrier de Lyon (The Lyons Courier) (1904)
Le Cake-Walk de la pendule (The Clock's Cakewalk)
Le Gourmand effrayé (The Scared Glutton)
Déménagement à la cloche de bois (Moving Out in the Night)

[longer films from her Gaumont studio]
L'Esmeralda (1905)—based on Victor Hugo's *Notre-Dame de Paris*
Fanfan la tulipe (1907)
Faust et Méphisto
Vendetta
L'Enfant de la barricade
Passion du Christ [aka *La Vie du Christ*] (1906; Foster gives 1905) This work is said to have required twenty-five sets and three hundred extras. Sets designed by Henry Menessier. (Often wrongly attributed to Victorin Jasset, who was hired by Blaché to put the huge cast together!!) Made to compete with the Pathé film, *La Vie du Christ*.

American films, some of which are [again consult Katz and Foster]:
Pierrot's Christmas
A Child's Sacrifice (1910) Starred Magda Foy. First production of Solax, a company Guy founded and presided over.
A Daughter of the Navajo (1911)

The Girl and the Bronco Busters (1911)
Rose of the Frontier (1911)
Rose of the Circus (1911)
The Sewer (production only; 1911)
In the Year 2000 (1912) Science fiction film in which women rule the world.
The Shooting of Dan McGrew
Falling Leaves (1912)
Face at the Window (1912)
The Pit and the Pendulum (based on Poe) (1913)
The Tigress (1913)
The Beasts of the Jungle (producer and *scénario* 1913)
The Monster and the Girl (1914)
The Million Dollar Robbery (1914)
Shadows of the Moulin Rouge (1914)
The Vampire (1915)
The Heart of a Painted Woman (1915)
The Making of an American Citizen (1916)
A Man and the Woman (1917)
Spring of the Year (1917) Shot in the Florida Everglades.
The Great Adventure (1918)
Tarnished Reputation(s) (1920)
A Soul Adrift (1920) (Foster gives 1918)
See Marquise Lepage below (Québec). Also refer to the video *Pioneers of the French Film.*

I have a video of her work made especially for me from her films by Glenn Video Vistas (Reseda , California). (No French, however.) It includes complete versions of *Canned Harmony; Burstup Homes' Murder Case; Officer Henderson; His Double; A House Divided* [1913]; *The Girl in the Arm-Chair.*

A quick view of Blaché's work is readily available on the video *Women Who Made Movies* (directed and written by Gwendolyn Foster-Dixon). Here you will see generous segments from *Little Tich and His Big Boots* (1904; attributed to Guy-Blaché; an early *French* film); *Canned Harmony* (1912); *A House Divided* (1913); *The Girl in the Arm Chair* (1913); *His Double* (1913); *Officer Henderson* (1913; officer puts on drag to catch a criminal and gets in trouble); *Tarnished Reputation* (1920).

[*La Vie du Christ:* see Video Yesteryear, 776, anonymous "The Life of Our Savior": Is this Blaché's work?]

Claudine Bories b. Paris, 1942. An actress in provincial theater and theater of Aubervilliers for many years, she began to make films at the onset of the feminist movement.

Femmes d'Aubervilliers (1975) Interviews made on 1/2-inch video.
Théâtre (1977) *Mise en forme* of the play *Coriolan*.
Juliette du côté des hommes (1981; 52 mins.) Men speak here of their experiences.
Lointains Boxeurs (1982) Short. Again it is men who speak.
Portrait imaginaire de Gabriel Bories (1983) Interlaces world history with the story of her own father.
Lejeune reports more recent work on a documentary about the life of the writer Bernard Noël.
See **Lejeune** 94–95

Catherine Breillat
Une Vraie Jeune Fille (1977)
Tapage nocturne (1979)
36 Fillette (1988; 86 mins.) Insightful drama about sexual politics and male hypocrisy revolving around a fourteen-year-old girl who falls in love with an older man. Stars Delphine Zentout, Etienne Chicot.
Available from Critics Choice for sale.
Sale comme un ange (1990)
Parfait amour (1996)

Jane **Bruno-Ruby** Primarily a novelist.
La Cabane d'amour (1927)

Joyce Buñuel b. in New York, 1944. She is, for the curious, the daughter-in-law of the famous director. She has written a number of *scénarios* for American films. She has directed
Jument Vapeur (Dirty Dishes) (1982; 99 mins.) "In this zany movie about the plight of the average housewife, things progress from crazed boredom to screaming hysteria. . . . **Carole Laure** lives in marital bliss with her husband, **Pierre Santini,** and their two sons. Well, almost bliss—after ten years of cooking, cleaning, and mending, life is dull. . . . This woman can't even get excited about an affair, or being a public heroine. An explosive encounter with a lecherous neighbor and a screaming fight with her husband bring it all to a head. And Carole finally learns just how to handle Dirty Dishes! Complete with unruly appliances, smart-aleck kids and a harassed husband, this hilarious look at the domestic scene is brilliantly real. It makes us wonder: Did my mother ever feel like this?" (from video jacket)
Juste la Seine à traverser (1980) Made for TV
Aéroport: Issue de secours (1983) Made for TV
La Dame des dunes (1984) Made for TV

Nicole de Buron
Vas-y Maman (1978–80)

Solange Bussi (Solange Térac) b. Paris, 1907. She collaborated with G. W. Pabst, Béla Balázs and Bertolt Brecht.

La Vagabonde (1931) Adaptation of story by Colette
Mon Amant l'assassin (1932)
Koenigsmark (adaptation; 1952)

Judith Cahen

La Croisade d'Anne Buridan (1994–5; 95 mins.)

Caro Canaille Mentioned in Kuhn's *Women's Companion* . . . , 165.

Annette Carducci b. Germany, 1947, she came to Paris when twenty. Has worked mostly on the production side of film, but wrote the *scénario* for and directed

Un Homme à ma taille (1982)
See Paule **Lejeune,** *Cinéma des femmes,* 100

Renée Carl

Un Cri dans l'abîme (1922) This, her only film, depicted some of the less desirable things about country life.

(Mentioned only in passing by **Foster** *Women Film Directors,* 26.)

Christine Carrière

Rosine (1995) A terrible family scene erupts when the mother, in hopes of marrying a former lover, tries on her wedding gown. Themes of incest in this film as well.

Camille de Casabianca b. Paris 1957. Daughter of the director Alain Cavalier and the film editor Denise de Casabianca. Studied at University of California in Berkeley. Then helped her father in writing of *Un Etrange Voyage,* in which she also acted, and in the writing of *Thérèse.*

Pékin Central (1986) Story of a girl who is in love with a married man, but filmed in Peking; partially cinéma vérité.
See Paule **Lejeune** 101.

Gisèle Cavalli b. Moselle, 1955.

Il n'y a aucune raison pour que je tremble ainsi (1983)
See **Lejeune** 102.

Denise Charevein Directed animated films in the 1960s.

[Claire Childeric?? directed *Automne 90* (1991)—listed under rubric Alekan-Cochet: ref. article: G. Colport, "Short Length," *Presence* 36–37 (January–February 1992): 58–59 (stills).]

Caroline Choumien

Les Lendemains qui chantent (1996)

Marie Chouraqui

Gaspard et Robinson (1991; 94 mins.) A homeless lady tests the bonds of two friends. Stars G. Darmon and Suzanne Flon.

Claire Clouzot b. Paris, 1933. Cousin to Henri-Georges Clouzot. Closely allied with other women directors: Varda, Akerman, and so on.

L'Homme fragile (1981) First shown at the Women's Film Festival at Sceaux. it was rejected, because the central figure was a man, and at that one shown to be fragile.
See **Lejeune** 103–4

Marie Colson-Malleville A friend and collaborator of Germaine Dulac. She directed the following films on her own:
Escale à Oran (shot in Algeria)
El Oued, la ville aux mille coupoles (Shot in Algeria)
Baba Ali (Shot in Algeria)
Du Manuel au Robot. On the industrialization of Algeria.
Solidarité
Les Doigts de lumière
La Route éternelle
Des Rails sous les palmiers
Les Tapisseries de l'Apocalypse
Pierre de Lune
Delacroix, peintre de l'Islam
Croyances
Une Simple Histoire d'amour

[**Christine Comencini:** *Les Amusements de la vie privée* (1992; 90 mins.). Version Française catalog cites this film as a "French Drama" about love and freedom during the French Revolution.) I have found no reference to Comencini elsewhere.]

Nina Companeez b. in Paris, 1937. Writes for TV.
Faustine, ou [et] le bel été (1972)
Colinot Trousse-chemise (1973)
Comme sur des roulettes (1976)
Un Ours pas comme les autres (1977)
Les Dames de la côte (1979)
Le Chef de famille (1981)
Deux amies d'enfance (1983) More or less the story of her parents, both Jewish; they had to move from city to city to avoid deportation (**Lejeune** 105).

Catherine Corsini b. in Dreux in 1956.
Le Mésange (1982)
Ballades (1983)
Nuit de Chine (1986)
Poker (1986–87)

Les Amoureux (1994; 108 mins.). Locale: small city of Monthermé, near the Belgian border. Marc, a fifteen-year-old high school student, ties up with Viviane, his half-sister, who gets Marc to go traveling with her. However, she falls in love with a Polish worker named Tomek. Marc feels betrayed and extremely jealous and, moreover, cannot understand why an old pal should drop him for a girl. Corsini gives the impression she doesn't know how to end her film. (Janick **Beaulieu;** *Séquences* 174 [September–October 1994]: 24.)

Jeunesse sans Dieu (1996) A professor in a lycée (high school) is bothered by Nazi ideology but does not have the courage to confront it. Adapted from a novel by Odön von Horvath.

A toute vitesse (co-directed by Gaël Morel)

Renée **Cosima** An actress who produced some short films and directed the documentary *Sur la Route de Key West*.

Ghyslaine Côté Actress and director.
Aux voleurs!

Jeanne Crépeau
Cartes sur table ... (1994?? 30 mins.?) Video. Illustrates, sometimes with humor, the often difficult relationship between mother and daughter. The discourse is transmitted through a bridge lesson degenerating into a surrealistic "charabia." Two television sets present alternately the faces of the two protagonists. Faces sometimes change television sets. Subtitles are used to convey the lesson. An "autoportrait." Reviewed by Johanne **Larue** (*Séquences* 176 [January–February 1995]: 53.)

Dominique Crèvecoeur b. Paris, 1947. Founded (with other interested parties) Adria Films, a small production house devoted to the creation of shorts.

A cloche-pied (1963) A short made with a rented 8 mm camera.

Une Approche (1976) A twenty-minute short made in her apartment; two women engage in a dialogue about the difficulty of being oneself, as they are cornered by received ideas and new dogmatisms (coming from 1970s feminism) (Lejeune 109).

Une Voix (1980; 30 mins.) Theme: a person, engulfed in silence and incapacity to communicate, falls in love with a voice.

Contes clandestins (1985) Again the theme is the difficulty of communication between a man and a woman of very different milieus.
See **Lejeune** 109–10

Colette Darfeuil
J'ai perdu mes bretelles (ca. 1935)

Danielle Darrieux
Quartet (1948) (Available from Evergreen on video.)

Hélène Dassonville
Mentioned in Kuhn *Women's Comp.*, 165.

Josée Dayan and Malka (or Malke) Ribowska
Simone de Beauvoir (1982; 110 mins.) A portrait of this author through the cinematic lens. Available from Evergreen on video.

Régine Deforges b. Montmorillon, 1936. Primarily a writer (*Blanche et Lucie; La Bicyclette bleue*), she has delved into erotica, and in 1975 published an interview with Pauline Réage, pseudonym of the author of *Histoire d'O.*
Contes pervers (1980) Banned to under eighteen; looked at several women's destinies.
See **Lejeune** 111.

Nathalie Delon b. 1938. Began career as actress. Spent quite some time in the United States.
Ils appellent ça un accident (1982) A child dies when a surgeon makes a mistake. Then it's a coverup by the powers that be. Delon wrote, acted in, and directed this film.
Sweet Lies (1987) A detective lands in Paris in search of a crook but is distracted by three women. Made in English.
See **Lejeune** 112.

Paula (Paule) Delsol b. Montagnac (Hérault), 1923. Spent her child-hood in Indochina. Moved to Montpellier in 1946. Made several shorts early on (*Dany, L'Hérault ce méconnu*).
La Dérive (1964) About a loose girl. Banned to under eighteen year olds, for at the time this was not a subject for film, especially if the film was made by a woman. Lejeune: "remains a beautiful work for its grasp of daily life and the fluidity of the writing."
Ben et Bénédicte (1976) Ben, the heroine accepts everything from a man who mistreats her; he prefers her "double" Bénédicte. Shown at Cannes in 1976 to mixed reactions.
L'Homme comblé (1984) Made for TV. Concerns the problem of sterility; a woman asks her mate to have a child with her best friend.
Augusta (1986)
See **Lejeune** 113–14.

Claire Denis Spent part of her childhood in Cameroon; on return to France lived near an American military base. Draws on her own lived experience for her films. (Colonialism; postindependence; anti-Americanism.) See *Journal Français d'Amérique* (4–11 August 1995): 10. Also see Pascaline **Dussurget**, "Claire Denis, entre noir et blanc,"

France-Amérique (5–11 August 1995): 12–13 (interview, primarily concerned with *J'ai pas sommeil*).

Chocolat (1988; 105 mins.) Set in Preindependence (colonial) Cameroon. Semiautobiographical; an engaging tale of a small white girl growing up in an isolated region of Cameroon, where her father, a French official, neglects her beautiful mother. The outcome is memorable. Foster: New Wave approach to the Bildungsroman, and a study of white guilt, racism, and oppression of women. Stars Giúlia Boschi, Issach de Bankolé, François Cluzet, and Cécile Ducasse.

S'en fout la mort. ([*No Fear No Die*] 1990; 97 mins.) Two Caribbeans are engaged in the illicit business of cockfighting in France. (S'enfout-la-mort is the name of one of the cocks.) Continues her examination of racism and colonialism. Stars Alex Descas; Isaach de Bankolé. Available Version Française subtitled.

J'ai pas sommeil ([*I Can't Sleep*] 1993) Shown at Cannes festival 1994?) Based on a true story very prominently covered by the French media (1987), this film concerns serial rape and murder of old women occurring in the XVIIIe arrondissement of Paris; it invites reflection on present-day society. Stars Richard Courcet as Camille and Katerina Golubeva as Daïga, with Isaach de Bankolé, Line Renaud and Alex Descas. Jean **Decock** (*French Review,*) March, 1994]: 763) finds this the best woman's film of the festival, having a "strange banalization of marginality and murder . . . A young black homosexual transvestite by trade also murders lonely little old women in Montmartre. His Martiniquaise mother does not understand. Nor do we."

[Denis maintains the above three constitute a trilogy: colonization; immigration; "integration."]

U.S. Go Home (1995) Made (to order) for TV. Set in the 60s, when the young French saw America as the *continent-phare,* but at the same time were completely anti-American (in part because of the Vietnam War).

[Denis is presently working on a film in Marseille (*Nénette et Boni*) with Jean-Pol Fargeau. It concerns trucks that sell pizzas.]
See **Foster** 108–10.

Lucy Derain
  Harmonies de Paris (1927)
  Désordre (1927?)

Claire Devers b. Paris, 1955.
  From 1982–84: *Pas à pas; Haut le coeur; Carré dégradé*
  A la mémoire d'un ange (1988)
  Chimère (1988)
  Zanzibar (1989)

Noir et blanc (1989; 89 mins.) (Lejeune gives 1985) Free adaptation of a short story by Tennessee Williams ("Desire and the Black Masseur," written in 1946, first published in 1948; found in the collection *One Arm,* New York: New Directions, 1967). The sadomasochistic homosexual relationship between a white and black male. Sordid. Can be rented from Facets; but is it worthwhile? (It is, however, highly praised in Sadoul; it took many prizes: Belfort, Grenoble, Cannes.)

Max et Jérémie (1992; 159 min) A story about the relationship between two gangsters, but also encompasses the problems of aging, the anguish of lovelessness, and the appearance of love in unexpected places. Producer: Alain Sarde, Les Films Alain Sarde. Stars Philippe Noiret, Christophe Lambert, and Jean-Pierre Marielle.

Suzanne Devoyod
L'Ami Fritz (1918; with René Hervil)

Germaine Dieterlen Ethnocinematographer and anthropologist. Close associate of and codirector with Jean Rouch of many films of the Dogon, especially the seven films concerned with the Sigui ceremonies. Compare Safi Faye. See accounts and sources in **Stoller.**

Sigui 66: Année zéro (1966; fifteen minutes) Collaborator
Sigui no. 2: Les Danseurs de Tyougou (1968; 50 mins.) Collaborator
Sigui no. 3: La Caverne de Bongo (1969; 40 mins. Collaborator
Sigui no. 4: Les Clameurs d'Amani (19790; 50 mins.) Collaborator
Sigui no. 5: La Dune d'Idyeli (1971; 40 or 50? mins.) Collaborator
Sigui no. 6 Les Pagnes de Yamé (1972; 40 or 50? mins.) Collaborator
Funerailles à Bongo: Le Vieil Anai (1972; released in 1979; 75 or 45? mins.) Codirector
Sigui no. 7: L'Auvent de la circoncision (1974; 15 mins.) Collaborator

Arielle Dombasle b. 1955. Of French parents, spent most of her childhood in the United States and in Mexico, but moved to Paris in 1974, when she was eighteen. She claims she thinks more like a South American (e.g., Borges) than like a French person (e.g., Balzac). She is an actress, as well as a director.

Chassé-croisé (1982)

La Novice (1987) Filmed in Mexico. Dombasle stars in this film that she also wrote and directed. Omar Sharif has a principal role. See **Lejeune** 116.

Liliane Dreyfus First began as an actress under the name Liliane David (small roles with Chabrol, Godard). Then married a businessman, Michel Dreyfus, and for a number of years left cinema.

August 16 (?)
Femmes au soleil (1974) Chronicle of 15 August in Provence. Re-volves around three couples, their children and their servants. The women, who appear to have everything, are consumed with boredom and dissatisfaction.
Schmattes
See also **Lejeune** 117.

Denise Dual
Mentioned in Kuhn, *Women's Comp.* 165.

Charlotte Dubreuil b. Paris, 1940.
Qu'est-ce que tu veux, Julie? (1976)
La Peine perdue (1977)
Ma Chérie (1978–80)
La Côte d'amour (1982)
Une Chance sur mille (1983)
A 50 ans elle découvre la mer (1987)
Mirage dangereux (1985)
Elles ne pensent qu'à ça (1994; 90 mins.) Elie **Castiel** [*Séquences* (April–May, 1994): 52] writes: "The family in this story wants to be a hymn to love but resembles a pyramid gathering up a strange fauna of characters directly tied to the mother as their point of origin. All are seeking love, the men in pleasure, the women in desire. All that is very well, but the director does not succeed in plumbing the hearts and souls of her protagonists, so preoccupied does she seem with affairs of the flesh, not in an illustrative fashion, but awkwardly suggested. If it weren't for the presence of Claudia Cardinale, always vibrant . . . , this film would risk falling quickly into oblivion."
Stars Claudia Cardinale, Carole Laure, Bernard LeCoq, Roland Blanche, and Heinz Bennent.
See **Lejeune** 118–19.

Danièle Dubroux b. Paris, 1947
L'Olivier (1973–76)
Les Deux Elèves préférés du Professeur Francine Brouda (1979) Short
Le Colosse et la fourmi (1982)
Les Filles héréditaires (1982)
Les Amants terribles (1984–85)
La Petite Allumeuse (1986–87)
Border Line (1992?; 90 mins.) A study of an unusual sort of mother-love that borders on the pathological. Dubroux looks up an old lover and finds he has died and left a grown son; the two are

drawn to each other in a passionate relationship that taps the woman's erotic and maternal instincts. Written by Danièle Dubroux; produced by Gemini Films/Paolo Branco. Stars Danièle Dubroux, David Léotard, and André Dussollier.

Le Journal d'un séducteur (1996)
See **Lejeune** 120–22.

Martine Dugowson

A bout de nerf (1981)
Les Cactus (1982)
Circuit fermé (1983)
En faisant le ménage, j'ai retrouvé Albert (1986)
Mina Tannenbaum (1994) This film stars Romane Boringer as Mina, and Elsa Zylberstein (also spelled Sylberstein) as Ethel Bénégui. They are friends, which does not eliminate a fundamental rivalry between the two. The film, constructed on a flashback, begins with Mina already dead. At first, Mina is on top as a talented painter; then Elsa loses weight and transforms her appearance, so she eclipses Mina in professional and amorous successes. In the end Elsa even steals the man with whom Mina was secretly in love.

See articles ("Elsa Sylberstein ..." and "Une amitié au féminin") by Anne **Sénéchal** in *France-Amérique* [4–10 March 1995]: 19.) "A first film which allows itself a few awkward passages and some clichés, but grants the actresses the true joy of acting."

Portraits chinois (1996) with Helena Bonham Carter and Romane Bohringer.

Germaine Dulac b. Charlotte Elizabeth Germaine Saisset Schneider

in 1882; d. 1942. Founded the film company Delia Film with her husband, Albert Dulac (divorced 1920) and writer Irène Hillel-Erlanger. Radical or avant-garde filmmaker, who had as friends such famous people as Abel Gance, Jean Epstein, Louis Delluc, and so on. During her career, she became increasingly interested in the relationship of film images and music (*Disque 927; Thème et variations*). When sound came to film (1927), people lost interest, at least temporarily, in the subtleties of purely visual imagery. Susan Smith (112): "From 1930–40 Dulac returned once more to commercial work, as head of newsreel operations, first for Pathé, then for Gaumont. Her career came to an end early in WWII, and in 1942 she died." Her goal was "pure cinema" (Katz).

Les Soeurs ennemies (1915; first film)
La Vraie Richesse ou Géo le mystérieux (1916)
Les Soeurs ennemies (1916)
Vénus Victrix, ou Dans l'ouragan de la vie (1917)

Martine Dugowson. *Mina Tannenbaum*. Courtesy Belgian Embassy.

Ames de fous (1918) (During shooting of this serial film, Germaine Dulac met Louis Delluc, with whom she subsequently collaborated for a long time.)

Le Bonheur des autres (1918)

La Fête espagnole (1919)

La Cigarette (1919)

Malencontre (1920)

Gossette (1920; six episodes) (Katz gives 1923; Foster, 1922–23) Heroine is kidnapped and drugged. Like most of Dulac's films, story is told from female point of view.

La Belle Dame sans merci (1921)

La Mort du soleil (1922)

Werther (unfinished) (1922)

Le Diable dans la ville (1924) (Treats medieval fanaticism.)

La Folie des vaillants (1925)

Ame d'artiste (1925)

Antoinette Sabrier (1927) (Katz gives 1926)

La Souriante Madame Beudet (1922–28?) (Katz gives 1923) "Dulac's masterpiece" (**Katz**). A woman who is domineered by her husband fantasizes and dreams of revenge over him. Readily available on video, together with: *La Coquille et le clergyman* (1927), a silent film of surrealist nature. *Scénario* by Antonin Artaud who denounced Dulac for having "feminized" his script. Male sexual fantasies of a frustrated clergyman who stalks a white-robed woman. **Sinyard** writes: "Surrealism at its most impenetrable was illustrated by Germaine Dulac's *The Seashell and the Clergyman* . . . , a film so obscure that it was refused a certificate by the British Board of Film Censors for that reason alone. 'The film is so cryptic as to be almost meaningless,' said the censor. 'If there is a meaning it is doubtless objectionable'" (168). Feminine and masculine desire are juxtaposed here.

Le Cinéma au service de l'histoire (1927) Compilation film.

L'Invitation au voyage (1927) (Based on Baudelaire's poem)

Disque(s) 927 (1928) (Katz & Foster give 1929) (Inspired by music of Chopin)

Thème et variations (1928) (Katz gives 1929) (Inspired by classical music. Dulac was seeking to achieve what she called "cinéma pur," on an analogy with "poésie pure.")

Germination d'un haricot (documentary; 1928)

La Princesse Mandane (1929)

Etude cinégraphique sur une Arabesque (1929)

See **Flitterman-Lewis**, *To Desire Differently: Feminism and the French Cinema* for three chapters on Dulac, especially concerned with *La Souriante Madame Beudet* and *La Coquille et le Clergyman*.

("For all their differences, [these two films] provide significant contri-butions to the development of a forceful new theory of sexual differ-ence in cinematic representation" [137].)
Also see **Foster** (115–18) who insists on Dulac's lesbianism; and **Lej-eune** 35–39.

Marguerite (Donnadieu) Duras b. 1914 in Indochina; d. France 1996. A novelist and screenwriter, she directed a number of films, many of which are based on her own writings.
[*Hiroshima mon amour* (*scénario* only; directed by Alain Resnais, 1960)]
La Musica (1966) (Collaborated on direction of this first film with Paul Seban)
Détruire dit-elle (1969) (Adaptation of her own novel)
Jaune le soleil (1971)
Nathalie Granger (1972)
La Femme du Ganges (1973) Set in a metaphorical India.
India Song (1973; 120 mins.) (Katz gives 1975) "Histoire d'amour que des voix sans visages essaient de reconstiuter" **(Duras).** Follow-up to *La Femme du Ganges*.
Concert pianist and the pampered wife of the French ambassador to Calcutta, Anne-Marie Stretter represents the "sovereignty of Woman's body." She is the only person in the film who pronounces the word 'intelligence.'" She has a knowledge of India and of oppression" (Porter 107–8). She has numerous affairs, which her husband chooses to ignore. The Vice-Consul and she both incorporate types of mad-ness. Other themes of film include erosion caused by passage of time, and the challenge of photographing death.
"This 'Last Year in Calcutta' evolves like a repetitious and poetic dream, the characters going through a strange, stylized ritual. Yet the physical distress of the beggar woman crying in the jungle and Anne-Marie's mental distress are palpable" (Bergan, 277).
Written and directed by Marguerite Duras; photography by Bruno Nuytten; edited by Carlos D'Alessio. Cast: Delphine Seyrig, Mathieu Carrière, Michel Lonsdale, Vernon Dobtcheff, and Claude Mann. Set in India of the 1930s but filmed in a house in Paris. See **Sadoul,** *Dictionnaire des films,* 158.
Des Journées entières dans les arbres (1976)
Son nom de Venise dans Calcutta désert (1976) New version of *India Song;* same sound track in a different setting.
Le Camion (1977) Studies multivalence of identity (Foster 118).
Baxter, Vera Baxter (1977) Story of a woman on the verge of suicide.

Aurélia Steiner (four-shorts omnibus; 1979)
Le Navire Night (1979)
Agatha et les lectures limitées (1981) *"limitées"* or see MOMA below: *"illimitées."*
L'Homme Atlantique (1981)
Dialogue de Rome (documentary; made in Italy; available in Italian [*Il Dialogo di Roma*]; 1981)
Les Enfants (1987) (Sadoul gives 1985)

A study of Duras's films might include *Hiroshima mon amour* (1959; Alain Resnais); *Un Barrage contre le Pacifique* (1958, René Clément; with Silvana Mangano); *Moderato Cantabile* (1960; Peter Brook); *Une aussi longue absence* (1961; Henri Colpi); *Le Marin de Gibraltar* (1967; Tony Richardson) *L'Amant* or *The Lover* (1992, Jean-Jacques Annaud; 103 mins.; with Jane March and Tony Leung);—films by other directors but based on Duras's writings.

An important festival, The Films of Marguerite Duras, showed at The Museum of Modern Art in May 1995. It included *The South Bank Show* (1984; with Marguerite Duras); *Les Enfants* (1984, with André Dussolier and Pierre Arditi); *Hiroshima mon amour* (1959; directed by Alain Resnais; with Emmanuelle Riva and Eiji Okada); *Le Camion* (1977; with Marguerite Duras and Gérard Depardieu); [*Apostrophes* (1984)]; *La Couleur des mots* (1984); *India Song* (1974, with Delphine Seyrig, Michel Lonsdale); *Agatha ou les lectures illimitées* (1981; 1hr. 30 mins.; with Bulle Ogier and Yann Andréa); *L'Homme atlantique* (1981; with Yann Andréa); *Le Navire Night* (1979; with Bulle Ogier and Dominique Sanda). Also *Césarée; Aurélia Steiner; Nathalie Granger* (with Jeanne Moreau); *Moderato Cantabile* (directed by Peter Brook, with Jeanne Moreau; Jean-Paul Belmondo). Cycle complemented by showing in New York of *La Mort du jeune aviateur anglais; Ecrite; Apostrophes* (in which Bernard Pivot speaks exclusively to MD; 1984). These are ways to come to know MD herself and her experiences as author and cinematographer. The show traveled from MOMA to Toronto; UCLA (July); Chicago at Facets (September). In conjunction with this show (*Fifteen Films and Documentaries;* "first time sub-titled") see article by Stéphane **Grand-Chavin,** "Le MOMA amoureux de Duras . . . ," *France-Amérique* (6–12 May, 1995): 13. Author stresses clarity of language, content, and form, making these films very accessible, with light dialogues, often presented in a slow rhythm. Contends that characters of MD are often narcissistic lovers, seeking happiness and marked by great loneliness; they are prey to resignation and cruelty. Emotion and messages are "universal." Finds that recurrent themes include glass of wine; piano sonata; rose; sea; crime of passion. *Récit* and narration have unconventional techniques (taken from the New Novel). Claims some people find they must leave the room (as was the case with *Nathalie Granger* when shown on 30 April).

Foster, *Women Film Directors* (118–20), sees Duras as a modernist filmmaker who explores silences and speech of women, subverts patri-archal language. Finds that many of her films address racism, colonial-ism, and imperialism. **Kaplan** (96) finds in Duras's films the portryal of the separation of female inner and male outer worlds. Also see **Lejeune** 123–26. One may find a great deal of information regarding Duras, including film synopses and credits, on the Internet.

Christine Ehm

Vue d'en face (1982) A girl waits for another girl while writing an essay on waiting.

Simone (1984) A young girl meets a woman of forty—perhaps a love story, but nothing physical occurs. Shown on French TV, but in 1985 in the middle of the summer at 11 P.M.

See **Lejeune** 127.

Claudine Eizykmann Often collaborates with Guy Fihman for holo-graphic work. Both have doctorates in philosophy.

L'Autre Scène (1969–72)

Maine-Montparnasse (1972)

Tours de Tours (1972)

V.W.-Vitesses Women (Jury Prize 1974 Belgian Festival, for France) Evocation of women in various places.

Bruine Squamma (1972–77) On perspective and movement

Moires Mémoires (1972–78)

Operneia (1976–80)

Lapse (1976–80)

Vols d'oiseaux (1982) Movement of gulls on a holographic plaque; birds appear to be in relief.

Un Nu (1985) Five-minute holofilm

See also **Lejeune** 128.

Monique Enckell b. in Neuilly, 1946. Has lived in Algeria and Fin-land. Has written *scénarios* (*Heureux comme des rois; Viva il cinema!*) and directed

Aller-retour (1978)

Si j'avais 1000 ans (1982) All Saints Eve in Brittany. Based on a Breton legend: Every year on this eve the island shakes, as it has for a thousand years, ever since Breton fishermen refused to rescue a young queen, condemned to die by fire and water.

Maria (or Marie) Epstein and Jean Benoit-Lévy

[Marie Epstein was Jean Epstein's sister and wrote scripts for him.]

Ames d'enfants (1928)
Peau de pêche (1928)
Maternité (1929)
Jimmy le bruiteur (1920)
Le Coeur de Paris (1931)
La Maternelle (aka *Children of Montmartre*) (1933 black and white; 83 mins.) Children of Parisian slums who find refuge at "La Maternelle." Centered on the story of Marie, the illegitimate daughter of a prostitute. Placed, by vote, in top ten films of 1933 by major film critics. For more information, see James Reid **Paris** 240–41. (Claims the film is realistic, psychologically valid, and unsentimental. Though a talkie, uses many silent film techniques.) Two other versions of this story have been made into film.

Cast: Marie—Paulette Elambert; Rose—Madeleine Renaud; Marie's Mother—Sylvette Fillacier; Superintendent—Alice Tissot; Madame Paulin—Mady Berry

Available on video (1992; Water Bearer Films 8025), hosted by Richard Peña.

See **Flitterman-Lewis,** *To Desire Differently: Feminism and the French Cinema* for three chapters on Epstein. "Over and above a new content that reworks patriarchal definitions of motherhood, the film resituates the viewer as producer of the fantasm not in terms of Oedipal desire but of female longing—both child for mother and mother for child—instead" (211).

Itto (1934) Filmed in Morocco with Jean Benôit-Lévy.

Altitude 3200 (1934–37) (Foster gives 1938)

Hélène (1934–37) (Foster gives 1936) Based on the novel of Vicky Baum and starring Madeleine Renaud.

La Mort du cygne (1937) A dancer-star played by Yvette Chauviré.

Altitude 3200 (many dates are given; Lejeune gives 1938)

Feu de paille (1939)

Les Ballets de France (1949–50) Documentary with Jean Benôit-Lévy.

La Grande Espérance (1953 w/ Léonide Azar). This is a documentary on atomic energy.

See **Foster** esp. 124–26. **Kuhn**'s *Women's Companion* (136–37) provides additional information on Epstein's life and career. Also see **Lejeune** 51–53.

Philomène Esposito

Mima (1991) Stars Virginie Ledoyen, a twelve-year-old girl who experiences the tragedy of her Cabrian immigrant grandfather's murder during a 1966 Christmas season. Extremely moving with background music during the funeral provided by the chorus of the Confrérie de la Santa Croce in Castelsardo, Sardinia, singing "La Misère de la Semainte Sainte." *Scénario* by Esposito. "With the help of the Languedoc-Roussillon region."

Toxic Affair (1992; 88 mins.) A difficult woman must try to cope when her lover leaves her. Stars Isabelle Adjani and H. Giradot. (Version Française catalog.)

Andrée Feix b. 1912, was involved in early sound films. Worked as editor for Gaumont from 1929.

Before returning to editing, she also directed:

Il suffit d'une fois (1946) *Scénario* by another director (Solange Bussi-Térac).

Capitaine Blomet (1947) Based on the play of Emile Bergerat.

See Paule **Lejeune** 63.

Pascale Ferran

Petits arrangements avec les morts (1994) First feature-length film by this director. A film at once grave and serene. Characters are bonded to one another either by familial ties or by those of place, a small swimming resort on the Breton coast. Explores how time and life do not heal the wound that came in childhood from separation caused by the death of a loved one.

Discussed by Jean **Vallier** in *France-Amérique* (8–14 April 1995): 12. He has a very good opinion of this film, which was shown at Cannes in 1994 and much noticed; it received the Golden Camera there. (This prize is for new talents.) It was also shown in 1995 at the Museum of Modern Art in New York.

Arrangement of space and time (as well as of the dead) are ludic, and in the manner of the Nouveau Roman (**Decock**, *French Review* [March 1994]: 764).

Triptych of three different points of view showing attitudes toward death. "C'est du grand art," says Janick **Beaulieu** in *Séquences* 174 (September–October 1994): 24.

L'Age des possibles (1995; 90 mins.) Made with ten student actors from the Ecole du Théâtre National in Strasbourg.

Joy Fleury

La Fête des pères (1990; 88 mins.) Two men look for a woman who will have their baby. Stars Alain Souchon and Thierry Lhermitte. (Version Française catalog.)

Tristesse et Beauté (?; 96 mins.) A man tries to relive the past by finding an ex-lover. Stars C. Rampling and b. Agenin. (Version Française catalog.)

Catherine Fol Scientist and prolific video artist; in twenty-six weeks she made twenty-three 4-minute videos on the explosive American earth, on gold seekers in Ecuador, on children in Bogota, and so on.

Tant qu'il y aura des jeunes (1993?) A positive, dynamic image of youth. Uses rap music.

See *Zoom sur elles*, 49.

Kathleen Fonmarty

Jalousie (1994; 89 mins.) A woman falls in love with a man who is a master in the art of seduction.

Anne Fontaine b. in Lisbon, Portugal of French parents, and came to France when sixteen. David **Doty** writes: "Her films adeptly extract humor from everyday situations, and her characters are often outsiders, complex dreamers whom we all recognize from the 'real people' all around us. She cites as her two biggest influences Buster Keaton and Jacques Tati." In that same place Fontaine is cited speaking of film in general and hers in particular. "In *Augustin* I took inspiration from one of my favorite places in Paris. The Hôtel Montalembert is quite close to where I live, and I often go to its dining room for meetings with friends and colleagues. . . . The hotel made its way into *Augustin* by way of a Chinese woman who works there in housekeeping. . . . Very different from the seventh *arrondissement* is the neighborhood of Belleville, which again figures in *Augustin*. I used some of its streets as a backdrop, and some mistook it for Portugal . . ."

Les Histoires d'amour finissent toujours mal (Or: . . . *finissent mal en général*)(*Love Affairs Tend to End Badly*) (1992–93; 85 mins.) Zina, a *beurette* (f. of *beur;* slang for Arab; a Maghrébin[e], or person [or descendant of a person] from the Maghreb in North Africa) hesitates between Slim (a night taxi driver and a law student) and an actor, and then departs. Stars Sammi Bouajil and Alain Fromager. Film took the Jean Vigo prize; Fontaine was the first woman ever to obtain this prize.

Fortune Smiles

Augustin (1995; shown at Critics' Week at the 1995 Cannes Film Festival.) A hilarious short film (60 mins.) inspired by *Candid Camera,* made up of a series of sketches revolving around the tribulations of a naif man (Augustin Dos Santos). Among these sketches: an improvised interview at a casting agency; a day in a great Parisian hotel as a "faux garçon d'étage"; and so on. Offered a role as a hotel waiter, he chooses instead a role in a documentary on the vaccination of rabbits. Stripped style, at the limits of fiction. Played by Jean-Chrétien Sibertin-Blanc, brother of Anne Fontaine. With Stéphanie Zhang,

Guy Casabonne, Nora Habib, Thierry Lhermite, and Jacqueline Vimpierre.

Janet Maslin in the *New York Times* calls this "a fine comic show-case." See also Carlo **Mandolini.**

Yona Friedman Maker of animated films.
Les Aventures de Samba Gana
L'Origine des Kabouloukou (1962)

Sylvia Gallaud [I have seen this written Sylvia **Jallaud**] Codirected shorts with her husband, Pierre Gallaud. (See **Erens.)**
Des Maisons et des hommes (1953) Short
Donfere-Mondragon (1954)
Fleuve-Dieu (1955)
Spirales (1956)
L'Age des Caravelles (1958)
Journal d'un certain David (1958)
47, rue Vieille-du-Temple (1960) Short
Comme un reflet d'oiseau (1961) Short
Les Six Jours de la Création (1962)

Nicole Garcia Actress (*Mon Oncle d'Amérique, Outremer, Les Mots pour le dire,* etc.) and director of
Le Fils préféré (1995; 110 mins.) An unsatisfied man learns a secret that turns his life upside down. Stars G. Lanvin and b. Giraudeau. (Version Française catalog.)
Un Weekend sur deux (1990; 100 mins.) In the hopes of recapturing their love, a mother kidnaps her children. Stars N. Baye, J. Serreau, and F. Pasotti. (Available: Version Française catalog.)

Lucette Gaudard
Paris-Berlin (1935)
L'Industrie du verre
Les Hôtes de nos terres (Wild animals of France)
Souvenirs de Paris (with Claudine Lenoir)
C'est un vrai paradis (with Claudine Lenoir)

Laurence Gavron
Envy : A segment of *Seven Sins, Seven Women* concerning the seven deadly sins. (1987)
Women Make Movies 1996 catalog, 76.

Anne Gillain

Claude Godard b. Paris, 1957.
Temps morts (1980; 80 minutes) To make this film, Godard spent

a long while doing research at Ivry hospice, where two thousand old people are housed.

Myopathie (1981)

Victor (1986) Seen from the perspective of a very young baby.

See **Lejeune** 131

Michka Gorki b. Paris, 1941.

Rendez-vous romantiques (1972) Short

Interprétations (1974) Short. A young actress coming face-to-face with her life, with men, with elements that throw her off balance, can dream only of poetry and dying of madness.

Les Femmes et le cinéma (1977) Short. Interviews on video with certain women present at the Cannes festival: Paula Delsol, Marguerite Duras, and Chantal Akerman.

Chamrousse (1978) Short

Ella, une vraie famille (1979) Themes of the couple, the family, and the means of freeing oneself from them. Shown not in France but in Italy, where it was received enthusiastically, and in Canada, where it raised a scandal. (It caused an upheaval in Gorki's own life, awakening in her the desire to have a child.)

See **Lejeune** 133–34.

Christine Gouze

La Rumba (?; 95 mins.) Rivalry and passion before World War II. Stars Roger Hanin and Michel Piccoli. (Version Française catalog.)

Dolorès Grassian b. Istanbul, 1925, of Jewish parents (father Turkish; mother Spanish). The parents moved to Paris when she was fourteen years old. She and her family all suffered at the hands of the Nazis. She was interned at Drancy, where she met her first husband. But it was her second husband, Mario Ruspoli (a director of ethnographic films: *Les Inconnus de la terre; Regard sur la folie*), who brought her to cinema.

La Surface perdue (1966) Short

Le Cadeau (1957) Short

Que ferait donc Faber? (1969) TV miniseries in eight episodes. Critique of consumer society; credulity of people who will fall for any sales pitch.

Le Futur aux trousses (1975) Feature length. Again a satire of the public's cultural habits; of prognosticators. Filmed in the computer room of the Crédit Lyonnais and other sites of high technology.

Le Dernier Baiser (1977) A comedy that deals with love at the point of break up. Two women meet and find themselves in the same situation: The husband has left with a younger girl.

From Paule **Lejeune** 135

Agnès Guillemot b. Agnès Perché in 1931. Known chiefly as an accomplished editor, esp. of New Wave films. Editing includes
    Le Petit Soldat (1960)
    Une femme est une femme (1961)
    Les Carabiniers (1963)
    Le(s)? Mépris (1963)
    Alphaville (1965)
    La Chinoise (1967)
    Weekend (1968)
    Cousin, cousine (1975)
    La Lumière du lac(1988)
    Every Other Weekend (1991)
But see **Katz** for more complete list.

Madeleine Guillon Wife of Jacques Guillon, with whom she made *Monsieur Rameau* and *Images sur les musiques françaises,* both of which she directed and for both of which she did the camera work.
    Souvenirs de cinématographie

Claudine Guilmain b. Poitiers, 1944. Received an *agrégation* (advanced degree) in classical literature in 1968, but never cared to teach. Instead, she went into movie production. Has been assistant to Eric Rohmer. In Italy between 1971 and 1973. Since *La Femme intégrale* she has directed a few made-for-TV movies.
    Colombe (1969) Short based on a novella of Katharine Mansfield. (*The Doves' Nest* [?].)
    En mai dernier A feminist film [of average length] that has femininity as its subject.
    Agamemnon (1971–73); 1 hr. 40 min.) Based on Aeschylus.
    Fellini-Città (1971–73) Study of the work of Fellini at the time he was making *Amarcord.*
    Véronique ou l'été de mes 13 ans (1975) First long fiction film; Véronique discovers the fragile and unstable world of adults.
    La Femme intégrale (1979–80) The heroine, Elizabeth, refuses to be repressed by her husband, so she takes a few lovers; she becomes pregnant (her panacea). Banned to under eighteen year olds.
See **Lejeune** 137

Alice **Guy** See Blaché (above)

Marion **Hänsel** [Haensel] b. 1952 in Marseille, France. (Lejeune says 1949.) Actress and film director who trained as a mime artist in France, studied at the Lee Strasberg Actors' Studio in New York and then returned to Europe, finally settling in Belgium. Portrays a brutal world in stark images. Projects a certain fatalism. Violence, but no moralizing. Characterizations of her in *Une Encyclopédie des cinémas de Belgique* are not flattering: She is said to have an *académisme malhabile*, that is, to be too academic, and unskillful at it besides (32); to be riveted on literary adaptation and to have the so-called *syndrome de Plateau* (221). There is considerable information regarding Haensel on the Internet under Cannes Film Festival 1995, some of which is reproduced here for your convenience.

Equilibre (1977)
Sannu Bature (1979)
Gongola (1979)
Hydraulip II (1979)
Bakh (1979)

Le Lit (*The Bed*) (1982), based on a novel by Dominique Rolin, concerns a "wife's deathbed vigil for her husband and is a deeply felt study of the ties that have bound the couple together, using expressionist lighting and sparing mise-en-scène to create a compelling vision of a shared existence" (Foster, 167). [*Internet Movie Database*] [Oscars.] *Lit, Le* (1988) Belgium / France 1988 Color; Produced by Man's Films. Cast (in alphabetical order): Heinz Bennent . . . Martin; Francine Blistin . . . Caroline; Johan Leysen . . . Brun; Patrick Massieu . . . Tardif; Natasha Parry . . . Eva. Written by Dominique Rolin (novel). Produced by Jean-Marc Hench.

Dust (1984) Stars Trevor Howard and Jane Birkin. Based on the novel of J. M. Coetzee. A woman yearns for her father's love and in the end finally kills him to have him to herself. Social setting is South African Apartheid. [*Internet Movie Database*] *Dust* (1985) Belgium / France 1985 Color; Produced by: Daska Films / Flach Films / France 3 Cinema (FR 3) / Man's Films. Cast (in alphabetical order) Jane Birkin . . . Magda; Rene Diaz . . . Jacob; Trevor Howard . . . The father; John Matshikiza . . . Hendrick; Nadine Uwampa . . . Klein Anna; Tom Vrebus . . . Piet. Written by J. M. Coetzee (novel *In the Heart of the Country*) and Marion Haensel. Cinematography by Walther Van den Ende. Music by Martin T. Pierre. Production design by Pierre Louis Thevenet. Costume design by Yan Tax. Film editing by Susana Rossberg.

Les Noces barbares (*The Cruel Embrace*)(1984?; 1987) Based on a novel by Yann Queffelec. A mother is murderd by her son, after he has been brutally raped. [*Internet Movie Database*] [Famous marriages, and some that lasted] *Noces barbares, Les* (1987) Belgium / France 1987 Color. Produced by Flach Films / Man's Films / TF1 Films Production. Directed by Marion Haensel. Cast (in alphabetical order): Marianne Basler . . . Ludovic's Mother; Yves Cotton . . . Ludo, child; Claudine Delvaux . . . Mrs. Blanchard; Thierry Fremont . . .

Ludo, young boy; Andre Penvern . . . Micho. Written by Marion Haensel and Yann Queffelec (novel). Cinematography by Walther Van den Ende. Music by Frederic Devreese. Production design by Veronique Melery. Costume design by Yan Tax. Film editing by Susana Rossberg. Other crew: Henri Colpi (art collaboration).

Il Maestro (1989; 90 mins.) [*Internet Movie Database; Version Française catalogue*] *Maestro, Il* (1989) Belgium / France 1989; aka: *Maestro, The* (1989); *Musical May* (1989). Cast (in alphabetical order): Charles Aznavour . . . Romualdi; Andrea Ferreol . . . Dolores; Francis Le Maire; Malcolm McDowell . . . Walter Goldberg; Pietro Pizzuti . . . Father Abbott. Written by Marion Haensel and Mario Soldati (story). Cinematography by Acacio De Almeida. Music by Frederic Devreese. Film editing by Susana Rossberg. Upon returning to Italy, a maestro comes to realize he is still haunted by events of World War II.

Sur la terre comme au ciel (1993; 80 mins.) [*Internet Movie Database*] *Entre el cielo y la tierra* (1992) Belgium / France / Spain 1992 Color. Aka: *In Heaven as on Earth* (1992) *Sur la Terre Comme Au Ciel* (1992). Cast (in alphabetical order): Didier Bezace . . . Tom; Jean-Pierre Cassel . . . Editor; Andre Delvaux; Johan Leysen . . . Hans; Carmen Maura . . . Maria Garcia; Samuel Mussen . . . Jeremy; Serge-Henri Valcke . . . Peter. Written by Marion Haensel and Paul Le. Cinematography by Jose Maria Civit. Music by Takashi Kako. Production design by Thierry Leproust. Costume design by Yan Tax. Film editing by Susana Rossberg. Produced by Michelle Troncon. [Copyright 1990–96 The Internet Movie Database Ltd.] Available from Version Française catalog.—without subtitles. A pregnant woman's foetus speaks to her of its reluctance to be born.

Li (*Between the Devil and the Deep Blue Sea*) (1995) (Mosley). [*Internet: Cannes Film Festival 1995*]. Belgium / France / UK 1995 Color Produced by Man's Films / Mark Forstater Productions / Tchin Tchin Productions; Genre(s)/keyword(s): Drama / china / hong-kong / opium; Runtime: Belgium: 92. Also known as: *Li* (1995)
See **Foster**, esp. 167–68. See also in **Kuhn**, *Women's Companion* . . . 187–88; and **Lejeune** 138.

Madeleine Hartmann-Clausset After studying literature and philosophy, she took her first teaching position in Brazzaville (Africa). She then taught in several other places in Africa, and returning to France in 1967, she met a group of people who wanted to make a film. So she wrote a *scénario*,
Villa les dunes, which she shot in 1972 in 16 mm black and white.
Du Côté des tennis (1976) About the lives of provincial women.

As this film was not well attended—probably due to poor publicity—, she decided to open her own movie theater: L'Epée de bois (opened in 1978) in the quartier Mouffetard (Paris).

Je parle d'amour (1979) About relations between man and woman, about sexuality.

Livret de famille (1983) Made-for-TV movie, based on the novel of Patrick Modiano. Legal problems ensued.

Aurore et l'Atlantique Themes of alcohol and loneliness.
See **Lejeune** 139–40.

Julie Hivon

Baiser d'enfant (1995; 16mm; 18 mins.) Short film that presents the sensual portrait of a woman's attraction to a boy-child, has drawn considerable attention. Not about incest or pedophilia. Inspired by a song of the same title by Kate Bush. Woman: Marie Lefebvre. With Rémi Laurin-Ouette. Photography directed by Frédérique Bolté; production: Productions Don Quichotte. She is apparently working on another short (7–8 mins.) whose working title is
Dans le parc avec toi.

Danièle Huillet b. in France in 1936, she works in New German Cinema with her partner and husband Jean-Marie Straub, whom she married in 1959. Was assistant director to Jacques Rivette in the making of *Le Coup du berger* (1956). All of her films are co-directed with Straub, and she does not usually get recognition for her contributions to the work. Selected Filmography

Not Reconciled, or Only Violence Helps Where Violence Rules) (*Nicht versôhnt . . .*) (1965)

Chronicle of Anna Magdalena Bach (*Chronik der Anna Magdalena Bach*) (1967). The life of J. S. Bach told through his wife's imaginary journals.

The Bridegroom, the Comedienne and the Pimp (*Der Brâutgigam, Die Komôddiantem und der Zuhâlter*)(1968) Prostitution in Munich.

Les Yeux ne veulent pas en tout temps se fermer ou Peut-être qu'un jour Rome se permettra de choisir à son tour: Othon (*The Eyes Do Not Always Want to Close or Perhaps One Day Rome Will Permit Itself to Choose in Its Turn: Othon*) (1969)

Toute Révolution est un coup de dés (*Every Revolution Is a Throw of the Dice*) (1977)

Class Relations (*Klassenverhâltnisse*)(1984) Based on Franz Kafka's novel *Amerika*.

See **Foster**, Gwendolyn Audrey. *Women Film Directors*: esp. 193–96;

and **Lejeune** (141–42) on her collaboration with Jean-Marie Straub and for the French titles of above listed films.

Caroline Huppert
Madame Sourdis (1976)
L'Apprentissage de la ville (1980)
Le Bonheur des tristes (1981)
Elle voulait faire du cinéma (1983)
Signé Charlotte (*Sincerely Charlotte*) (1986; 92 mins.) Bitter-sweet romantic drama about a rock singer (Isabelle Huppert, sister of director) who is blamed for her boyfriend's murder. She escapes with her former lover Mathieu. Their travels through the French country-side are memorable. Written and directed by Caroline Huppert; Luc Beraud; Joelle Goron. Photography by Bruno de Keyzer. Music by Philippe Sarde. Produced by Adolphe Viezzi. Stars Isabelle Hupper, Neils Arestrup, and Christine Pascal.

(Marie-)Louise Iribe Began as an actress (role in Feyder's *Atlantide*). Founded a production company in 1927 and also directed
Hara-Kiri (1928) Interracial love between a Japanese man and a European woman. Depicted a woman's suicide.
Roi des aulnes (1930) Based on a ballad by Goethe of the same name. The codirector was the German director Peter-Paul Brauer. French, German and English versions appeared in 1931, one year after Iribe's death.
See **Foster**, *Women Film Directors:* mentioned en passant, p. 26; and also **Lejeune** 54.

Marielle Issartel (w/ Charles Belmont)
Histoires d'A (1973) Famous documentary on abortion.

Aline Isserman [Sometimes the first name is incorrectly given as Alice!] b. Paris, 1948
Le Destin de Juliette (1982; 75 mins.) (See **Buss** 161) Version Française catalog: To escape the streets, a woman marries a man who becomes abusive. Stars Richard Bohringer and L. Duthilleul.
L'Ombre du doute (with Alain Bashung)
L'Amant magnifique (1986; 100 mins.) Having fallen head over heels in love with a man, the "heroine" gets rid of her current boy-friend. Stars Didier Agostini and Michel Fortin. (Version Française catalog.)
See **Lejeune** 144–45.

Sylvie Jallaud See Gallaud

Irène Jouannet b. in Roanne, 1945.
L'Intrus (1983–84) Concerns Anne, a robotlike woman in her

forties, engulfed in solitude, bordering on neurotic mysticism; one of those people Jouannet calls "social suicides." She meets a man (l'in-trus); the film ends in tragedy (Lejeune).
See **Lejeune** 148.

Tana Kaleya b. Poland, 1939.
Principally a photographer who has produced important albums (*Hom-mes* [1975]; *Femmes* [1980]), Kaleya has made a film where the images are gripping; but this film has drawn little attention.
Femmes (1983)
See **Lejeune** 149.

Nelly Kaplan b. in 1931 in Buenos Aires, Argentina, of Russian and Jewish parents, but when eighteen moved to France where she has lived since the 1950s. She began her career as assistant to Abel Gance (*La Tour de Nesle;* and the triple screen production of *Magirama, Austerlitz, Cyrano et D'Artagnan*). Began directing such shorts on art as
Gustave Moreau; (1961) *Rudolph Bresdin; Dessins et merveilles* [art by Victor Hugo]*; Abel Gance: hier et demain;* (1963) *A la source de la femme aimée* [about the erotic drawings of André Masson]; and a 60-minute film, *Le Regard Picasso* (1967), which took the Golden Lion at the Venice Film Festival.
She has also done some writing: *Le Manifeste d'un art nouveau: la polyvision* (1955); *Le Sunlight d'Austerlitz* (1960); *Le Collier de ptyx* (1972); and *Un Manteau de fou-rire ou les mémoires d'une liseuse de draps* (1974; an erotic tale). After 1979 she wrote several *scénarios,* made into TV movies by Jean Chapot: *Un Fait d'hiver; Livingstone; Ce fut un bel été.*
La Fiancée du pirate [*A Very Curious Girl* aka *Dirty Mary*] (1969; 105 mins.) Written by Nelly Kaplan, Claude Makovsky. Pho-tography by Jean Badal [Badard?]; music by Georges Moustaki. Stars Bernadette Lafont, Georges Géret [Genet?], Michel Constantin, Julien Guiomar, Jean Paredes, and Claire Maurier.
Marie, a beautiful gypsy woman, engages in sexual acts with several men of the village, and finally gets her revenge over the whole town by exposing the men and the hypocritical pettiness of all the townspeople. Sharon Smith (120): Picasso described this film as "insolence raised to a fine art." "Kaplan's film has verve, some good gags, and lively music, but it leans too far towards stereotypes, including that of a Lesbian," says **Bergan** (158). "A jolly feminist send-up of Catholicism and bourgeois conformism" (**Buss** 68). See also **Buss** 158.
Papa, les petits bateaux (1971) Cookie is being held by kidnappers who are demanding a ransom. They find out she is not so stupid as

they think, for in the end she has managed to have killed all seven of her kidnappers and to have gotten the ransom of two million francs for herself. Sharon Smith (121): "the emphasis on [Cookie's] dizzy-blonde Betty Boop characterization somewhat spoils the film, especially after the initial surprise at her resourcefulness fades away."

Il faut vivre dangereusement (1974–45?) *Scénario* of Claude Makovsky.

Néa (1976) A young woman (girl) actively seeks sexual knowledge, and, in writing a novel, becomes famous, then falls in love with an older man who betrays her. Based on a novella by Just Jaeckin, the author of *Emanuelle*. *Néa* has had greater success in the United States than in France; it is Kaplan's best, in my opinion. See Georgiana M. M. **Colvile** who describes this as a fairy tale: Sibylle the main character is a 'sorceress'—combined to the princess of the fairy tale. Accompanied by her cat, Cumes, she gets her prince charming. (Colvile doesn't say that prince charming leaves the princess in this story, but Colvile's interest is in "scoptophilia," as she writes it.)

La Satellite de Vénus (1977)

Charles et Lucie (1979; 98 mins.) *Scénario*, Claude Makovsky and Jean Chapot; photography, Gilbert Sandoz; music, Pierre Perret. Stars Daniel Ceccaldi, Ginette Garcin, Jean-Marie Proslier, Samson Fainsilber, and Georges Claisse. An antique dealer, Charles (Ceccaldi), has been reduced to selling trinkets and junk, and a chanteuse, Lucie (Garcin), no longer beautiful, is a cleaning lady. They fall for a con and find themselves in the Midi pursued by gangsters and police. "Picaresque fantasy . . . charming, poignant and sometimes witty, but remains little more than a light-weight divertissement," says **Bergan**. [See also **Johnston**, Claire, ed., "Nelly Kaplan, An Introduction," in *Notes on Women's Cinema* (London: British Film Institute, 1973).]

Abel Gance et son "Napoléon" (1983)

Plaisir d'amour (1994)

See **Foster**, esp. 204–6; and **Lejeune** 151–52. See also Herman G. **Weinberg**, "Manifeste d'un Art Nouveau: la Polyvision," *Film Culture* 2, no. 2 (1956): 31.

Anna Karina b. in Copenhagen, 1940. Besides her film career, she has written one detective novel, *Golden City* (1983).

Vivre ensemble (1973) A love story that takes place in the Quartier Latin (of Paris). Karina, a famous actress, who is in particular a star in the films of Jean-Luc Godard, wrote the *scénario* to this film and directed it.

Liliane de Kermadec

Le Temps d'Emma (1963) Short about an old lady, a painter; won the Lion de Saint-Marc in Venice.

Home, Sweet Home (1971) Feature length; black and white. Two boys meet a girl, and the three of them go wandering together; they stop in a house, and there the past mixes with the present (Lejeune).

Aloïse (1974) Tells the true story of a soprano, confined for forty years and living in her own world of writing, drawings, and paintings. Stars Delphine Seyrig.

Sophie et le Capitaine (1978) Story of a transvestite. Shooting of this film interrupted by financial problems.

Le Petit Pommier (1980) TV movie. Story of three "flights": a little boy, a girl, and a mother who escapes the real world and recreates the world through dreams and photographs (Lejeune).

Mersonne ne m'aime (1986) Also made for TV; story of a police investigation in feminist milieus.

See **Lejeune** 154.

Maria Koleva b. in Sofia (Bulgaria), studied in the United States, in Germany, and finally went to France in 1971. Here she became active in cinema (having studied it in Vincennes).

Chères amies On cosmetics ("le commerce de la beauté")

L'Enfant aux yeux morts (1973) Short. Satire of the use of children in advertising.

Cinq Leçons de théâtre d'Antoine Vitez (1978)

La Fête aujourd'hui, la fête demain (made in 1972; shown in 1974–75) A sociopolitical essay on the Leftist Union.

L'Etat de bonheur permanent (1981)

Fragments pour un discours théâtral: Vitez, le conservatoire (1983)

La Voiture (1983)

Lettre à l'ami suisse n° 7 (1986)

See **Lejeune** 156.

Germaine Krull

6, pour 10 francs (1932?)

Diane Kurys b. 1948; married to director-producer Alexandre Arcady (b. 1947, Algiers). As an actress she has appeared in *Elle court, elle court la banlieue* (Gérard Pirès); *Casanova* (Fellini); *F comme Fairbanks* (Maurice Dugowson).

Diabolo Menthe (*Peppermint Soda*) (1977; 101 mins.) (**Katz** gives 1978.) *Scénario*, Diane Kurys; photography, Philippe Rousselot; music, Yves Simon. Stars Eléonore Klarwein, Odile Michel, Coralie Clément, Marie-Véronique Maurin, Anouk Ferjac, Michel Puterflam, and Yves Renier. Two sisters, Anne (Klarwein) and Frédérique (Puterflam), are very different: the first introverted; the other, extroverted. "Examination of early adolescence, complete with disciplinarian teacher, parents' divorce, menstrual cramps, first love" (**Maltin**). The daughters of a divorced Jewish couple, they live with their mother and go to a very deadly school. Their holidays are spent with their father. "Gentle, observant and nostalgic ... [at times] somewhat clumsy [in its] handling of social and political climate; ... admirable command of excellent cast—notably Klarwien—and is sensitive to the school milieu" (**Bergan** 442–43). Indeed, the portrayal of the school is most memorable, and the life of Jewish people in France is of some interest. (See also *Entre Nous* for another portrayal of Jewish life in France.)

Cocktail Molotov (1980) Same theme as above; reworked thirteen years later as *C'est la vie*. After having a fight with her mother, Anne runs away from home with a boy from the working class, whom her mother does not approve of. Anne has many bad experiences, including abortion and "existential wandering" (Foster 211).

Entre Nous (*Coup de Foudre* or *At First Sight*) (1983; 110 mins.) Kurys examines an intense relationship between her mother and a friend. Said to be sweeter than *Thelma and Louise,* more erotic, and more audacious (Sarasota French Film Festival Program Book, 1992). Bergan: "Lesbianism is dealt with somewhat coyly" (42). Producer: a Partners Production, Alexandre Films, Hachette Première/ Ariel Zeitoun. *Scénario,* Diane Kurys and Alain Le Henry; photography, Dernard Lutic; music, Bacalov. Stars Isabelle Huppert, Miou Miou, Guy Marchand, Robin Renucci, Jean-Pierre Bacri, and Patrick Bauchau.

A Man in Love (*Un Homme amoureux*) (1987; approx. 110 mins.; in English) A young man comes to Rome to play the Italian poet Cesare Pavese, who committed suicide. The actor (Coyote) ends up in an overpowering affair with the leading lady. Written by Diane Kurys; music by Georges Delerue; photography by Bernard Zitzermann; sound by Gerard Lamps; produced by Diane Kurys and Michel Seydoux. Stars Peter Coyote, Greta Scacchi, Peter Riegert, John Berry, and Vincent Lindon, with Claudia Cardinale and Jamie Lee Curtis.

This film has not had a good reception. **Acker** (326) speculates that it has been a "bid for commercial success." This is not necessarily a bad thing; but the film lacks sharpness and profundity.

La Baule-les-Pins (*C'est la vie*) (1990; 100 mins.) The marriage of the parents of two sisters, Sophie and Frédérique, is disintegrating. A film that presents a Jewish household in 1950s Lyons, with studies of male desire to control and of domestic violence. With Nathalie Baye as mother. Also stars Richard Berry, Vincent Lindon, and Zabou.

Après l'amour (1991–92; 100 mins.) (*Love after Love*) A novelist with writer's block oscillates between David—with whom she lives and who is buried in his work—and Tom, a musician with whom she falls in love. Both men are married and are fathers. All vow to accept the situation as is. But their modernity is caught up short in jealousy and other age-old emotions. Love Parisian style in the late twentieth century. Stars Isabelle Huppert, Bernard Giraudeau, Hippolyte Girardot, Lio, and Yvan Attal. Says Sonia **Benjamin,** "They all need a good slap, or else psychoanalysis" (*Journal Français d'Amérique,* [1–14 April 1994]: 17; my trans.).

A la folie (or *Six Days and Six Nights*) (1995; 100 mins.) A woman disrupts the life of her sister and her sister's husband.
See **Foster,** esp. 211–13.

Jeanne Labrune

De Sable et de sang (*Sand and Blood*) (1987; 101 mins.) Set in Southern France, this film focuses on the erotic and on human intimacy. "Using the mystique of bullfighting as a stepping-stone to broader issues, Labrune explores the friendship between Francisco, a gifted matador, and Manuel, a cultivated doctor and musician" (Facets). Stars Sami Frey and André Dussolier.

Sans un cri (1993; 86 mins.) Love story and jealousy of a young couple, badly matched. Version Française catalog: "A boy from an unloving family befriends a dog to ease his solitude. Stars Lio; Rémi Martin."

Martine Lancelot b. Neuilly, 1948.

Images de Gilles de Rais (1975) Documentary on the work of actors during rehearsals.
S'il vous plaît . . . La mer (1979)
Portrait de Chantal Akerman (1983) Short. Shown on TV-FR3.
Danse et sculpture (1984) Short
[*Jenébana ou la maladie des esprits* (1984; filmed in Bamako, Mali. Lancelot participated in the making of this film.)]
See **Lejeune** 161–62.

Annick Lanoë Began as a journalist and documentarist. Short films

such as: *Pour le meilleur et pour le pire* (1977); *Rita, la plus grosse femme du monde* (1978).
L'Ephémère (1960) Short. Is about her grandmother.
Les Nanas (1985) Four years in the making, this is a satirical comedy about modern women and their experiences with the backlash from the feminist movement.
See **Lejeune** 163. [She mentions here a film Lanoë was writing about the gangster Bruno Sulak.]

Christine Laurent b. 1944. Began in costumes and décors.

Alice Constant (1977) A *scénario* drawn from her own childhood, which she then filmed. Two sisters "investigate" a servant woman who committed suicide at twenty-five.

Vertiges (1981) The double life of an operatic soprano.

Eden Miséria. Documentary feel. Filmed on the desert (Cape Verde); stars Daniouta Zaruzic and Kader Bakanef.
See **Lejeune** 164–65.

Yvonne Leenhardt Worked with her husband Roger [q.v., Sadoul]; she directed:

Jacques Coupeau A film about the pioneer French theatrical producer of the early 1900s. The couple gets a child, then a dog. The child is the narrator.

Geneviève Lefèbvre [Kuhn spells Lefèvre (166)] b. in Lens, 1949.

Le Jupon rouge (1987) On the destiny of three women, each of a different generation.
See **Lejeune** 166.

Nicole Le Garrec b. in Plougastel-Saint-Germain, 1942.

Plogoff, des pierres contre des fusils (1980) Le Garrec, from Brittany (and wife of Félix Le Garrec who was the photographer for this film), is concerned with the struggles of the Bretons in most of her work.

Le Maître des chevaux (Lejeune mentions this as in progress.)
See **Lejeune** 167–68.

Claudine Lenoir Producer and also director of the following:
La Belle au bois dormant
La Prisonnière
Le Rendez-vous sauvage
L'Aventurière des Champs Elysées (1956)

Monique Lepeuve
Animation:
La Chanson du jardinier fou (1960)
Concerto pour violincelle (1962)

Maud Linder
L'Homme au chapeau de soie Film is in homage to Max le Dandy (1883–1925), a father she did not know but whom she is intent upon pulling out of oblivion. (An actor and director of silent films, he was precursor to Charlie Chaplin.)

Christine Lipinska b. Algiers 1951, but following her parents' divorce, she moved with her mother to Normandy.
Après nous, le désert (1972) Short
Je suis Pierre Rivière (1975)

Folie suisse (1986) Directed and written by Lipinska, based on the novel of the same name by Jacques Perry.

Papa est parti . . . maman aussi (1988; 104 mins.) A young girl takes care of her siblings when her parents leave them. Stars S. Aubry; J. Kircher, and A. Subra (Version Française catalog.)

Le Cahier volé (1993; 106 mins.) A girl discovers three different people are in love with her. Stars Elodie Bouchez and Edwige Navarro (Version Française catalog).
See **Lejeune** 169–70.

Marceline Loridan b. Epinal 1928, descended from Polish Jewish emigrants from Lodz. She knew the horror of the concentration camps, where her father, in fact, died. Longtime collaborator with Dutch documentarist Joris Ivens. First appeared as actress in *Chronique d'un été* (1961; directed by Jean Rouch/Edgar Morin). Style: cinéma vérité or cinéma direct.

Algérie année zéro (1962) Codirected with Jean-Pierre Sergent. Short. Later censored.

Le 17e parallèle (1967) Filmed with Ivens in Vietnam just after the American involvement began. The "militant" filming of this war was dangerous, underground work.

Le Peuple et ses fusils (1968) Filmed with Ivens in Laos.

Rencontre avec le Président Ho-Chi-Minh (1968) Filmed with Ivens.

Comment Yu-Kong déplaça les montagnes (*How Yukong Moved the Mountains*) (A 12-hour film on China; 1973–76) Filmed with Ivens on many locations: footage on a factory, barracks, an artisan's workshop, a fishing village, a pharmacy, a school, a worker's home, the opera, the circus. "Une oeuvre d'enthousiasme et d'un réalisme familier [a work of enthusiasm and familiar realism]" (Lejeune 171).

Une Histoire de vent (1988; with Ivens) With Ivens's failing health, this film may have been more the work of Loridan than of Ivens.
See **Lejeune** 171.

Noémie Lvovsky (Lvosky)
Oublie-moi (1995; first film) Concerns the existential flight of a young woman who is not able to anchor her own reality in a stable love relationship.

Babette Mangolte b. 1941 in France. An important photographer who has shot several classic feminist films, including a couple of Akerman's. Came to New York intending to stay only a short while, but wound up staying for several years.

Maintenant entre parenthèses (*Now*) (1976)

She has also made the important and rather well-known film
The Camera: Je or La Camera: I (1977)
See **Foster,** *Women Film Directors.*

Laetitia Masson b. in Nancy.

Nulle part
En avoir (ou pas) (1995) Alice, a young girl (played by Sandrine
Kiberlain), leaves her small town for a bigger one (Boulogne-sur-Mer
for Lyon) in search of a job, a boy friend, a new way of seeing things.
She becomes a singer.

Nine Mayo

L'Arbre (1961)
Les Six Jours de la création (1962)

Patricia Mazuy

Peaux de vaches (1988; 95 mins.) Shown at the forty-ninth
Cannes film festival, 5/12/96. (Version Française catalog: "1990"; 90
mins. Cut version?) Two brothers commit a crime, but only one is
convicted. The latter's return creates powerful tensions in his
brother's family setting. Stars Sandra Bonnaire and J.-F. Stevenin.

From the internet, re Cannes 1996: Palais des Festivals—A French
university professor has just given an endless and profoundly boring
speech, citing in passing a book that he wrote some fifteen years ago.
His conviction: A film must reflect the social milieu it is evoking. To
that Agnès Varda responded that the French cinema was a bourgeois
cinema, after which the young woman director, Particia Mazuy
("Peaux de Vaches") began to imagine out loud being considered as a
director (woman director) of the "rural milieu," and said her only
pleasure would be to film tractors. Volker Schlöndorf and Ettore Scola,
as francophile directors, changed the conversation to their youthful
work placed under the sign of French cinema. Then Nicole Garcia,
actress ("Mon Oncle d'Amérique") and director ("Le Fils préfére")
said in essence that a film is the reflection of what happens in your
head and has nothing to do with what society is. Clearly some after-
noons seem very long! (My trans.)

[Un universitaire français vient de faire un discours interminable
et d'un profond ennui, citant au passage un livre qu'il avait écrit il y
a une quinzaine d'années. Sa conviction: un film doit refléter le milieu
social qu'il évoque. A cela Agnès Varda répondit que le cinéma français était un cinéma bourgeois, après quoi la jeune réalisatrice Patricia
Mazuy ("Peau de vaches") se prit à rêver d'être considérer (sic) comme
une cinéaste du "milieu rural", et que son seul plaisir serait de filmer
des tracteurs. Volker Schlöndorf et Ettore Scola, en cinéastes fran-

cophiles, détournèrent la conversation au profit du récit de leur jeunesse placée sous le signe du cinéma français. Puis Nicole Garcia, actrice ("Mon Oncle d'Amérique") et réalisatrice ("Le Fils préféré") dit en substance qu'un film est le reflet de ce qui se passe dans votre tête et que cela n'a rien à voir avec ce qu'est la société! Décidemment, certains après midi paraissent très longs.]

Travolta et moi (1994; 90 mins.) A teenage girl dreams of the actor John Travolta and conjures up *Saturday Night Fever* in her imagination. She then meets a morbid young man who has bet a friend he can seduce her. Mazuy captures the youth culture and its anguish. Producer: IMA Productions; La Sept/ Arte, SFP Productions; Sony Music/ Georges Benayoun and Paul Rozenberg. Stars Leslie Azzoulai and Julien Gerin.

Pomme Meffre b. Lion-en-Sullias (Loiret) in 1933.

Venial Sin, Mortal Sin An eleven-year-old girl's sexual awakening. Set in a post-WWII small French town.

Le Grain de Sable (Grain of Sand) (1984; 90 mins.) Stars Delphine Seyrig as Solange, an unemployed woman in Paris who is trying to reconcile her past and her present. The past unfolds in Corsica, where she expects to find the only man she ever really loved. Whatever opportunities come her way, she is not prepared to take advantage of them, and the result is quite bleak. I found the music especially haunting and the scenes of Corsica, including Le Grain de Sable Rock, picturesque. Also starring Geneviève Seyrig and Michel Aumont.

Agnès Merlet b. 1959.
Artemisia (1983)
L'Arcane sans nom 1984
La Guerre des pâtes (1989)
Poussière d'étoiles (1985)

Le Fils du requin (1993; 85 mins.) First full-length feature of Merlet, likened to Truffaut's *Quatre cents coups* and, by Martin **Delisle** (*Séquences* 176 [January–February 1995]: 41), to Jean-Claude Lauzon's *Léolo* for the oneirism and and use of imagination by which Martin [in *Fils* . . .] and Léolo escape reality. Both create a mantra from their favorite book; here Martin's is "I am the son of the female of the shark species," drawn from *Les Chants de Maldoror* by Lautréamont. No Hollywood sentimentality here. Delisle praises the mise-en-scène and Merlet's discovery of the two young actors. Actors: Ludovic Vandandaele, Erick Da Silva, Sandrine Blancke, Maxime Leroux. Distributed by Action.

Florence Mialhe b. Paris 1956. Animated films.

Hammam (1991; 8 mins.) Young women go for the first time to the *hammam:* steam baths, fountains, feminine beauty, voluptuous bodies. Shown in June 1996 at the Centre Rabelais in Marseille.

Schéhérazade (1995; 15 mins.) The story of *A Thousand and One Nights.* Shown in June 1996 at the Centre Rabelais in Marseille.

Anne-Marie Miéville [Mielville] A modernist. Collaboration with Godard; her name always subsumed to his (**Colvile,** 75: " . . . l'idéologie féministe, comme la marxiste, s'intéresse avant tout à dénoncer le discours de l'autre." [. . . feminist, like marxist, ideology, is above all interested in denouncing the discourse of the Other].) (My trans.)

2 × 50 Years of French Cinema (1995; 52 mins.; w/ Jean-Luc Godard)

Lou n'a pas dit non (1996)

Nous sommes tous encore ici (1996) With Aurore Clément et Bernadette Lafont.

Ariane Mnouchkine b. Boulogne-sur-Seine, 1939. Had her beginnings in theater; founded the Théâtre du Soleil. After filming Molière, she returned to the theater, producing in particular the plays of Shakespeare, but also a work of Cixous (*L'Histoire terrible . . .*).

1789 (1974; 150 mins.)

Molière—Le Théâtre du Soleil (1977; 4 hours) Sumptuous film that evokes the entire epoch, including painters. Not well received by critics but is appreciated by the public. Shown in episodes on PBS TV in United States. (See Version Française catalog; 140 min.[?]) See **Lejeune** 177.

Patricia Moraz. See Swiss directors

Jeanne Moreau b. Paris 1928.

Lumière (1976) "A film of ambiguous charm" (**Katz**). I find that this film has a tone and atmosphere that are memorable; but the plot or situation is not quite so much so.

L'Adolescente (1978)

Lillian Gish (1984) Documentary

Portrait d'un séducteur See **Lejeune** (180) concerning this adaptation of Henriette Jelinek's novel.

Solstice (1996) In progress. An adaptation of a work by Joyce Carol Oates; Moreau closely collaborates with Oates on this project, traveling often to Cambridge, where Oates teaches.
See **Lejeune** 180.

Monique Muntcho Wife of J. J. Raymond-Millet with whom she often collaborated, though she made films on Madagascar without him.

Réalités malgaches
Tamatave la marine
Il était une montagne

Musidora b. Jeanne Roques in Paris in 1889; d. 1957. Best known as a "vamp" actress (esp. *Les Vampires,* 1915–16; a series), whom Louis Aragon, the famous French poet, called "The Tenth Muse," although she also directed or codirected and often scripted films. She traveled to Spain in 1924 to shoot *La Terre des taureaux* (*La Tierra de los toros*), for which she also wrote a feminist screenplay demonstrating that women's courage warranted their having the vote. "During the filming she tested her courage in the bullring to demonstrate that women were brave enough to deserve the vote" (Sharon **Smith** 114). She sometimes directed stage plays too (e.g., *La Vie sentimentale de George Sand* [1946]).

Les Misères de l'aiguille (1913)
Le Calvaire (1914)
Minne, or *L'Ingénue libertine* (1915)
Le Grand Souffle (1915)
Fille d'Eve (1916)
Le Maillet noir (*The Black Leotard*) (1917)
La Vagabonde (1918). From Colette. Musidora directed, produced, and acted in this film.
Vicenta (1918) (Katz gives 1920; Lejeune 1919.) Musidora also scripted and starred in this film.
La Flamme cachée (made in 1918; released in 1920–23; with Jacques Lasseyre) Colette wrote the screenplay.
Mam'zelle Chiffon (1919)
Pour Don Carlos (1920–23; with Jacques Lasseyre; Sp.)
Une Aventure de Musidora en Espagne (1922)
Soleil et ombre (1920–23 [Lejeune gives 1922]; with Jacques Lasseyre)
La Geôle (1921)
La Tierra de los toros (1924)
Le Berceau de Dieu (1926)
Les Ombres du passé (1926)
La Magique Image (1951) Clips from her early films are seen here.
See **Katz** 990 for more films. See also **Cazals** as well as **Foster,** esp. 273–76; filmography; bibliography; and **Lejeune** 40–42.

Rose (Lacau-)Pansini b. Orthez 1890 d. Paris 1985. From the silent era. Sometimes codirected with Georges Monca. In Italy (1915–18) she directed several films (*Manon; Graziella, Mascanor*). Returning to France she established a company and made several more films between 1918 and 1922.

Chantelouve (1920; with Monca) Pansini also wrote the *scénario*.

Esclave (1921; with Monca)

Un Drame d'amour (1921)

La Puissance du hasard (1921)

Le Sang des Finoël 1922

Judith (1922)

See **Lejeune** 44.

Christine Pascal b. 1953 in Lyon. She is an auteure director, as well as an actress and a screenwriter. "Commercial cinema with a New Wave flourish; films tend towards the melodramatic à la Fasssbinder" (Foster 304). Commited suicide early September, 1996.

Félicité (1979)

La Garce (1984; 92 mins.) A police officer rapes the seventeen-year-old girl he had gone to help. Stars Isabelle Huppert and Richard Berry.

Zanzibar (1989; 95 mins.) Subject is auteur cinema. A tyrannical director (Maréchal; reminiscent of Godard) insists that actress Camille Dor take a role in his film; there is no script, and it is to be filmed in a haphazard manner. The producer, Vito, helps Maréchal to convince her, but then Vito falls in love with Camille, who, despite his love, and despite her use of drugs, does not find her experiences with Maréchal any less painful. (*Séquences* [April 1994]: 48.) A French-Swiss film. Written by Pascal with Catherine Breillat and Robert Boner. Stars Fabienne Babe, André Maracon, Francis Girod, and Dominique Maurin.

Le Petit Prince a dit (1991; 105 mins.) The story of a divorced father's despair when his little girl Violette (Marie Kleiber) develops cancer. He flees with her on a journey through Switzerland, Italy, and Southern France as if he hopes to make time stop. (The girl's parents are divorced.) Producer: French Production/Emmanuel Schlumberger. Stars Richard Berry, Anémone, Marie Kleiber.

Reviewer Pierre **Lecarme**, writes: "What is more unfair or more unbearable than the death of a child. Violette, ten years old . . . has beautiful black hair and deep eyes. She seems to bear up under the separation of her parents. Her father, Adam (Richard Berry), is a physician. Her mother (Anémone) is an actress. These beautiful people live in Switzerland, without problems, until one day everything gets shaken: Violette, tired, undergoes examinations that reveal a brain tumor. For the director, Christine Pascal, nothing soothes in the face of death. And particularly not the child's refrain that gives the film its title and announces that all will begin over again tomorrow. Here, emotion is intelligent and hesitant. Adam and Violette are light-hearted, because living is above all laughing and sharing. Richard Berry is outstanding, as are Anémone and Marie Kleiber who plays the role of Violette." Reviewed in *L'Actualité* 36–37 (Thursday 24 December 1992–Wednesday 6 January 1993): 14. (My trans.)

Adultère mode d'emploi [*Adultery (A User's Guide)*] (1995; 95 mins.) An erotically charged day in the life of a young couple. Stars Vincent Cassel.

See **Foster,** esp. 303–4; see also **Lejeune** 183; and *Séquences* 186 (September–October, 1996): 6.

Marie Perennou

Microcosmos (with Claude Nuridsanty; 1996; 80 mins.) Shown at the Cannes film festival. From the Internet: Un voyage d'une heure vingt dans une prairie, redécouverte à l'échelle du centimètre. Chaque touffe d'herbe devient une forêt impénétrable, chaque insecte une créature fantastique. Cette micro-aventure se déroule sur une seule journée, l'équivalent d'une saison pour les insectes dont la durée de vie se mesure en semaines. Les lois de la physique y semblent nouvelles et sans limites: on sait y marcher sur l'eau, ou la tête en bas. . . . Un micro-monde dont les réalisateurs montrent régulièrement la relativité, avec l'introduction d'images à une échelle très large (paysages entiers, vues aériennes de nuages ou d'orages), voire cosmique (le soleil, la lune, les étoiles).

A trip of twenty hours in a prairie brings the rediscovery on the scale of centimeters. Each blade of grass becomes an impenetrable forest, each insect a fantastic creature. This microadventure unfolds in a single day, the equivalent of an entire season for insects whose life span is measured in weeks. The laws of physics seem new here, and without limits: These insects know how to walk on the water or with their heads down . . . A microworld whose relativity is regularly shown by the directors, with the introduction of pictures on a very wide scale (entire landscapes, airplane views of clouds or storms), indeed, cosmic (the sun, the moon, the stars). Principal roles (by order of appearance on screen): the seven-pointed ladybug, the butterfly Machaon, the caterpillar, the bee pillaging the sage flower. . . . Production: Directed and filmed by Claude Nuridsany and Marie Perennou, with Hughes Ryffel and Thierry Machado. Sound: Philippe Barbeau. Executive producers: Michel Fauré, Philippe Gautier, André Lazare, and Patrick Lancelot. Delegate producers: Galatée Films, Jacques Perrin, Christophe Barratier, and Yvette Mallet. (From the Internet; my trans.)

Léonce Perret

Madame Sans Gêne (1941; 100 mins.) An eighteenth-century

woman becomes famous for her frank speech. Stars Arletty. (Version Française catalog.)

Denise Piazza-Tual b. Paris 1906. First worked under name Denise Batcheff, her first husband having been the actor Pierre Batcheff, who was leading man in *Le Chien andalou* (Salvador Dali; Luis Buñuel). She later collaborated with her husband, Roland Tual. She was involved in the production of many important films of her period, but, using the compilation methods of *Paris 1900* (directed by Nicole Védrès, q.v.), she also directed:

Ce siècle a 50 ans (1949)
Le Jeune Homme et la mort (1969) Short
Olivier Messiaen et les oiseaux (1973)
L'Imagination surréaliste: André Masson (1977)
Souvenirs surréalistes: Luis Buûuel (1977)
See **Lejeune** 65–67 under Tual.

Chantal Picault b. in Nice, 1954. Made several shorts for industrial uses on order (for Régie Renault (automobile company); the SNCF (railroad system), and so on, between 1975–85.
Accroche-coeur (1987) Based on the novel *Les Platanes* by Monique Lange.
See **Lejeune** 184.

Béatrice Pollet b. Paris, 1964.
Visions et image (1984) Short, in Super 8
Mim'hic (1985) Short
Coeur à barbe (1985) Short
Véra (1987) A heart attack strikes the heroine; after this, happiness should follow in her married life. Based on a novella of Villiers de L'Isle-Adam. However, according to Lejeune, he told a more macabre story of love after death.
See **Lejeune** 185.

Elisabeth Rappeneau
Fréquence meurtre (1988; 100 mins.) A man who killed a girl's parents menaces her after twenty-five years. Stars Catherine Deneuve and André Dussollier.

Jackie Raynal
Editor of *Paris vu par . . .* (1964) and of *La Collectionneuse* (directed by Rohmer, 1966). As director her first feature film was *Deux fois.*
Deux fois (1971) (Erens gives 1970; Lejeune 1969.) Filmed in Barcelona.

New York Story Filmed in New York; camera work by Babette Mangolte.

Hôtel New York (1984) Camera work by Babette Mangolte.
See **Lejeune** 186.

Pauline Rebuffat

Fuites [with Baptiste Kleitz] Short that was an audience choice at the seventeenth International Festival of Women's Films held April 1995 in Créteil.

Marguerite Renoir An important **editor** of the 1930s. Included among her works are
   Madame Bovary (1934)
   Le Crime de Monsieur Lange (1936)
   Les Bas Fonds (1936)
   La Grande Illusion (1937)
   La Règle du jeu (1939)

Claude Révol

Retour de bonheur (1930; with René Jayet) [*Retour du???*]
L'Enfant de minuit (with Egyptian singer Réda Caire)

Malka (or Malke) Ribowska—See Dayan

Marie-Geneviève Ripeau b. Versailles, 1949.

We Will Remain Indians (1970) Codirected with Liliane Korb. Interview with a Red Power woman who happened to be in Paris.

Histoire d'un crime (1972) Short concerned with building renovations in Paris (Belleville and Montparnasse).

Si tu t'imagines (1973) Short
Patrick Pons, pilote professionnel (1975) Short
Nuit, une guerre (1976) Short
La Voie de la main vide (1977) Short
Entrevu par l'indiscrétion d'un Judas (1978) Short

Adieu, voyages lents (1978) Three shorts that can be threaded together to give a full-length film. Theme: Difficulty couples have communicating; need to break up.

The Cloisters Museum New York (1980)

En l'absence du peintre (1982) Full length. About the German artist Paula Modersohn-Becker. Also about the difficulties two artists run into when they become a couple.
See **Lejeune** 187–88.

Caroline Roboh

Hélas! il n'y a plus de jeunes filles! (1979) Short

Clémentine Tango (1983) The story is set in Pigalle (site of Parisian nightlife). A young man falls in love with a girl who turns out to be his sister.

See Lejeune 189; and also **Kuhn** 166 (who says Roboh is postmodern).

Françoise Romand
Passé-Composé (1994; 95 mins.)

Jeanne Roques See **Musidora**

Michelle Rosier b. Paris 1930. Her mother was Jewish and a journalist; Michèle came with her to the United States at the outbreak of WWII; she, therefore, spent her childhood in New York, where she developed a passion for the cinema. After the war, she returned to Paris, where for ten years, she was a journalist (*France-Soir; Le Nouveau Fémina*); then she turned to fashion.

George qui? (1972) About George Sand.

Mon coeur est rouge (1977) Fiction filmed in 16 mm. A woman conducting an investigation has several encounters. All these take place in one day.

Le Grand Jour (1978) The first day in a couple's life (the wedding day).

Mimi (1979) Story of a grandmother who takes care of her grandson, although she is ill from a very serious and very painful cancer.

Un Café, Un! (1980) Captures the life of a Parisian café.

Le Gros Départ (1982)

[*Une Enfant amoureuse*]
See **Lejeune** 190–91.

Brigitte Rouan
Outremer (or *Overseas*) (1990; 98 mins.) Traces fortunes of three wealthy sisters living in North Africa during Algerian war. Stunning! The three enjoy sexual pleasures in colonial Algeria while social change and political upheaval surround them. Styled as a triptych, this is a startling, stylistically audacious first film by Rouan, a proven actress. Photographed by Dominique Chapuis, starring Nicole Garcia (q.v.), Brigitte Rouan herself, and Marianne Basler; also Philippe Galland. (Available from Facets; for sale at Critics Choice).

Françoise Sagan b. Cajarc, 1935. Well known for her novels, and especially for *Bonjour Tristesse,* written when she was only eighteen years old, Sagan has also done camera work (*Encore un hiver*) and even directed:

Les Fougères bleues (1977), which is her own adaptation of her novel *Les Yeux de soie.*
See **Lejeune** 192.

Nikki [Niki] de Saint-Phalle b. New York in 1933.
Daddy (1973; with Peter Whitehead) Violent portrayal of the father, bent on possession; childhood memories clash with images of the present.
Un Rêve plus long que la nuit (1977) Also a violent film, this time about her own daughter's various initiations, undergone while becoming an adult.
See **Lejeune** 193.

Valeria Sarmiento See Chile

Suzanne Schiffman b. Paris, 1923. A Truffaut protégée.
Le Moine et la sorcière (*Sorceress*) (1985; 98 mins.; Lejeune says 1986) Based on an authentic memoir from the time of the Inquistion (thirteenth century). Clash between a dedicated healer and a pursuer of heretics that raises questions regarding the Church and its oppression of women. Produced and cowritten by Pamela Berger. This was a Franco-American production, with financial support contributed by the National Endowment for the Humanities.
See **Lejeune** 195.

Isabel Sebastian
La Contre Allée (?; 85 mins.) A young girl and a prostitute become good friends. Stars Caroline Cellier and J. Covillault. (Version Francaise catalog.)

Coline Serreau b. Paris, 1947 (Lejeune says 1948.) Rejects the label "woman director"—but here she is, just the same!
Le Rendezvous (1977) Short TV film
Mais qu'est-ce qu'elles veulent? (*What Do These Women Want?*) (1975-77; Foster: 1977)
Pourquoi Pas? (*Why Not?*) (1979)
Qu'est-ce qu'on attend pour être heureux? (1982)
Trois hommes et un couffin (*Three Men and a Baby*) (1985; 100 mins.) Three bachelors have to change their life style when they become parents overnight. Stars Roland Giraud as Pierre; also André Dussolier.
Romuald et Juliet (*Mama, There's a Man in Your Bed*) (1989; 111 mins.) An unlikely romance between a CEO and his (black) cleaning woman who has five children to support. Also written by Serreau, the film stars Daniel Auteuil, Firmine Richard, Pierre Vernier, and Maxime Leroux.

La Crise (The Crisis) (1992; 95 mins.) A lawyer finds a note from his wife who has run away with someone else; he then learns he has been fired. There follow other crises, occurring in the lives of the two very different men who, oddly enough, become friends. Producer: Les Films Alain Sarde, TF1 Films Production; RAI2; Eniloc; Leader Cinematografica/Claude Albouze. Stars Vincent Lindon, Patrick Tim-sit, and Zabou.

Lapin, Lapin Among Serreau's most recent films.
See **Foster**, esp. 337–38. Also see **Lejeune** 196–98 and **DalMolin**.

Charlotte Silvera b. Paris, 1954. Her parents, of Jewish origins, had come to Paris from Tunisia in the 50s; in Paris her father ran a book-store. She took some courses in the Film Studies Department at Vincennes (1974) and at that same time discovered video (tapes on abortion, rape, boycott of the Olympics, etc.).

Subjint (1982) Video Short A lonely woman, trying to break out of her isolation in an unexpected way.

Louise, l'insoumise (written in 1979; shot and released 1982–84) Theme of entrapment of women. Louise, the little girl, sees her mother trapped in the house and rebels against this kind of prison. Interwoven is the war in Algeria and the depiction of three soldiers deserting. Took the Georges Sadoul prize.
See **Lejeune** 199; see also **Kuhn** 166.

Gabrielle Sorère

Le Lys de la vie (1921) Made in collaboration with the American dancer Loie Fuller. A fairy tale. A negative print was used to set reality apart from illusion or imagination. One of the first uses of this technique.

Sotha A member of the band of the Café de la Gare. The group is featured in *Le Graphique* . . . , with its usual gags and sketches. Sotha takes a lead.

Au long de la rivière Fango (1975) A utopia in which men live in harmony with one another and nature.

Le Graphique de Boscop (1976)
See **Lejeune** 201.

Irène Starevich [Starewicz] and her father Ladislas [Wladyslaw Starewicz, 1892–1965] created films with puppets, animated cartoons, and live-action films.

Zanzabelle à Paris (1949)
Fleur de fougère (1950)
Gazouly, petit oiseau
Nez au vent

After her father's death (1965), Irène, having gone blind, could not continue their work.

Nicole Stéphane Founded the Ancinex Production Company and directed:
   La Génération du désert (1957)
   Les Hydrocéphales (1965)
   Le Tapis Volant A Zionist tale in which a tractor becomes a flying carpet and transports Jewish wanderers to Israel.
She has also produced:
   Mourir à Madrid (*To Die in Madrid*) (1965) directed by Frédéric Rossif
   Phèdre (by Racine)
   Promised Lands, directed by Susan Sontag (1974)

[Daniele Suissa
   Prince Lazure (1982; 84 mins.) French comedy. A severe hypochondriac falls in love with a young woman. Stars Patrick Fierry and Mitsou. Listed in Version Française catalog.]

Sarah Taouss b. Algiers (Algeria), 1948, Taouss (of very strict Jewish parents) went to live in Montpellier with her family when fourteen years old (1962). When the events of 1968 broke out, she was able to get to Paris, where she met and lived with a young man who was not Jewish. Thus, she supposedly achieved full rupture with the "clan." In 1971 she left him and became an assistant editor for the film *Kashima Paradise* (directed by Bénie Deswarte; Yann Le Masson). Also worked with Loridan (q.v.) and Ivens when they made their documentaries on China. Editing, marriage, departure from Paris, return. Finally, she made a long film:
   La Journée continue (1980)
According to Lejeune, nothing has appeared since then, but she is planning a film on the 60s, including a narrative about her own life, her departure from Algeria, the culture shock she experienced upon arriving in France, the effect of her stern father and the family milieu on her life.
See **Lejeune** 202.

Elyana Tayer (Kuhn: **Tayar**) A silent film actress, she turned director of documentaries with the advent of sound.
   Versailles

Solange Térac See Solange Bussi

Tilda Thamar b. in Argentina in 1921, she became a highly successful actress in that country, before going to France around 1948. There she played in commercial productions, such as *Les Pépées du Service Secret* and *Une Nuit au Moulin Rouge*. Then she wrote, directed, and acted in

L'Appel (1974), which features three people in the afterworld, sharing their experiences.
See **Lejeune** 203.

Virginie Thévenet b. Paris, 1957. First an actress (*L'Argent de poche* [François Truffaut]; *Les Nuits de la pleine lune* [Eric Rohmer]).

La Nuit Porte-jarretelles (1984) A ludic film about sex, revolving around Paris at night.

Jeux d'artifices (1987) A brother and a sister seek to free themselves from their childhood and to pass into adulthood. "A high relief portrayal of the difficulty present-day young people have in living life" (Lejeune).
See **Lejeune** 204.

[**Alice Tissot** Actress who apparently directed the film *Si tu vois mon oncle* (ca. 1935)].

Titaÿnia (1929–67). She was a novelist (*Voyage autour de mon amant; La Bête cabrée*) and a journalist (*Mon tour du monde; Nuits chaudes*), who made the following three films in the 1930s:

Indiens, mes frères (1932) Filmed in Mexico in the Yucatan. An ethnocinematographic effort at filming the work of the natives: shaping of calebasses; weaving of fibers.

Tu m'enverras des cartes postales, which is about a cruise on a steamer going from Marseilles to Saigon.

Bonjour la terre
Loin chez les mangeurs d'hommes
Promenade en Chine (1937)
See **Lejeune** 57.

Fina Torres
Oriana (1985) In Spanish; shown at Cannes festival.

Mécaniques Célestes (1995–6) First film in the French language by this Venezuelan director living in Paris. Concerns a Venezuelan singer, Ana (Ariadna Gil), who has come to France to make a career as an opera star. Themes of alienation and exile; problems with the French immigration officers.
See Jean Vallier, "Des films pour l'été," in *France-Amérique* (31 August–6 September 1996): 10. Also see Anne Sengès, "Mécanique céleste: Un conte de fée des temps modernes," in *Journal Français* 18: 13 (September 1995): 31.

Marie-Claude Treilhou b. Toulouse, 1948.
Une Sale Histoire de sardines (1983) 60-min. TV offering.

Simone Barbès ou la vertu (1980)
Lourdes, l'hiver (1983)
Il était une fois la télévision (1985)
Et cric, et crac (1987)
Le Jour des rois (1991) With Danielle Darrieux, Paulette Dubost, Micheline Presle, and Michel Galabru
See **Lejeune** 205–6.

Annie **Tresgot**

Tableau (1957) Short
L'Age bête (1959) Short
Folle Passion (1966) Short
Les Enfants du néant (1967; with Marcel Brault)
Tour du monde des marionnettes (1968)
El Ghorba (*The Passengers*, 1971) Concerns Algerian immigrants in France.
Elia Kazan, Outsider (1982)
Visages de l'émigration
See **Lejeune** 207.

Nadine [Marquand] **Trintignant** b. 1934. Sister of actors Serge and Christian Marquand. Has been script girl, scriptwriter, editor, and director. Wife of Jean-Louis Trintignant, who usually stars in her films.

Fragilité, ton nom est femme (1965) Short
Mon amour, mon amour (1967)
Le Voleur de crimes (1969)
Ça n'arrive qu'aux autres (1971; 90 mins.) Semi-autobiographical, this film is related to the death of N.T.'s own child, and portrays the shock and pain of parents at the loss of their child in a very poignant fashion. Stars Catherine Deneuve and Marcello Mastroianni.
Le Voyage de noces/Jalousie (1976)
Défense de savoir (1978; 120 mins.) A lawyer is assigned to defend a prostitute accused of killing her lover. Stars Jean-Louis Trintignant and Bernadette Lafont.
Premier Voyage (1979)
Un Innocent (1983)
L'Eté prochain (*Next Summer*) (1986; 100 mins.; Lejeune gives 1984) Concerns various couples' lives, depicting middle-aged marriage. Quart: "it is no feminist film, built instead on age-old French truisms about unfaithful husbands, men and women's needs for one

another, and the battle of the sexes. It does remarkably little with the central middle-aged mother and wife, who conveys only vacancy, with much reassurance from others about how beautiful she looks and how young, as if those are the only or the central issues for an older woman. Dino/Fanny Ardant's grief over the hero's brain disease feels uncomfortably like an exploitation of her relation to Truffaut at the end of his life."

Produced by Alain Sarde (A Ronald K. Goldman European Classics Release). Written by Nadine Trintignant; photography by William Lubtchansky; music by Philippe Sarde. Stars Philippe Noiret, Claudia Cardinale, Fanny Ardant, and Jean-Louis Trintignant. Costars Marie Trintignant, Jérôme Ange, Pierre-Loup Rajot, Riton Liebman, Dominique Rousseau, Benoît Régent, and Christian Marquand.

Le Tiroir secret (1986)
Qui c'est ce garçon? (1986)
La Maison de Jade (1988)
See **Foster,** where this director is mentioned only in passing [p. 27], and where her name is spelled Tritignant. See especially **Lejeune** 208–10.

Marion Vandal
Monsieur le vagabond (1933)

Christine Van de Putte b. Nancy, 1954.
La Vie très brève de Joseph Bizouard (1976)
Poker menteuses et revolver matin (1978) "Joyously desperate and 'ludicly' suicidal, Marianne and Agostina decide to reinvent their lives, while escaping a world which is not made for them" (Van de Putte's summary).
Une Pierre, un arbre, un nuage (1981) Short Adaptation of a Carson McCullers novella. Shown on FR3 in 1982 and then came out in Paris theaters in 1983.
Et si je ne réponds pas c'est que je suis mort (1983) Inspired by the death of the filmmaker Jean Eustache and by the attempted suicide of C.V.'s own uncle. The uncle recounts his life and Van de Putte incorporates his story into Eustache's "universe." (Eustache: Gérard Blain).
See **Lejeune** 211.

Agnès Varda b. in Brussels, Belgium (1928), to a Greek engineer
father and a French mother. After World War II she went to Paris, where she studied art and photography. (Katz says she was "raised in France.") She founded a filmmaking cooperative with Alain Resnais as producer and Carlos Vilardebo as technical advisor in 1954. She is

concerned with portraying the truth—the truth of woman's "inner contradictions." She has made a clear contribution to "the changed image of women on the screen" (**Acker** 308). Considered the "Mother of the New Wave" (and sometimes labeled *Grandmother*—rather than Mother—of the New Wave), Varda's philosophy is that a filmmaker must exercise as much freedom as would a novelist. This became Rule Number One for all New Wave directors (**Heck-Rabi** 322–33). She, like Chris Marker and Alain Resnais, espouses the "dilemma of filming the subjectivity of the individual as related to the objectivity of the environment" (**Heck-Rabi** 324). A social pioneer as well as a film pioneer (**Acker; Mario Cloutier**). See also **Flitterman-Lewis, Sandy.** *To Desire Differently: Feminism and the French Cinema,* for four chapters on Varda, including *Cléo* . . . and *Sans toit.*

La Pointe-Courte (1954 [**Sadoul** gives 1956]; 75 mins.) *Scénario:* Varda; photography: Louis Stein; music: Pierre Barbaud; ed.: Alain Resnais. Actors: Silvia Monfort and Philippe Noiret.

First feature film. Filmed near Sète in the neighboring village of La Pointe Courte, where Varda spent her childhood (cf. Paul Valéry). A low-budget short that used revolutionary techniques. A young couple (Noiret and Montfort) tries to save their marriage; the plot is set against the fight of the fishermen in the village against big combines. The simplicity of village life draws the couple closer together. Sharon **Smith** (121): "This very personal film is considered one of the forerunners of the *nouvelle vague,* though it received limited distribution at the time."

Georges **Sadoul** (*Dict. des Films,* 1990): "Une vision aigüe, très personnelle, des choses et des gens, le sens du drame éternel, lié à l'actualité la plus directe . . . cette femme est quelqu'un, et l'une des meilleures révélations de la Nouvelle Vague." (**Heck-Rabi** treats this film at length.)

Varda tells of the first showing of this film in Belgium (**Head** 94).

O Saisons ô châteaux (1957) Documentary about the chateaus of the Loire Valley. In this film, gardeners dance ballets on the chateau grounds. Does that make you think of Jacques Demy? (Demy was later to be Varda's husband.)

Du Côté de la côte (1958) Documentary about the French Riviera, in which Varda contrasts wealthy estates with shops and streets visited by tourists.

L'Opéra Mouffe (1958; 19 mins.) Documentary. Black and white. Said to be the best of these three documentaries, this film won the International Federation of Film Clubs Prize in Brussels (1958). A portrait of the Mouffetard district of Paris with its famous market, the film concerns a poor woman who is pregnant. Varda uses vegetables—

pumpkin, cabbage—to sign the pregnancy. The cabbage sprouts re-
volve; a hen becomes a glass bubble; a girl is shown running—in slow
motion. There is a section called "Drunkenness," in which a pregnant
woman's fears unfold, and a section called "Desires" that translates
the cravings of a pregnant woman.

La Cocotte d'Azur (1959)

Cléo de 5 à 7 (1961) Second feature film, uses binary constructs
of *La Pointe Courte* and *L'Opéra Mouffe*. A superficial pop singer
awaits results of a cancer diagnosis. The two hours mark an evolution
in her character, as she "realizes she must confront life—and death—
entirely alone" (Sharon **Smith** 121) and "arrives at her own emancipa-
tion in the face of death" (**Acker** 107). For **Heck-Rabi**, Cléo's "rest-
less walking and waiting takes her . . . from self-conceited ignorance
to incipient understanding of private self and public image" (327). For
some, the film is verbose; for others, it echoes the techniques of the
films of Jacques Demy—especially *Lola*. The exterior shots of Paris
that surround the "story" are considered stunning. [See also
Flitterman-Lewis 28–32: "In accepting the possibility of death, Cleo
accepts life, and in accepting herself, Cleo begins to accept others. . . .
The film demonstrates a concern with questions of identity, sexuality,
and vision that substantially predates their contemporary status as
the currency of critical debate." (See also Buss 155.)

Les Fiancés du Pont MacDonald (1961)

Salut les Cubains! (1963)

Le Bonheur (1965) This third feature film won a top prize at
Cannes. First film in color, a pursuit of the palette. Told from the
"male point of view," this is a powerful film about woman as sufferer
and martyr subjected to the betrayal of her husband, "whose pleasures
are immediate and whose appetite for affection is insatiable" (quoted
by **Heck-Rabi** 333). One scene—in which the wife is found
drowned—is unforgettable. It is preceded by a "Picnic on the Grass"
scene, which—like other scenes in other Varda films—evokes impres-
sionism, especially that of Renoir.

Misunderstood by some critics, the film and even the title are sardonic: There is little true happiness portrayed here (except as it may
be immorally manifest in the husband, who claims that happiness may
be submitting to nature, though Varda herself takes no position). With
Varda's usual binary approach, we are first shown bucolic or pastoral
vignettes, then thrust from bedroom to bedroom, and back again to
the slow motion of the outdoor setting. Sharon **Smith** (121) claims
the main theme is that "happiness is a 'given' of life and can never
really be lost." On the other hand, Varda herself says, "Happiness is
like the delicious combination of melon with smoked ham, or grapes

with roquefort cheese—always slightly paradoxical" (**Heck-Rabi** 333).

Savaged by Elizabeth **Sussex** in *Sight and Sound* (autumn 1965): 200–1, who found the film imitative of Jacques Demy. For a rather complete critical account of *Bonheur,* see **Heck-Rabi** 332–39). (See also **Buss** 97.)

Les Créatures (1966) Stars Catherine Deneuve. Two stories are interlaced: one is grounded in reality, whereas the other is being woven in a novelist's imagination. Set on the island, Noirmoutier, in the Bay of Biscay. Black and white with red tinting. See **Heck-Rabi** (340–41) for extensive details.

This film was not well received by critics.

Loin du Vietnam (collaboratrice) (1966) (**Katz** gives 1967)

Elsa (1966) (Katz gives 1967) **Heck-Rabi** (340): "Positively reeking with the kinds of technical effects that originally made the New Wave such a controversial happening." A film portrait or cinematic essay. Subject is Elsa Triolet and her husband, Louis Aragon; deeper subject is love.

Oncle Janco (1967) (Katz gives 1968)

Black Panthers (1969) (Katz gives 1968)

Lion's Love (1969; 115 minutes) Stars Viva, Jerome Ragni, James Rado, Shirley Clarke, and Edith Constantine, gathered in a rented house in Hollywood. Sharon **Smith** (121): "The absence of a recognizable plot might not be a weakness in this free-flowing film if the people were more interesting."

Nausicaa. (Katz: 1970; Foster: 1976) Semidocumentary about Greeks in France.

Daguerréotypes (1975) (Released in 1975–76.) A short about the street on which Varda lived. She claimed the film showed how people really talked to each other on her block. A documentary made for German television during a decade from 1967–77 that was especially unsuccessful for Varda. The title involves a pun: These are portraits of people living on the rue Daguerre where Varda herself lived; they are a tribute to the city of Paris and to the inventor of the photo portrait.

Mon corps est à moi (after 1975) The subject of this film is abortion.

Réponses de femmes (1975)

Plaisirs d'amour en Iran (1976)

L'Une chante, l'autre pas (1977) Brought Varda international acclaim. But she could not find a producer, and so founded her own company, Ciné-Tamaris.

A film about inner contradictions. About two friends who find that each must follow her own destiny. Issue of abortion and other reproductive controversies are treated in this film. Stars Valérie Mairesse and Thérèse Liotard. For abundant critical commentary see **Heck-Rabi** (346–50).

Documenteur (1981) A French woman in Los Angeles is separated from her lover; a study in nostalgia.

Murs murs (1981) Documentary (Lejeune lists this as *Mur murs*)

Ulysses (1982)

Une Minute pour une image (1984)

Les Dites Cariatides (1984)

Sans toit ni loi (1985; 105 mins.; in English, *Vagabond*) (**Buss** 163) A woman outside the safety of domesticity attempts to maintain herself. Varda probes deeply into the woman's condition of darkness and pain. A bleak account of the adventures of a waif who drops out of Parisian society to wander and to die in the southwest corner of France, where she learns she is not "free." Stars Sandrine Bonnaire (*A nos amours*). Again, the title is sardonic, referring to the French expression "sans foi ni loi." But who are those without foi or loi? The film is not only an analysis of Mona, but also a dissection (a vivesection) of French society.

Mario Cloutier in "Agnès Varda: Une Jeune Femme très digne." ([Interview.] *Séquences* 177 [March–April 1995]: 25–27) claims Varda feels she has something in common with Mona. . . . Being half Greek, she states that she has no roots. She also says that the portrait of Mona was impossible to do, as it was painted by one thousand people; she invented her, but does not know all there is to know of her. She compares it to the title of Godard, *Deux ou trois choses que je sais d'elle* (*Two or three things that I know about her*) (1967). See also **Flitterman-Lewis** 312–14, where she studies the "gaze" through a window and shows analogous techniques in Jean Epstein's *Coeur Fidèle*, Maya Deren's *Meshes of the Afternoon*, and Jean-Luc Godard's *Alphaville*. For Flitterman-Lewis, it is a defining moment. For her, too, this film addresses not only Mona herself who always eludes us, but also "The 'Mona effect' on those she came in contact with and inevitably affected. She is a catalyst, someone who forces others to react and adjust themselves in relation to her. . . . In *Vagabond*, Varda's *Ulysses,* the 'impossible portrait' reverberates with possibilities."

Much has been written about this film; Mona's name, for example, means alone, lonely, and other things besides. Criticism can be found through international directories.

T'as de beaux escaliers, tu sais . . . (1986)

Le Petit Amour (first called *Kung Fu Master!*) (1987; 80 mins.) (or 1989) A forty-year-old divorcée falls for a fifteen-year-old boy who adores video games. He has difficulty getting away from her. Stars Jane Birkin and Mathieu Demy (son of Agnès Varda); also C. Gainsbourg. Compare the reverse situation in *La Petite Sirène* (forty-year-old man and fourteen-year-old girl). Some found both these films "sensitive"— I found *Le Petit Amour* unrewarding and somewhat bizarre.

Jane B. par Agnès V. (1987)

Jacquot de Nantes (1991) Tribute to Varda's late husband— Jacques Demy, director of *Les Parapluies de Cherbourg*. Acclaimed as a "masterpiece" by Roger **Ebert**. Read his short and glowing essay on this film. Foster (361) sees this film as comparable to *Sans toit . . .* in its handling of identity issues. See also the film *L'Univers de Jacques Demy*.

Les Demoiselles de Rochefort ont eu 24 ans (1993?) Deals with a film of Demy (*Les Demoiselles de Rochefort*—in which twin sisters strive to find the perfect romance). Films the joy of filming ("d'être là"). Forgetfulness, old age, time, and death are "evacuated." (*French Review* [March 1994]; 714.)

Les Cent et une nuits (de monsieur Cinéma) (1995; 125 mins.) A mythomaniacal old man (Simon or M. Cinéma) looks back on his childhood and recalls certain movies and stars. Written, directed, and produced by Agnès Varda; photography by Eric Gauthier; editing: Hughes Darmois; music, taken from films by others; sound: Jean-Pierre Duret and Henri Morelle; sets: Cyr Boitard and Cédric Simoneau; costumes: Rosalie Varda. Cast: Michel Piccoli, as Simon Cinéma; Julie Gayer, as Camille; Mathieu Demy (son of director) as Mica; Marcello Mostriani; Henri Garcin as Firmin; Emmanuel Saliner, as Vincent; Carole Benôit and Weiwei Melk as servant women; Romane Bohringer; Gérard Depardieu; Jean-Claude Brialy; Alain Delon; Sandrine Bonnaire; Jeanne Moreau. Distributed by Astral. Available from Version Française with subtitles.

Varda insists that this film is not about the death of cinema; that it is in no way symbolic. She also states that the film has as its basis, point of reference, and master Buñuel, in his short pieces, his golden age. There is some reflection, too, of the old René Clair short films in the dadaiste style, such as *Entr'acte*.

For review of this film, see Mario **Cloutier**, "Agnès Varda: Une Jeune Femme très digne" (interview). *Séquences* 177 (March–April 1995): 25–27. Varda asserts that this film is a "divertissement"—much lighter than her other recent work. See insert by Johanne **Larue** (*Séquences* 177 [March–April 1995]: 27), who did not find the film convincing. "Varda's point of view left me dissatisfied." [Le point de vue de Varda m'a laissée sur ma faim.]" I found it did not stand up to Varda's best.

For another discussion of this film, see Stéphane **Grand-Chavin,** "La Mémoire percée d'Agnès Varda." *France-Amérique* (30 March–5 April 1996): 13.

Additional selected bibliography on Varda:

Mario Cloutier. "Agnès Varda: Une Jeune Femme très digne." *Séquences* 177 (March–April 1995): 25–27.

"Daisy Lamothe et Agnès Varda." *BREF* 13 (summer, 1992): 12. Still.

Edelman, Rob. "Travelling a Different Route: An Interview with Agnes Varda." *Cinéaste* 15, no. 1 (1986): 20–21.

Filmographie. filmags. 11 *Segnocinema* 55, no. 36 (May–June 1992).

Floret, M. C., et al. "Agnès, par Varda." filmag. *Jeune Cinéma* 214 (April–May 1992): 4-17. Stills.

Milet, C. "La Cinécriture d'Agnès Varda: 'Je ne filme jamais des gens que je n'aime pas.'" *Cinemaction* 41 (January 1987): 132–36. Stills.

Revue belge du cinéma 20 (feté indien 1987). On Agnès Varda.

On Les Demoiselles . . . see *The French Review* 67, no. 4 (March 1994): 714.

Varda, Agnès. "Vers le visage de Jacques." **Cahiers** 438 (December 1990): 30–33.

Bassan, R. "Jacquot de Nantes." *Revue du Cinéma* 412 (June 1991): 220–21, Credits; filmographie; stills.

Cortellazzo, Sara, and Michèle Marangi. *Agnès Varda Script* 11 (spring 1991): 12.

Delvaux, C. "Entretien avec Agnès Varda." *24 Images* 55 (summer 1991): 53–53.

"Evocation d'une enfance heureuse." *24 Images* 55 (summer 1991): 52.

On Le Bonheur. Filmfacts 9 (1966): 138. Credits given.

Blair, Sallyann. "Le Bonheur." Movie 14 (autumn 1965): 24–25.

Gow, Gordon. "Le Bonheur." *Films and Filming* 11, 12 (September 1965): 30–31.

Kozloff, Max. "Le Bonheur." *Film Quarterly* 22, no. 2 (winter 1966–67): 35–37.

Rubin, Elizabeth, and James Mallory. "Le Bonheur." *Cinema* 3, no. 4 (December 1966): 48.

Sussex, Elizabeth. "Le Bonheur." *Sight and Sound* 34, no. 4 (autumn 1965): 200–1.

Wellington, Frederick. "Le Bonheur." Film Comment 3, no. 3 (summer 1965): 32–33.

On "Cléo de 5 à 7." Film 34 (winter 1962): 24.
On "Cléo de 5 à 7." Filmfacts 5 (1962): 232.

Manvell, Roger. *"Cléo de 5 à 7." Films and Filming* 9, no. 3 (December 1962): 38.

Roud, Richard. *"Cléo de 5 à 7."* Sight and Sound 31, no. 3 (summer 1962): 145–46.

Shivas, Mark. *"Cléo de 5 à 7."* Movie 3 (October 1962): 32.

See also **Lejeune** 213–16 and **Foster,** esp. 360–62, including filmography and bibliography; as well as the book *Varda par Agnès*, Editions de l'Etoile, *Cahiers du Cinéma*, 1994.

Nicole Védrès b. 1911; d. 1965. Made her first compilation film with the great woman editor Myriam and with Alain Resnais (then unknown). Concerned with the life of the city at the turn of the last century, it was called *Paris 1900* (made in 1947). Because this film was so successful, she went on to direct other works.

Paris 1900 (1947) A compilation film, using archival footage made before 1914; news items, documentaries, and a few sets. Paris in the time of fiacres, Paris of the boulevards, but also the common people of the faubourgs (outlying areas of Paris). In the last part, more serious: the floods of 1910, the strikes, the workers' demonstrations, the great maneuvers of the two sides of the Rhine, the Balkan wars, and finally general mobilization, the departure of the *pioupious* in red pantaloons, in August 1914, from the gare de l'Est in Paris. (Freely trans. from **Sadoul,** *Dict. des Films,* 249.)

La Vie commence demain (1950) This film contains interviews with J.-P. Sartre, Jean Rostand, and Pablo Picasso. It was a commercial failure.

Amazone (a segment of *L'Encyclopédie filmée*) (1951)

Aux frontières de l'homme (1953; with Jean Rostand)

In **Foster,** Védrès is mentioned only in passing (26); but see **Lejeune** 64.

Aude Vermeil
Corps et âmes (1996)

Marion Vernoux b. 1967.

Personne ne m'aime (1994; 95 mins.) French-Swiss. First feature-length film by this director. Directed and written by Vernoux. Actors: Bernadette Lafont, Bulle Ogier, Lio, Michèle Laroque, Jean-Pierre Léaud, André Marcon, and Boris Bergman. A "road movie" whose principal protagonists are two women past forty. The film does not in any way resemble *Thelma and Louise*. In *France-Amérique* (8–14 April 1995): 12, Vernoux claims she wanted to break with the chic Parisian naturalism found in most French films. Pascal **Boutroy** finds that the film surfs gracefully over the remains of New Wave. Even with debts, the film at no moment suffers from the shadow of the elders. (*Séquences* 174 [September–October 1994]: 45.)

Marguerite Viel 1894–1976.
La Jungle d'une grande ville (1929; wtih Léon Marten)
Occupe-toi d'Amélie (1932)(with René Weissbach; adapted from Feydeau's play)
La Banque Némo (1934)

Sandrine Veysset
Y aura-t-il de la Neige à Noël? (1996) See *Séquences* (January–February 1997): 20.

Rachel **Weinberg**
Pic et pic et colegram (1972)
L'Ampélopède (1973)
La Flambeuse (1980)
La Gambler (?; 95 mins.) A woman loses her job, turns to gambling, and risks losing her family, too. Stars L. Massari, L. Terzieff, and G. Blain. (Version Française catalog.)
See **Erans;** see also **Lejeune** 218–19.

Anielle Weinberger b. Paris 1946. (Has written adaptations of several literary works, including two of Diderot's works.) She has directed
Jémina, fille des montagnes (1970) Short. Adapted from the short story "Jemina, the Mountain Girl" (1916; 1921, 1922) by F. Scott Fitzgerald.
L'Honorable société (1980)
Les Enfants du jazz (1980) Made for TV
Le Temps d'une chanson (1982) Made for TV

Yolande Zauberman
Moi Ivan, Toi Abraham [*Ivan and Abraham*] (1993; 105 mins.) Written in French and then translated into a combination of Yiddish, Polish, Russian, and Rumanian. (It is listed as a French event in *France-Amérique*.) About the intercultural friendship of two children, one Christian, the other Jewish, in 1933 Poland, before the holocaust. Stars Roma Alexandrovitch. (See *French Review*, March 1994: 715). Also Version Française catalog.
La Petite Lola

Addendum: See **Kuhn** who lists Black European women directors, including Véronique Mucret and Harmel Sbraire.
Also note: Sharon **Smith** (119) adds to her list the following names of women who were or are directors of short films: Francine Premysler, Sylvia Hulin, Vergez-Tricom, Lucile Costa, Colette Harel-Lisztman, Anne Dastrée, Simone Crozet and Yolande de Luart.

She also mentions several women producers (123), including Mag Bodard (*Les Parapluies de Cherbourg*, 1964; *Je t'aime, je t'aime*, 1968; *Peau d'âne*, 1970); Christine Gouse-Rénal (*Les Amitiés particulières*); Nicole Stéphane (q.v.); Lucy Ulrych; Jenny Gérard; Vera Belmont (q.v.).

Iceland

Kristin Johannesdotter An Icelandic filmmaker born in 1948. She made several short films in French while studying in Paris in 1978, including
Arthur et Rosa, in which she imagines what it would have been like for Rimbaud to meet Rosa Luxemburg.
Lendemains moroses, in which she treats the subject of depression from hangovers.

Lebanon

Joceline Saab A documentarist.
Le Liban dans la tourmente (Lebanon in Turmoil) (1975)
Beyrouth ma ville (Beirut My Town) (1982)

Monaco

Sabrina Joris See under Belgian directors

Québec

Anne Ardouin
Une Rivière imaginaire (1993–94?) Roméo Céré, a legendary prospector in the mining industry of Québec, tells about his job. This man, eighty-three years old, is both a passionate person and, indeed, a hero. Ardouin (*Séquences*, [April 1994]: 10) relates her experiences in making this film and explains how the film is a kind of documentary on the world of prospectors: "They are fascinated by everything there is beneath the earth."

Paule Baillargeon b. 1945. Actress (*Entre tu et vous, Les Vautours, La Femme de l'hôtel, I've Heard the Mermaids Singing*), producer, and director of
Anasthasie, oh ma chérie (1977) (Carrière spells: *Anasthasie;* Coulombe *Anastasie.*) A woman has decided to cut herself off from

the world; she shuts herself up in an apartment; masculine power tries to recuperate her.

La Cuisine rouge (1980; codirected with Frédérique Collin) Men and women back-to-back: During a wedding the men drink and wait to be served by the women who are in the kitchen. The women rebel. A controversial film, perhaps B.'s most famous and certainly one of the first important feminist films of Québec. See Coulombe for credits.

Sonia (d., 1986) A portrayal of Alzheimer's disease, and the effect of it on the mother-daughter relationship. Sonia played by Kim Yaroshevskaya; daughter by Baillargeon. Themes are creativity, loneliness, and aging. Took André-Leroux prize. See Coulombe for credits.

Le Complexe d'Edith (1991) A TV film for which B. did not write script.

Bulle (1991) A TV film for which B. did not write script.

Le Sexe des étoiles (1993) The story of a man whose daughter grapples with his sex change. The role of daughter is well played; but that of "father" is overdone. As a woman he seems a parody of a woman—overplaying arm and leg movements; he is nothing but a man in drag. Yet in the end when he or she appears in male clothes in effort to please the daughter he or she is repulsive; the daughter gives up struggling against the change and at the same time gives up the (quest for the lost) father.

Josée Beaudet b. 1938. Producer, editor, director, and researcher. Edited *Jules le magnifique; Les Servantes du Bon Dieu; On n'est pas des anges.*

Le Film d'Ariane [Ariadne's Movie](1985) The history of Québec's women (1925–80) through the story of one woman, Ariadne. Early scenes in the film show a rapid history of the Québécoise, including nuns baling hay. The strong role the Church played in the lives of the women of Ariadne's generation is emphasized. Ariadne explains that in those days women were told not to mix into politics; the Church was against women's suffrage. In the second part, we learn that Ariadne is interested in being a wife/mother. Women "in those days" got married and then they did as they were told. A man's voice—that of Ariadne's husband—explains that "in those days there was no divorcing." Ariadne tells how the war brought on marriages. Moreover, women became "soldats de l'industrie." Between the two wars, then, came the exodus of women from the home and into the workforce.

In the third section we are informed men were no longer innocent, thanks to the war; but women still were. At thirty-eight, says Ariadne, she had had eight children within ten years. Every sexual encounter was high risk. Yet, when she told the priest she had denied her husband sex just after her baby was born, the priest told her, "I'm going to excommunicate you." There were other blatant prejudices against women. Ariadne tells about the advances made by her daughters who appear to have surmounted the obstacles. The final segment of this fascinating documentary deals with the "generation of change," 1965–80, when women achieved more freedom. Took four prizes, including two Gerbes d'or.

See Coulombe (under Beaudet) for her work as producer of Office National du Film's Regard de femmes (or, in English, National Film Board [of Canada]).

Diane Beaudry Has been employed by the Office National du Film (du Canada) (or National Film Board) since 1979 as editor, producer, and director.

An Unremarkable Birth Describes the dehumanization of giving birth.

L'Ordinateur en tête Impact of information on women's employment.

L'Autre Muraille Filmed in China; depicts women torn between ancient heritage and modernity.

La Double Histoire d'Odile Fiction

Apprendre . . . ou à laisser Fiction

See *Zoom sur elles*, 51. Also see Pratley's list of films in English, 271.

Brigitte Bergman

Bix (1983) Documentary Recollections of the jazz artist Bix Beiderbecke.

Sara Bézaire

Sophie Bissonnette b. 1957. Editor, producer, and director. Works primarily with the "engaged" or committed social documentary.

Une Histoire de femmes (1980; codirectors, N. Duckworth and J. Rock) A documentary restricted to special concerns. It specifically treats the wives of strikers who questioned their traditional support role at the time of the 1978 INCO of Sudbury (Ontario) strike that involved the copper and nickel mines, foundries, and refineries. Bissonnette has written an essay about making this film entitled "Exploration féministe du documentaire" (in *CinémAction: Aujourd'hui le cinéma québécois*, ed. Carrière, 1982: 255–61). Consciousness-raising. *Une Histoire de femmes* is in the tradition of the *cinéma direct*. Bissonnette states that this is a "*cinéma d'intervention*."

This film took the Prix de la critique québécoise for 1981, but it lacks the profundity and electricity of *Les Terribles vivantes* (q.v.) or *Les Filles du Roy* (q.v.). *Une Histoire de femmes* receives ample treat-ment in Coulombe under Bissonnette.

Luttes d'ici, luttes d'ailleurs (1982) Documentary that reflects on relations and international solidarity.

Quel Numéro? or *What Number?* (1985; 81 mins.) Documentary that explores the condition of women who must work with computers, but feel they are controlled by these machines.

L'Amour à quel prix? (1987) Feminization of poverty in North America. Three long *récits* by women who had waited for marriage with idealized notions based on romance novels and telenovels. They are, of course, disillusioned.

Des Lumières dans la grande noirceur (1991) Gives homage to a eighty-six-year-old militant of union and feminist milieus, Léa Roback. (See Coulombe.)

Nicole Boisvert
Pourquoi l'étrange M. Zolock s'intéressait-il tant à la bande dessinée? (1983) Documentary about comic strips and cartoons in France and Belgium.

Hélène Bourgault with Helen Doyle
Chaperons rouges (1979)

Marilyn Burgess
Une Fille de ma gang (1989)

Iolande Cadrin-Rossignol
L'Art populaire (1976)
L'Espace intérieur (with F. Dansereau and F. Pilon) (1976)
L'Eglise traditionnelle (with G. Cousineau) (1976)
Thetford au milieu de notre vie (1978)
Musique outre-mesure (1982)
Rencontre avec une femme remarquable, Laure Gaudreault (1983) A study of Gaudreault, journalist, teacher, and union organizer in the 30s and of her work for the women's movement (Pratley, 265).
Contes de mille et un jours, ou Jean Desprez (1986)
See entry in Coulombe under Cadrin-Rossignol for complete listing of her works. Here it is stated that she is preparing an adaptation of *Menaud maître draveur,* a classic of Québec literature by Félix-Antoine Savard.

Diane Cailhier
Une Vie comme rivière (1996; ONF) Video, codirected with her husband Alain Chatrand.

Louise Carré b. 1936. Producer (La Maison des Quatre), administrator, scriptwriter, and director.

Ça peut pas être l'hiver, on a même pas eu d'été (It Can't Be Winter; We Haven't Had Summer Yet) (1980; also scripted by Carré) Adèle Marquis, a woman of fifty-seven (played by Charlotte Boisjoli), finds herself alone when her husband Albert dies. She decides to take stock, and in so doing, she concludes she has been served a great injustice. She has waited on a selfish husband and eight children for forty years. On the verge of a severe depression, she resists, and instead opens up to the world. She finds friendship, digs into her past for explanations, and discovers a meaning for her existence and her frustrations. With Céline Lomez. Took the Prix de la Presse Internationale (1980).

Qui a tiré sur nos histoires d'amour? (A Question of Loving) (1986; also scripted by Carré) The story deals with the relationship between a mother (Monique Mercure), who is a sophisticated director of radio, TV, and film, and her daughter. (Certain autobiographical aspects here.) The daughter, Renée, has come to look upon her mother—who is full of life and enthusiasm—with humor, tenderness, and irony. The latter has become for the young woman a model of passion and courage, but the daughter experiences, nonetheless, some hesitation in her admiration. The two women spend one last summer together in a small provincial town (Sorel). They come to appreciate each other and to discover their love is indestructible and invaluable.

Germaine (1991) Made in memory of her mother who died of Alzheimer's disease. Revolves around a poem by Carré and a letter her mother had written.

Ghyslaine Côté

Aux voleurs! Took prize for her **scénario** at the International Festival of shorts at Montréal (1993).

Aimée Danis b. 1929. Producer, editor, and director.

Maryse, pile ou face (1967)

KW (1969)

Gaspésie, oui j'écoute (1971)

La Croix du Mont-Royal (1971)

L'Evadé (1971)

L'Adieu au lys (1971)

Souris, tu m'inquiètes (1973) (En tant que femmes series). Loss of woman's identity. (Principal role played by Micheline Lanctôt.) Produced by Anne Claire Poirier. See Coulombe (Génériques) for credits.

Joie de vivre (1973)

Mesdames et messieurs la fête (1976)
Le Stock du futur (1979)

Mireille Dansereau b. 1943. Editor, producer, scriptwriter, and direc-
tor. Seventeen years as a dancer before turning to film.
  Moi un jour (1967) A young girl questions her bourgeois milieu.
  Compromise (1969; 28 mins.) Took first prize at National Student
Film Festival in London.
  Forum (1969)
  La Vie rêvée (*Dream(ed) Life*) (1972) The core meaning conveyed
here is that "dream life" is representative both of the nightmare and
of the "ideal" imposed upon the female psyche by advertising and by
socialization processes, including dreams of incest and extermination.
To be free, the dream must be dissipated. The nightmare content of
these dreams is a theme represented by images of barbed wire, clothes
strung on clothes lines, and so on.
  The two girls in the film (Isabelle, of wealthy parents—that is, of
a very constrained background—and Virginia, of a middle-class, less
affluent family whose freedom is envied by Isabelle) are in advertising.
They, like the viewer, are barraged with images and imaging. Some
of the products alluded to—seemingly largely American (made in the
United States)—include 7-Up; Coca-Cola; Coffeemate; Heinz tomato
ketchup; Pepto-Bismol. And during this film the two enter the "real
life" free of fantasy and, at the end, are delirious over their liberation.
  Received the Wendy Michener Award for Outstanding Artistic
Achievement.
  Louise **Carrière** (*Femmes* . . . [1983], 164–65) claims that *La Vie
rêvée* is inspired by sociological reflections on youth and the contradictions of *québécois* society. Commenting on the technical features of
Dream(ed) Life, Carrière points out that Mireille Dansereau, using
slow motion, long shots, pastel tones to denounce and to visualize the
women's fantasies, makes her film somewhat blurry. The question is,
therefore, raised (by Carrière, by the viewer) about what exactly
Dansereau intends?
  For credits, see Coulombe's Génériques 599.
  J'me marie; j'me marie pas (1973) Four women artists seek to recon-
cile their careers with their family life. [In *style direct.*] For credits,
see Coulombe's Génériques 574.
  Rappelle-toi (1975; codirected with V. Cholakian) Stars Luce
Guilbeault.
  Famille et variations (1977) Documentary The evolution of family
reality in the context of Québec society. Collaboration with Claire
Leduc. [In style direct.]

L'Arrache-coeur (1979) (Pratley gives 1980) Uses the structure of psychoanalytic discourse. A young woman (played by Louise Marleau) frees herself from a conflict with her mother (played by Françoise Faucher) and is, therefore, better able to love her husband and child. For credits, see Coulombe's *Génériques* 555. Incidentally, Louise Marleau took a prize at the FFM (Festival des films du Monde [Montréal]) for her role in this film.

Le frère André Documentary for television

Le Sourd dans la ville (1987) Adaptation of Marie-Claire Blais's novel. Depicts the suffering and despair of a rich woman (played by Béatrice Picard), abandoned by her husband, as well as those of a sick child (played by Guillaume Lemay-Thivierge) whose mother (played by Angèle Coutu) fills his head with dreams of California. The two worlds come together in a sordid hotel. For credits, see Coulombe's *Génériques* 592.

J'aime, j'aime pas (1997)

(For further information see Coulombe under entry for Dansereau, Mireille)

Irène Demcauk

Une Maison de naissances (1987)

Francine Desbiens b. 1938. Producer, animation artist, and director.

Le Corbeau et le renard (1969; codirected with P. Hébert et al.)

Les Bibites de Chromagnon (1971) [*The Little Men of Chromagnon*]

Du Coq à l'âne (codirected with P. Hébert et al.)

Dernier envol (1977) About loneliness.

E (1981; codirected with Bretislav Pojar)

L'Art de l'animation (1982)

Ah! vous dirai-je maman (1985)

Dessine-moi une chanson (1990) Using the music of Robert M. Lepage, Desbiens traces the culpability of parents who leave their children in day care.

(*La Plage; This Is Me* [Pratley, 279])

Marguerite Duparc

La Turlute des années dures (1983) Documentary about the years between the two world wars, referring mostly to Québec.

Viviane Elnécavé b. in Egypt in 1945, but came to Canada when quite young. It was in Canada that she learned her art; she studied in the Ecole des Beaux-Arts of McGill University. Director and animation artist.

Notre jeunesse en auto-sport (1969) Based on the song of Claude

Gauthier, this film was made for the ONF series "Chansons contemporaines."

L'Oeil (1972)

Rien qu'une petite chanson d'amour (1974) Relationship of children to parents.

Moi, je pense (1978) E. created two animated sequences for this film, directed by R. Tunis.

Luna, luna, luna (1981) This film used a new and original animation technique (q.v., Coulombe). Prize-winning film.

Caravane Parody.

Michèle Favreau

Monique Fortier b. 1928. Editor (*Les Voitures d'eau*, 1970; Pierre Perrault; *L'Acadie, l'Acadie*, 1971, Michel Brault and Pierre Perrault; *Le Crime d'Ovide Plouffe*, 1984, Denys Arcand) and director. Worked for ONF during the 1960s. She has edited many other works of *cinéma direct* with the masters (Perrault, Brault, Dufaux, Gosselin, and Arcand); on this see Coulombe.

A l'heure de la décolonisation (1963)

La Beauté même (1964) Fortier seeks to show in this documentary what beauty is to a woman.

Fermont, P.Q. (1980; codirected with C. Perron)

Jeanine Gagné

Drôle de fille The story of the woman clown, Sonia "Chatouille" Côté.

Louise Gendron

Femmes de rêve (1979)

Suzanne Gervais-L'Heureux b. 1938. Animation artist; director. Began work with the ONF in 1969.

Cycle (1971) Short

Du Coq à l'âne (1973; codirected with F. Desbiens and P. Hébert)

Tchou-Tchou (1973; directed by C. Hoedeman) Gervais created the characters painted on wooden blocks. For credits, see Coulombe's Génériques 594.

Climats (1975) Reveals desire of Gervais(-L'Heureux) to grasp feelings buried in the deepest part of the heart.

La Plage (1978) Adaptation of a Roch Carrier long short story. For credits, see Coulombe's Génériques 585.

Premiers Jours (1980; directed by Lina Gagnon) Gervais helped complete this film after the death of Clorinda Warny, q.v. For credits, see Coulombe's Génériques 587.

Trêve (1983)

L'Atelier (1988) A woman artist questions her relationship to her male model. For credits, see Coulombe's Génériques 555.

Le Tableau noir (1990; directed by J. Giraldeau) Gervais participated in the creation of this feature-length film.

Les Iris (1991)

Hélène Girard b. 1945. Editor and director. Worked on the program "En tant que femmes" for the ONF (Office National du Film) from the time of its inception. Edited many of the important films of Québec (see listing, Coulombe).

Les Filles c'est pas pareil (1974) Themes of feminine identity during adolescence. For credits, see Coulombe's Génériques 568.

La P'tite Violence (1977) In direct style; relationship of man to work.

Fuir (Flight) (1979) Suicide is subject of this film.

Charlotte Gobeil

Sylvie Groulx b. 1953. Distributor; director. In 1991 she adapted from English into French a series of short pedagogical films on sex education. She also became a permanent film director for the ONF.

Une bien belle ville (1975; codirector; Groulx a part of a collective that made this film). Deals with problems of housing in undesirable Montréal locations.

Le Grand Remue-ménage (1978; with Francine Allaire) This is a "fierce expedition" into the question of stereotypes as projected by media and by other forces rampant in a preconditioned society.

Jean-Pierre **Tadros** claims the directors of *Le Grand Remue-ménage* intend to present a film in which men are recognized as victims. Not only men, then, but women also, are shown in the film to be victims. Tadros states that for Allaire and Groulx, it is a question of demonstrating the social mechanisms that make man what he is and make woman a creature of desire or the mother of a family. ("Grand Remue-ménage . . . ," 1978; see bibliography.)

But is the film so objective as Tadros claims? The images flashed before our eyes, and the testimonials of the interviewees seem a trifle biased toward women.

[For credits of *Le Grand Remue-ménage,* see Coulombe's Génériques 570.]

Entre deux vagues (1985; codirected with Richard Boutet)

Chronique d'un temps flou (1988) A documentary that presents a portrait of young people in Québec today. For credits, see Coulombe's Génériques 560.

"Qui va chercher Gisèle à 3h45?" (1989) A documentary on problems of motherhood.

Un Enfant à quel prix? Accumulates anecdotes around children,
daily catastrophes, and so on. "The dynamism and freshness of the
film owe much to the use of gags and of Odile's 'double'" (Louise
Carrière, *Zoom sur elles*, 38).

Luce Guilbeault b. 1935; d. 1991. An important Québécoise actress,
she had roles in Denys Arcand's *Maudite Galette* (1971); Jacques
Godbout's *IXE-13* (1971); Francis Mankiewicz's *Le Temps d'une
chasse* (1972); Jean Beaudin's *J. A. Martin, photographe* (1976), and
many other movies, including several feminist films (see Coulombe,
under Guilbeault). With Paule Baillargeon she was a protagonist in
Le Temps de l'avant (1975; directed by Anne Claire Poirier; q.v.) But
she was also a director (see below). In 1991, the year of her death,
she received the first Iris award from the ONF for her life's work.

Denyse Benoît comédienne (1975) A young actress takes care of old
people while she waits for a part.

Some American Feminists (1977; 56 mins.; with Nicole Brossard
and Margaret Wescott) Highlighted in this documentary—which is
not meant to offer a definition of feminism, but rather a document on
the experiences, feelings, and theories of a select group of feminists—
are such porte-parole(s) of American feminism as Bella Abzug (the
American congresswoman, a vigorous proponent of women's rights
and a pacifist, who helped found the Women's Strike for Peace in
1961); Rita Mae Brown (author and poet); Margo Jefferson (writer
and critic); Kate Millett (author and sculptor); Lila Karp (writer and
professor); Ty-Grace Atkinson (feminist theoretician and activist) and
Betty Friedan (author). The film (produced at the ONF) is described
by Michel **Euvrard** as "a gallery of portraits and an anthology of
feminist discourse . . . ; as an attentive and riveting film, serious and
animated . . . because the people are presented 'in action'" (Coulombe
249). For credits, see Coulombe's Génériques 592.

D'abord ménagères (1978) **Euvrard**, comparing *D'abord* . . . with
Some American Feminists, finds that "there is more fantasy, good humor, atmosphere and warmth here [in *D'abord* . . .] . . ." (Coulombe
249).

Dorothy Todd Hénaut [Sometimes listed under *Hénaut;* sometimes
under *Todd.*] b. in Ontario in 1935. Producer, researcher, scriptwriter,
and director. Mother of the producer Suzanne Hénaut. Much of her
work has been done in English, but *Les Terribles Vivantes* (available
in both French and English) and *Québec . . . un peu . . .* (made in
French) are to be noted here.

Les Terribles Vivantes (*Fire Words*) (1986; 84 mins.) Portrays the work and the inner nature of three renowned women writers of Québec: Louky Bersianik, Jovette Marchessault, and Nicole Brossard. *Fire Words,* or *Les Terribles Vivantes,* is a documentary not to be overlooked. Its value lies in particular in the segment on Marchessault.

Québec ... un peu ... beaucoup ... passionément (1989) concerns the singer Pauline Julien and her poet-politician husband, Gérald Godin, both of whom were very much involved in history-making events during the "Quiet Revolution" and the 1980 referendum.

Also in Pratley 283–84: directed—*Horse Drawn Magic; The New Alchemists; Sun, Wind and Wood; VTR Saint-Jacques;* produced—*Temiscaming, Québec.*

Carole Laganière See Belgian directors

Evelyn Lambart

She is an anglophone Québécoise, and one of the greatest animation artists of the world; virtually all her works are available in French as well as in English.

Les Femmes parmi nous
See Pratley 289–90, for list of ten works in English.

Micheline Lanctôt b. 1947. Animation artist, actress, scriptwriter and director. In *Châtelaine* (February 1996:14) she states that the cinema is not a man's trade, nor a woman's, but that of a single person, man or woman, since when one has children (as she does), they should come above all else. As actress, Lanctôt played the lead in *La Vraie Nature de Bernadette* (directed by Gilles Carle; 1972), had a role in *The Apprenticeship of Duddy Kravitz* (Ted Kotcheff, 1974), *Mourir à tue-tête* (Anne Claire Poirier, 1979), *Les Liens de sang* (Claude Chabrol, 1977), and so on. (See Coulombe under Lanctôt.) She also wrote scripts for: *Le Grand Air de Louise* (for which no producer was found) and *La Ligne de chaleur* (H.-Y. Rose, 1988). One of her most recent acting roles was in *L'Oreille d'un sourd,* opened 10 February 1996. But as director she has made

Trailer (1976)

A Token Gesture (1978 says Coulombe; 1975 says Foster; 1976 says Kuhn.) Animated film on female stereotypes (ONF).

L'Homme à tout faire (1980; 99 mins.) A naif man (played by Jocelyn Bérubé) keeps getting involved with women, especially a beautiful bourgeoise (played by Andrée Pelletier), for whom he is the homme à tout faire or handyman.

Sonatine (1983) Set against the background of an impending public strike, this three-part story is one of two alienated adolescent girls—

Chantal and Louisette—who are convinced that the world is full of nothing but aloof and indifferent people. They try to escape from the indifference they encounter in their daily lives by "discovering" Montréal—one of the girls (Chantal) with a bus driver whose route she always takes—until he gets transferred—and the other girl (Louisette) with a Bulgarian sailor as a stowaway—until he exposes her. But thanks to him, she experiences a fleeting moment of tenderness. The third part shows the two girls joining forces to try to get the world to prevent their suicide.

This film was a failure, according to the public and to some critics (though it appealed to others, and also took the Silver Lion at Venice). **Donohoe** compares the structure of the film to three movements in a musical piece, with Chantal as movement one; Louisette as movement two, and Chantal/Louisette plus coda as movement three. He also finds debts to Antonioni's *Deserto Rosso* in the second movement, and sees the third movement as reminiscent of Truffaut's *Quatre Cents Coups*. Above all, he sees the suicide of the two adolescents in the metro as attributable to the lack of moral sustenance that the girls receive in a society that even so has arrived at considerable technological sophistication and material prosperity. **Foster** finds parallels here with Varda's *Sans toit ni loi* (q.v.). [For credits, see Coulombe's Génériques 592.]

La Poursuite du bonheur (1987) Made for the ONF series *l'Américanité*. It examines happiness within a consumer society, and in the process bitterly portrays the Americanization of Canadian culture. This effort was put under a critical cloud.

Onzième Spéciale (1988) A television film, based on a *scénario* by Louise Roy and Marie Perreault, in which a woman painter, in her thirties, examines, the failure her life seems to be (Marcel **Jean**, in Coulombe 1991: 309).

Deux actrices (1993; 94 mins.) The reality of the lives of two actresses is intercut with parts they are playing as two sisters whose intense and bitter confrontations with their mothers are portrayed on video, from which the two actresses view their "progress." Directed, produced, written, and edited by Lanctôt; photography: André Gagnon; music: Kate and Ann McGarrigle. Characters: Solange—Pascale Bussières; Fabienne—Pascale Paroissien; mother—Louise Latraverse; Charles—François Deslisle; Florist—Suzanne Garceau.

This film, *Deux actrices,* gets a strongly positive review from Mario **Cloutier** in *Séquences* 168 (January 1994): 41–42. See also p. 12 of same issue.

La Vie d'un héros (1994) Film made with Rock Demers. Story of relations of a mother and daughter over time. Marked by rare sense

of humor. Mario Cloutier (in *Séquences* 174 [September–October 1994]: 9) states that the film was made on a small budget but is skillfully edited. "Micheline Lanctôt has an unusual vision, unique in realistic cinema. Cynical she is, probably, but certainly not more so than the sad epoch in which we live" (my trans.).
See in bibliography: Denise **Pérusse**, *Micheline Lanctôt: La Vie d'une héroïne*, 1995. See also **Foster**, esp. 214–16

Nicole Lavallée

Monique LeBlanc b. 17 December 1960 in Richibouctou, New Brunswick, Canada. She wrote the script for the award winning animated short, *Maille, Maille (Stitches in Time)*.
Le Lien acadien (The Acadian Connection)
She is currently working on a feature script and on a documentary on cigarettes.

Marquise Lepage b. 1959. Became a permanent director at the Office National du Film in 1991.
Prince pas prince ... (1981) Lepage made this first film (a short) while studying communications at the University of Québec at Montréal (UQAM).
Jacques et Novembre (1984; with Jean Beaudry and François Bouvier) Lepage was director of production and adjunct director of this very fine film.
Marie s'en va-t-en ville (Marie in the City) (1987) Having been assaulted by her older brother, Marie, still an adolescent, leaves their home in rural Québec and departs for the city, where she meets an aging and disillusioned prostitute named Sarah. Marie would like to move into Sarah's apartment and insinuate herself into Sarah's life, but Sarah is not interested in Marie's affection and not touched by her admiration. However, Marie's naïveté and the tenderness finally penetrate Sarah's hard surface, and the two women bond. Stars Frédérique Collin. (For credits, see Coulombe Génériques 577.)
Un Soleil entre deux nuages (1989) A documentary about children with fatal illnesses.
Deux femmes en voyage Mother-daughter theme.
Le Film d'une vie
Ce qu'il en reste (1991?) Documentary about immigrants and the American dream.
Mon Amérique à moi (1992)
Dans ton pays (1992)
La Fête des rois (1994) A family celebration. Second of the ONF's series on "Familiarité." (Five more to come.) The film is in part a

caricature of the new generation, in which children become adults sooner than expected, due to new technological methods of communication.

Directed and written by Marquise Lepage. Photography: Jean-Pierre Lachapelle; editing: Yves Chaput; music: Michel Rivard; sound: Richard Besse; artistic direction: Gaudeline Sauriol; cast: Marc-André Grondin (Benjamin); Monique Mercure (Flore); Marie Elaine Berthi-aume (Charlotte); Marcel Sabourin (Anthony); Marc Messier (Denis); Denis Bouchard (Daniel).

See interview with Marquise Lepage in *Séquences* (May–June 1994): 12–13. She states that the family is a small community where different members amuse one another, love one another, tear one an-other apart, quarrel, make up, and perpetuate themselves by having children. It is also a group of persons who gather around a table for a meal. In same issue, review of film by Janick Beaulieu (34–35).

Le Jardin oublié: La Vie et l'oeuvre d'Alice Guy-Blaché (1995; 53 mins.) Documentary narrated by Blaché's granddaughter Adrienne Blaché-Channing, sometimes in the company of her mother, in which we have archival scenes from works of Blaché, including some from *Les Fées aux choux;* photos; documents; an analysis of *La Vie du Christ* by Prof. André Gaudreault. Review: Louise-Véronique Sicotte in *Séquences* 181 (November–December 1995): 44–45.

See also *Zoom sur elles*, 48–49.

Diane Létourneau b. 1942. Began her career with two or three docu-mentaries co-directed with Georges Dufaux (*A votre santé* [1964]; *Au bout de mon âge* [1975] and *Les Jardins d'hiver* [1976]).

A Force de mourir (17 mins. 30 secs.; in the series La Bioéthique: une question de choix; ONF) Dying from cancer, the father is something of a burden to his daughter. About euthanasia.

Les Oiseaux blancs de l'île d'Orléans (1977)

Les Statues de monsieur Basile (1978)

Les Servantes du Bon Dieu (1978; 90 mins.) Offers a portrait of a community of nuns formed to serve priests and living according to social and religious traditions inherent in the Québec historical heri-tage. Does not seek to show these women in any ironic light, but with honesty and respect. For credits, see Coulombe Génériques 591.

La Vie de couple (1980) About the life of a married couple. Show-cases political and societal realities.

Le Plus Beau Jour de ma vie (1981) Meditation on marriage as an institution (industry and life choice).

La Passion de danser (1982; ONF)

En scène (1982; ONF)

Une Guerre dans mon jardin (1985) Studies the situation of members of a family following the accidental death of a man. They relive the tragic event, occurring in 1980 as a result of a military *obus* being tossed into the flames of a fire on the feast day of Saint John the Baptist, historically Québec's most important holiday. The resulting work is pacifistic in tone. For credits, see Coulombe Génériques 597.

A force de mourir . . . (1987) Here Létourneau (a nurse) used her medical knowledge to look at the question of euthanasia in a somewhat fictional cadre.

Comme deux gouttes d'eau (1988) About twinning.

Pas d'amitié à moitié (1991) About friendship among women.

Tous pour un, un pour tous (1993; 75 mins.) ONF Film paying homage to friendship and solidarity, depicted through participation of four "musketeers" (fencers) in the Barcelona Olympics. Directed by Létourneau. *Scénario* by Létourneau, Georgette Duchaine, François Renaud. Cast: Stephen Angers, Nicholas Bergeron, Benoît Giasson, Luc Rocheleau, and Jean-Pierre LeCoz.

Review by Denis Desjardins in *Séquences* 168 (January 1994): 50. In same issue (p. 60) this film is rated as *passable* (one star out of five) by the only two critics to rate it.

Jacqueline Levitin

Pas fou comme on le pense (1984) Documentary in which a group of former psychiatric patients meet to compare notes.

Marilú Mallet b. Santiago Chile, 1944. Editor and director. Studies in anthropology and architecture, then in film. Made her first films in Chile under the Popular Unity regime. Her Canadian films are characterized by portrayal of problems of the immigrant in adjusting to present and accommodating his or her past.

Amuhelai-Mi (1971)

A.E.I. (1972)

La Première Année (1972; as member of a collective under direction of Patricio Gusman)

Donde voy a encontrar otra Violeta (1973)

Lentement (1974)

Il n'y a pas d'oubli (1975; with R. Gonzalez and J. Fajardo)

L'Evangile à Solentiname (1979)

Musique de l'Amérique Latine (1979)

Les Femmes de l'Amérique Latine (1980)

Les "Borges" (1978) Here Mallet documented a family of Portuguese immigrants in Montréal. Because of a language barrier, the father of this family cannot communicate with his coworkers and, therefore, feels exiled; he dreams of returning to die in his little house in Portugal. The more realistic mother, on the other hand, is attached to Montréal through her children and grandchildren. In this family, one of the sons has become an anglophone, the other a francophone; it is the latter who offers the explanations, information, and commentaries on the family, while "the camera is both familiar and respectful." (Michel Euvrard in Coulombe 359) For credits, see Coulombe Génériques 558.

Journal inachevé (*Unfinished Journal; Unfinished Diary*) (1982–83) In 1980 Mallet cofounded with Dominque Pinel les Films de l'Atalante. One of the most outstanding productions of this company was Mallet's own *Journal inachevé* (55 mins.), a film that portrays the life of a young Chilean filmmaker who lives in exile in Montréal. Analyzes Québec society from the perspective of the alienated immigrant. Also examines the coup d'état of Chile. Perhaps most important, we have in this work the clash of the filmmaker and her husband, also a filmmaker, and their conflicting value systems.

Neither documentary nor fiction (though in Coulombe [1991, 574] it is called "fiction")—*Journal* partakes of private correspondence, an intimate journal, and memories. It translates the need to reconstruct a life still hesitating between childhood and adolescence in Chile—a past that is still present in Montréal—and also portrays the problems of present-day life: a weak marriage, a difficult child, and the problematical integration into *québécois* society. The 1992–93 catalog of Women Make Movies quotes Julian Burton [of the University of California at Santa Cruz] as saying: "The displacements and disjunctions of exile have never been more poignantly conveyed. Mallet uses her domestic space as mirror of the self struggling to find a place to call home. A compelling, resolutely tentative exploration of female subjectivity." For credits, see Coulombe Génériques 574. Available Women Make Movies 1996 catalog, 45.

[Carrière's study of this film is important. But Mallet also gets ample treatment by Michel Euvrard (Coulombe 1991: 318–19).]

Mémoires d'une enfant des Andes (1986) A Peruvian village seen through the eyes of a little girl who is handicapped. More directly a documentary than any other work of Mallet.

Chère Amérique (1990) Continues the examination of the condition of the immigrant, again the Portuguese. Céleste is the owner of several apartment buildings that she administers, though she is also doing housework. She is successful in the new milieu, but she has had to leave her husband and children behind.

See **Foster**, Gwendolyn Audrey (esp. 238–39). See also **Pick** (biblio).

Nancy Marcotte
Reportage Brésil: 1 (1986) A women's police station in Brazil.

Jane Marsh
Alexis Tremblay, habitant (1943; 30 mins.; ONF)
Terre de nos aïeux (1943; in the documentary film series on Québec's history and contemporary society entitled *Nostalgie*; ONF)

Catherine Martin Editor and director.
Du jour au lendemain (1981) Short
Odile ou les réminiscences d'un voyage (1985) Short
Nuits d'Afrique (1989) Made on a budget of $38,000 Can. A collective work; the crew even deferred their salaries to make this film, but the editing was suspended for lack of money.
Les Fins de semaine (1996) "Conceived in vignettes, filmed on weekends with pieces of string, good will and a lot of imagination. Filmed thoughts about love whose humor reminds one of Eric Rohmer." (Johanne Larue, "Coutes et moyennes folies . . . ," *Séquences* 183 (April–May 1996): 7–8. My trans.)
See *Zoom sur elles*, 49.

Lise Noiseux-Labrèque

Maxine Nunes

Suzanne Olivier
Des Ensembles (ONF)
(See Pratley 295)

Maryka Omatsu

Yvette Pard

Monique Pardis (with Lucie Ménard)

Claire Parker American-born, but codirected animated films with her husband Alexandre Alexéieff for the National Film Board; also worked in France.
Une Nuit sur le Mont Chauve (1933?) Uses the screen of pins technique invented by her husband.
Le Nez (with her husband) This film took Belgian Festival Prize in 1963.

Liliane Patry
Plus qu'imparfait (1980) Description of feminine oppression; roles

of men and women are inverted, so the men are secretaries, for example, and sex objects too, while the women are macho bosses.

Lynda Peers
Le Plaisir (1987)

Andrée Pelletier b. 1951. Actress (Rita Sauvage in *Les Mâles* [Carle, 1970]; *Homme à tout faire* [M. Lanctôt, q.v., 1980]; *Bach et Bottine* [Melançon, 1986]; *Les Noces de papier* [Michel Brault, 1989]; Idola St.-Jean in *Nelligan* [R. Favreau, 1991]), writer (*The Peanut Butter Solution* [Rubbo, 1985]) and director of

Petit Drame dans la vie d'une femme (1990) A feminist short from Studio D (the National Film Board's women's studio), this is a fable about a thirteen-year-old girl who has locked herself in the bathroom and refuses to become a woman.

Michèle Pérusse
L'Humeur à l'humour (1989; 48 mins.; with Nicole Giguère) Tells the story of the Québécoises struggle for their rights.

Raymonde Pilon (with Guy Beaugrande-Champagne)

Anne Claire Poirier b. 1932. Arguably the greatest woman director of Québec. She took the Albert Tessier Prize awarded by the Québec government in 1988. Also a producer ([*J'me marie, j'me marie pas* [M. Dansereau, q.v., 1973]; *Souris, tu m'inquiètes* [A. Danis, q.v., 1973]; *Les Filles, c'est pas pareil* [H. Girard, q.v., 1974]), scriptwriter and editor (*Jour après jour* [C. Perron, 1962]). Had planned to go into law (which she received a degree in), but started writing and interviewing for radio; then began to work in 1960 for the National Film Board (ONF) in various capacities (Sharon Smith 97; see also Coulombe under Poirier).

30 Minutes, Mister Plummer (1962; Coulombe gives 1963) A documentary about Christopher Plummer.

La Fin des étés (1964) Fiction film cowritten with Hubert Aquin.

Les Ludions (1965)

Impôt de tout . . . de tout (1968; five 5-minute films made for the Department of National Revenue) (Coulombe gives 1969.)

De mère en fille ("Mother to Be") (1967–68) This was the kickoff film for the feminist movement in Québec. Reflections on pregnancy and on maternity.

Le Savoir-faire s'impose (1971; five 5-minute films for the Department of National Revenue)

En tant que femmes nous-mêmes (with Jeanne Morazain) A manifesto for films by and for women submitted to the ONF 29 March 1971. Lay behind the establishment of the En tant que femmes series.

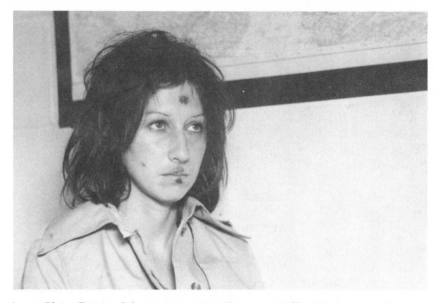

Anne Claire Poirier. *Mourir à tue-tête.* Courtesy Office National du Film.

Les Filles du Roy (1974) (*They Called Us: "Les Filles du Roy"*)
Les Filles du Roy is one of Poirier's best-known films and one of her
most poetic: A durasien film that translates the state of *attente* (or
patient waiting) in which women, like Blacks, must find themselves;
it seems their opportunity for true participation in humanity's "history" is forever projected into the future. The film features eight
women through whom the servitude of all Québécoises is shown; each
personal history is the history of Québec, and that is the point. The
arrival of the *filles du Roy* is also invoked here. (These were the
strong French women the king sent in 1760 for the settlers, "robustes,
courageuses, de bonnes moeurs"—as the film narrator states.) All in
all, the film deals with the largely unwritten history of the Québécoise. Marcel Jean (in Coulombe 438) appreciates the rhythm and
"*distanciation*" of this film, which will come to characterize Poirier's
future work. For credits, see Coulombe Génériques 568.

    Le Temps de l'avant (1975) This work (ONF; En tant que
femmes series), about abortion in a lower-class family, caused a good
deal of controversy. It aimed to shake up the masculine population.
For credits, see Coulombe Génériques 594.

    Les Instants privilégiés (Filmed between 1975 and 1988) About
friendship between two women.

    Mourir à tue-tête (or *Scream from Silence;* aka *Primal Fear*) (1979)
No other film of Poirier's can compare with this graphic and troubling

work about rape. The director has de-eroticized and universalized rape in this film that oscillates between documentary and fiction. "Editorials" interrupt the story, and panning, tracking, and freeze-frame are used most effectively; the ultimate realization of the viewer, who sees the entire rape from the point of view of Suzanne (played by Julie Vincent), and thus is forced into the position of identifying with her, is, in a sense, that the rapist can be anyone, as also the victim. It is a highly political film, which criticizes the society and its institutions for further victimizing, even criminalizing, the victim.

As a frame to *Mourir à tue-tête* —which contains several levels of diegesis—Anne Claire Poirier has used the concept of two women making a documentary on rape. Their film focuses on Suzanne, a nurse, who is going home from her night shift. Throughout the rape scene, the rapist drinks beer, urinates on the woman, and talks steadily. Through his monologue we learn that he is a failure and that for him, this is a power trip.

What makes the scene especially frightening and ferocious is that the rapist faces the viewer . . . it is the viewer who is raped. Then the director of the documentary explains to her colleague that the rapist and his victim must not be shown together, for "rape forms no couple." We are subsequently presented with the aftermath of the rape, which constitutes a series of mental rapes. *Mourir à tue-tête* is a film to be seen, and once seen it will not be forgotten. It is not like any other film on rape. [The film is minutely analyzed by Denise **Pérusse** in *Le Cinéma aujourd'hui*.] For credits, see Coulombe Génériques 580.

La Quarantaine (produced by the ONF; 1982) Ten forty year olds, once childhood friends, meet in their former haunts in a small québécois village. There they tell of the things, good and bad, that have happened to them over the years. "[T]he whole [is] skillfully held together by the marvelous ensemble acting, the direction, and the very real expression of feelings and emotions" (**Pratley** 254). For credits, see Coulombe Génériques 588 or Pratley 253.

Salut, Victor! (1988; 85 mins.) Stars Jacques Godin and Jean-Louis Roux. Film about two aging homosexuals in a rest home. Some have found this a quite touching tale; I thought it weak in comparison with *Mourir à tue-tête* or *Les Filles du Roi*, for example. (Written in collaboration with Marthe Blackburn.)

Il y a longtemps que je t'aime (1989; directed by Poirier/Sicotte) An extraordinary amalgam of scenes (a montage or compilation film) from many Québec films showing the evolution of the image of woman in *québécois* ONF films. It might be hard to follow for one who is not familiar with the cinema of Québec, but the narrator warns us not to try to identify film clips; for that is not the point.

Done under the auspices of the ONF (Programme: Regards de femmes), this work offers an accurate picture of woman and woman's life. Drawing from old newsreels, women at war, women at beauty contests are depicted. We hear the opinions of men on physicality versus femininity in women; we see the socialization processes coming in the early primer (reader), where Guy likes sports, while Yvette helps in the house, and always pleases her parents. Contains one hundred excerpts from sixty films, all intertwined. Among the most stunning scenes are those drawn from certain animated films. This portrayal of woman in film appears, in the long run, to provide a history of Québec film in general. The excerpts are taken from ONF productions covering a span of fifty years (1940–88).

Souvenir d'une enfant perdue (1995) Produced by the ONF. The sad story of the death of Yanne, Anne Claire Poirier's twenty-six-year-old daughter, who was a heroin addict, is narrated in this film. In *Châtelaine* ([January 1995]: 84–86) one can see pictures of the daughter, or Poirier, and read the full account of this sorrowful affair. Poirier has researched the subject from several angles and thought a great deal about Québec society's treatment of addicts and the lack of resources and programs in that province.

[Some of Poirier's films are treated in the April 1990 issue of *La Châtelaine*.]

Diane Poitras

La Perle rare (1980) About pink-collar workers.

Pense à ton désir (1984) Fiction film about women at the age of menopause.

Comptines (1986) An Irish woman's protest against a prisoner's death.

Léa Pool b. 1950 in Soglio, Switzerland. Scriptwriter and director.
From 1978 to 1983 taught film courses at UQAM. Of Jewish background. An immigrée to Québec in 1978.

Laurent Lamerre, portier (1978) This film was directed while Pool was a student.

Strass Café (1980) Voice is the main element of narration in this film about desire, loneliness, emptiness, exile, men and women searching for, and not finding, each other. Walls form an important metaphor here.

La Femme de l'hôtel (1984; NFB [ONF]) Stars Louise Marleau and Paule Baillargeon (q.v.). Built around three characters one of whom is making a film and seeking an ideal actress; she makes

Léa Pool. *Anne Trister.* Courtesy Office National du Film.

friends with a strange woman who is a wanderer, and from her she draws new inspiration for her film. This excellent film, well received by public and by critics, took seven prizes! and made Pool one of the most famous filmmakers of Canada, at least among women.
See Donohoe, or else Pallister, *The Cinema of Québec.*

Anne Trister (1986) Said to complete the triptych begun by the above two films. Problems of exile, lesbianism, identity. This film, in which a young Jewish woman leaves Israel (Coulombe says Switzer-land) and settles as an artist in Québec, made an auteur(e) of Pool. See Pallister (in Donohoe) or Pallister (*The Cinema of Québec*), for complete study. For credits, see Pallister (*The Cinema of Québec*).

A corps perdu (*Straight to the Heart*) (1988) Based on Yves Navarre's *Kurwenal.* Pierre Kurwenal, a photographer-reporter (played by Matthias Habich), after doing a stint in Nicaragua, returns to Montréal, where he decides to visually incorporate his own city in the film. On his return, too, he finds that his two lovers (David and Sarah) have abandoned him. Gnawed by violent jealousy, he begins following them and photographing them. This is one of the most visu-ally oriented films I have ever seen; the photography is at times lumi-nous and shows that Pool's fame as a photographer of Montréal is truly deserved. The suffering of Pierre Kurenwal is translated through closeups of his face and backgrounded by the beauty of early classical music. Pool's preoccupation with the connection between art and reality continues here. For credits, see Pallister (*The Cinema of Québec*).

Hotel Chronicles (1990) Formed part of the collection on "*L'Americanité*" or the ONF's series "Parler d'Amérique." Pool had made a series of documentaries for Radio-Québec before making *La Femme de l'hôtel;* she also made, as a student at the University of Quebec, a short documentary entitled *Laurent Lamerre, portier,* about a doorman at a large hotel, standing at the door of two worlds. But *Hotel Chronicles* (a road movie) is Pool's first full-length documentary. By Pool's admission, it presents a satirical vision of the American dream. It projects a story of separation. And the "person" addressed could be a human or a personified America.

Note: is there not a problem with a "documentary" presenting a "satirical view"?

La Demoiselle sauvage (1991; with Laurent Gagliardi and Michel Langlois) (Swiss/Québécois) Adapted from a novella by S. Corinna Bille. In this film, the dialogue is again at a minimum, indeed, is reduced to such an extent that the characters speak less than in any other work of Pool's. Here she insists even more than ever on the iconographic power of cinema. *La Demoiselle sauvage* opens with the flight of a young woman (played by Patricia Tulasne) after she has committed a murder. In desperation she has attempted to commit suicide, but, having failed, only finds herself all the more lonely and impoverished. She takes refuge in the magnificence and immensity of the Swiss landscape. There she confronts an enormous dam that cuts off her escape route. She also meets a man, Elysée (Matthias Habich), who will change her life by coming to her assistance and by "taming" this "wild girl." Their ways of dealing with the past are, however, at odds: He wants to dig into the past as a form of understanding and knowing; she wants to forget the past. Her sole desire is to live in the present. Toward the end, it seems she will face the law. However, she commits suicide instead, thus extinguishing the past—just as she had earlier killed her lover. Contains some of Pool's favorite themes: solitude, wandering, and desire. (Madness, also.) For credits, see Pallister (*The Cinema of Québec*).

Mouvements du désir (1994?) A beautiful film about love. The action has locus on a train, during a trip of four days. Pool claims to have been inspired by *Discours amoureux* of Roland Barthes. Birth and rise of a *coup de foudre* (of love at first sight). Catherine, a pianist, with an illegitimate daughter, Charlotte, is afraid of being alone and confronting her feelings for Vincent, a married man who is en route for Vancouver, where he will meet his wife at the station. Catherine does the crab dance (two steps forward and one step back). Catherine and Vincent make love in front of an audience, seated in a row as if in front of a TV. Tadzio, seventeen years old, one of the travelers, has lost his first love in an accident; he sows confusion on the train, as the coup de foudre also sows confusion: Pool says (*Séquences* [March-1994]) she wanted the train itself to become the site of confusion and a reflection of the *intériorité* of the characters.

Stars Valérie Kaprisky and Jean-François Pichette.

Montréal vu par . . . (1991, says Foster) Contains a sketch called "Rispondetemi (Répondez-moi)." The city sees a young woman (played by Anne Dorval) in an ambulance struggling for her life. The idea is that Montreal is in a death agony, struggling for survival. Codirected with Michel Brault, A. Egoyan, J. Leduc and Patricia Rozema.

Femmes: une histoire inédite (TV documentary; co-directed with Anne Henderson and Tom Puchniak; 4 Dec. 1996 through 22 January 1997.

See *Zoom sur elles,* 50–51. See also Pallister; M. J. Green; as well as Foster 306–8.

Johanne Prégent b. in Saint-Lambert in 1950. Costume director (*Contrecoeur* and *Elvis Gratton*); scriptwriter (*Sonia,* q.v. Baillargeon; *Le Crime d'Ovide Plouffe; Pouvoir intime*); director of
La Peau et les os (Skin and Bones) (1988; 90 mins.; ONF) A documentary on eating disorders. "Poignant appeal to thousands of adolescent girls lost in the jungle of advertising images and in their difficult relationship to those around them" (Vidéo Femmes catalog: see Film Sources). While making this film, Prégent developed a passion for these poor girls, sacrificed to a societal illness. See *Zoom sur elles,* 50.

Blanche est la nuit (1989) Based on a scénario by Yvon Rivard, this film tells of a woman (played by Léa-Marie Cantin) who decides to live after meeting her "guardian angel" and lover (played by Jean L'Italien).

L'Irréparable outrage (1989–90) Documentary about the fear of growing old.

On a marché sur la lune (1990) Based on a script by Josée Fréchette, it deals with adolescence.

Les Amoureuses (1992) The story involves the intersecting actions of two couples—David-Léa and Nino-Marianne—the first in its decline; the second embryonic. As the title suggests, the two women bond.

Rossignol See Cadrin-Rossignol

Yolaine Rouleau
Le Futur intérieur (1980–81; with Jean Chabot)

Brigitte Sauriol b. 1945. Scriptwriter; director of
Le Loup blanc (1973)

L'Absence (1975) Absence of the father. Stars Frédérique Collin, Monique Mercure, Jean Gascon, and Guy Thauvette.

Une Ville que j'aime (1981)

Bleue brume (1982)

Rien qu'un jeu (Just a Game) (1983) Made with the financial participation of L'Institut Québécois du Cinéma; Ciné II (1982); La Société du Développement de l'Industrie Cinématographique Cana-dienne; and Famous Players. Dealing with the problem of incest, this film shows considerable sensitivity and unusual frankness. It ranks with, or may even be superior to, another highly regarded Canadian film on the same subject, *Loyalties* (Anne Wheeler).

Perhaps because this work is filmed and scripted by women, the importance of power structures and manipulation in the unfolding of this "psychological drama" are not to be underrated. André Vézina, whose marriage to Mychelle is sadly wanting on many levels—it hav-ing been forced by Mychelle's pregnancy fifteen years earlier—is shown in the beginning as a man enlisting his authority role to force his daughter, Catherine, to have sexual relations with him. (One scene is especially lurid and graphic.) "J'ai le droit; je suis ton père," he claims. And besides, he adds, "C'est pas grave. C'est rien qu'un jeu. [I have the right; I am your father; and besides, it is nothing serious; it's just a game.]" He warns her not to tell; he bribes her with gifts, as is characteristic of the child molester. (His long suit is, in fact, offering gifts to his daughters and to his wife.) But as Catherine becomes more and more resistant, he turns to her younger sister, Julie. The mother, who is abusive and intolerant, finally sees her husband with Julie, and this forces a turn of tables. When Mychelle confronts him, he breaks down. But she seems to pardon him, telling him he is not sick, and that it is just a matter of not touching his daughters any longer.

Subsequently, we see that these acts—even if they are to stop—have destroyed the very fabric of the family. While the mother begs the older daughter to think of the episodes as "a bad memory," the girl is submerged in the abyss of depression and shame incest is said to foster even in the victim.

Quite near the end, we have a traveling shot that takes in gulls, sea, and rocks off the coast of Percé on the Gaspé Penninsula. (Some scenes were shot on the Ile Bonaventure.) The girl is contemplating a leap to her death. I would have been willing to accept a suicide as one final turn of events in this sad tragedy. Instead, the film ends with a freeze-frame, with a cracked glass effect coming over her face. There can be no good future for her; and, of course, that is another way in which the "shattering" experience of incest leaves its mark.

The makers of this film have shown the role alcohol plays in such a troubled household, and the mother's frequent abdication of duty when the cancer is brought to the fore: she, being weak and unhappy in her marriage, nevertheless seems to forgive the husband and to blame her daughters. For credits, see Coulombe Génériques 589.

Laura Laur (1989) Shows a taste for psychological exploration. It is based on the novel by Suzanne Jacob, which is well worth reading. Laura (played by Paula de Vasconcelos) is an elusive woman whom the men in her life cannot understand or capture. But the film is rather weak; it was not well received. For credits, see Pallister, *The Cinema of Québec.*

Doubles jeux (1989)

Dagmar Gueissaz Teufel
L'Intelligence du coeur
"Madame, vous avez rien" ("Mrs., you don't have anything") (1982) Credits in Coulombe Génériques 576.

Clorinda Warny b. Gand, Belgium 1939—d. Montréal 1978. She was a great animation artist, her finest work being

Premiers jours (in English, *Beginnings*) (1980; 8 mins. 2 sec.) A dreamy animated film in which "abstract landscapes evolve into strange, godlike figures, whose images revert into landscapes."

It is a must. Also
The Egg
Petit Bonheur (Happiness Is)

SWISS

Olga Baillif See Belgian directors

Yaël Bitton See Belgian directors

Clarisse Gabus b. 1949. Studied ethnology in Neuchatel, then went to Brussells, where she specialized in audiovisual techniques. She then became a film editor and worked both in France and in Switzerland in this capacity.

La Fragilité des choses (1976) Short
Melancoly Baby (1979) A bourgeoise housewife decides to throw it all over and make a life for herself.
See **Lejeune** 131.

Danielle Jaeggi b. Lausanne, Switzerland, 1948. Cinematographic training at the IDHEC in Paris. Became a member of the Musidora group. Author of a polemical book: *Me sentir femme.*

Questionnaire (1970s)

Pano ne passera pas (1970s)

Deux dans une (1970s)

Cérizay, elles ont osé (1971) Short concerning working women on strike.

Sorcières-Camarades (1971) Short

Un Geste en moi (1972) Short

L'Appartement au carré (1976) Short

La Fille de Prague avec un sac très lourd (1978) Full-length feature, fiction but using documentary techniques. The glance of a woman from the East is cast over French society, which she compares with her own (communist).

Le Dépanneur (1979) Short

Sollers et Guégan ont deux mots à dire (1980) Video

Bernard Frank est insupportable (1981) Video

Beuve-Mery par lui-même (1982) Video

Tout près de la frontière (1982) Video

Mon tout premier baiser (1984) Video

See **Lejeune** 146–47

Patricia Moraz b. of Swiss father and Egyptian mother in Kartoum (Sudan, Africa) 1941. Grew up in Switzerland (Lausanne); spent time as young adult in Algiers. Returning to Switzerland in 1966, she became involved in TV and took up video. In 1970–75 she went to Blois, France, shooting film about life in a psychiatric clinic. Shown two years later under the title *Voyage dans le Loir-et-Cher* (1977). Moraz has also taught film in Vincennes and at the Sorbonne. She wrote *scénarios* for Swiss filmmakers Jean-Louis Roy and Francis Reusser.

Les Indiens sont encore loin (1977) Based on a fait divers occurring in Lausanne: the suicide of a young girl who leaves home and dies alone in the snow.

Le Chemin perdu (1980) The child's vision of the world.

See **Lejeune** 179.

Jacqueline Veuve b. Payerne, Switzerland in 1930.

Le Panier à viande (1966) Short

Les Lettres de Stalingrad (documentary) (1972)

La Grève de 18 (1972)

Genève le 9 novembre, 1932 (1972) Short

No More Fun and No More Games (1973–74; made in the United States)

Susan, Susan (1973–74; made in the United States)

Mais vous, les filles (1974–78; made in Switzerland)

Swiss Graffiti (1976; animated short; made in Switzerland)

Angèle Stadler, ou la vie est un cadeau (1974–78; short; made in Switzerland)

Chronique d'une ville: Fribourg (1974–78; made in Switzerland)

La Mort du grand-père (aka *Le Sommeil du juste*) (1978)

Parti sans laisser d'adresse (1982)

See **Lejeune** 217.

VENEZUELAN

Fina Torres See under French directors

Core Concepts and Themes

ABORTION

Where Are My Children (1916; Lois Weber)
Histoires d'A (1973; Issartel-Belmont)
Le Temps de l'avant (1975; Anne Claire Poirier [Québec])
Abortion Stories, North and South (1984; Gail Singer [Canadian])
Les Silences du Palais (1994; 116 mins.; Moufida Tlatli [North African])
Jane: an Abortion Service (d. Kate Kirtz and Nell Lundy)

By men

Une Affaire de femmes (The Story of Women) (1988; 110 mins.; Claude Chabrol)

ADOLESCENCE

Diabolo Menthe (Peppermint Soda) (1977; Diane Kurys)
Pauline à la plage (1983; Eric Rohmer)
On a marché sur la lune (1990; Johanne Prégent)
Mima (1991; Philomène Esposito)
Tant qu'il y aura des jeunes (1993?; Catherine Fol)

ALIENATION AND EXILE

Les "Borges" (1978; Marilú Mallet [South American; Québec])—identity and exile
Documenteur (1981; Agnès Varda)
Sonatine (1983; Micheline Lanctôt [Québec])
Journal inachevé (1982–83 ; Marilú Mallet)—chief subject is identity (and exile too).
La Femme de l'hôtel (1984; Léa Pool [Québec])
Sans toit ni loi (1985; Agnès Varda)

Anne Trister (1986; Léa Pool)—identity and exile

An Autumn's Tale (1987; 98 mins.; Mabel Cheung [Hong Kong/United States])

The films of Valeria Sarmiento (Chile)—exile

By a man

A nos amours (1993–94; 100 mins.; Maurice Pialat)—a young girl (played by Sandra Bonnaire) goes from man to man, seeking the love her family does not give her. (She is abandoned by her father and beaten by her brother.)

THE BODY "POLITIC" (INCLUDING AGING AND ILLNESS)

Cléo de 5 à 7 (1961; Agnès Varda)

La Beauté même (1964; Monique Fortier)—seeks to show in this documentary what beauty is to a woman

Taking Our Bodies Back (1974; Cambridge Documentary Films)

Vital Statistics of a Citizen Simply Obtained (1977; Martha Rosler)—about measurements; uncannily relates to certain passages in Virginia Woolf's *A Room of One's Own.*

Charles et Lucie (1979; 98 mins.; Nelly Kaplan)

Ça ne peut pas étre l'hiver (1980; 90 mins.; Louise Carré [Québec])—aging

Tell Me a Riddle. (1980; 94 mins.; Lee Grant)—After many years of marriage and a resulting indifference, a Jewish couple rekindles their love—in the light of the woman's lethal cancer.

Des Saints et des anges (1984; Elsie Haas)—symbolism of hair and hairstyle

The Electronic Diary (1985–89; Lynn Hershman)

Sonia (1986; Paule Baillargeon [Québec])—aging (Alzheimer's)

La Peau et les os (1988; Johanne Prégent [Québec])—documentary on eating disorders; esp. anorexia

Perfect Image? (1988; Maureen Blackwood [Haitian])—concern for image of black body and black hair (See also Women Make Movies Catalog [64]: *Hair Piece, A Film for Nappie-Headed People,* d. by Ayoka Chenzira, 1985.) [See Foster, Gwendolyn Audrey. *Women Film Directors: 23–24; 44–46 and elsewhere.*]

Irréparable Outrage (1989–90; Johanne Prégent [Québec])—fear of aging

A Company of Strangers (1990; Cynthia Scott [Canada])—aging

Germaine (1991; Louise Carré [Québec])—aging (Alzheimer's)

Nitrate Kisses (1993; Barbara Hammer)—septuagenarian lesbian love-making among other things; *Optical Nerves* (1984–85)—aging

By men

Sugar Baby (1985; Percy Adlon [German])
Tatie Danielle (1991; 114 mins.; Etienne Chatliez)—bitter comedy about a nasty elderly woman and her problems with her "family"; aging

BREAKING AWAY (CRISIS)

Jument Vapeur (1978; Joyce Buñuel)
Patricia's Moving Picture (1978; Bonnie Klein)
Ça ne peut pas . . . (1980; Louise Carré)

By men

The Color Purple (1985; Steven Spielberg)
Thelma and Louise (1991; Ridley Scott)
Fried Green Tomatoes (1991; John Avnet)

CLITORDECTOMY; CLITORIDOTOMY

Mourir à tue-tête (1979; 96 mins.; Anne Claire Poirier)
Warrior Marks (1992; Pratibha Parmar and Alice Walker)
Femmes aux yeux ouverts (1993–94; video, 52 mins.; Anne-Laure Folly [Togo])
L'Excision (1994; Salifou Yaye [Niger])

By men

Finzan (1990; 107 mins.; Cheick Oumar Sissoko—Mali)
[See article by Laura DeLuca, "Representation of Female Circumcision in *Finzan*," *Research in African Literature* 26, no. 3 (fall 1993): 83–87.]
Ramparts of Clay (1970; Jean-Louis Bertucelli)

COLONIAL LIFE; POSTCOLONIALISM; DECOLONIZATION

Sambizanga (1972; Sarah Maldoror)—the struggle of native Africans against Portuguese rule

Kaddu beykat (or *The Voice of the Peasant;* or *News from My Village;* 1975; Safi Faye)—concerns, among other things, peasants' refusal of colonialism

Cananea (1976; Marcela Fernandez Violante [Mexico])

Selbé et tant d'autres (or *Selbe: One among Many;* 1983; 30 mins.; Safi Faye)

Dust (1984; Danièle Haensel)—based on the novel of J. M. Coetzee; concerns apartheid in South Africa

Chocolat (1988; Claire Denis)—pre-independence life in Cameroon

Farewell to Africa (1989; Helena Nogueira [South Africa])

S'en fout la mort ([*No Fear No Die*] 1990; Claire Denis)

Outremer (*Overseas*) (1990; 98 mins.; Brigitte Rouan)—pre-independence life in Algeria. Not everything about the life of the wealthy, swinging pieds-noirs was so wonderful!

Films of Marguerite Duras

Trinh T Minh-ha (an authority on postcolonialism and feminism) See her books (*Woman, Native, Other*) and **films**
Rassemblage (1982)—ethnocinematographic portrayal of women in Senegal. "A film that challenges the role of the colonialized 'other' (Third World women) as subjects of the filmmaker's gaze" (Foster).
Naked Spaces; Living Is Round (1985; 2 hrs.)—poetic study of vernacular architecture in five West African countries

By men (There are many; I cite only a few here.)

L'Etat sauvage (1978; Francis Girod)

Where the Green Ants Dream (1984; Werner Herzog)

An African Dream (South African) (1987; John Smallcombe)

Indochine (1992; Régis Vargnier)—powerful film in which mother and adopted daughter love the same man, a film set against French colonialism. But see L. Maltin (1994), where this film is called "tripe" and given two stars!

CRIME

Mikey and Nicky (1976; Elaine May [United States])

Charles et Lucie (1979; 98 min.; Nelly Kaplan)—comic entanglement with crime

Scrubbers (1982; Mai Zetterling)

A Question of Silence (1984; Marlene Gorris)

Mrs. Soffel (1984; Gillian Armstrong [Australian auteure])

Signé Charlotte (*Sincerely Charlotte*) (1986; Caroline Huppert)

By men

Susana (1951; 87 mins.; Luis Buñuel [Mexican; in Spanish])
Kamouraska (1973; Claude Jutra [Québec])
Cordélia (1979; Jean Beaudin [Québec])
Pouvoir intime (1986; Yves Simoneau)
Une Affaire de femmes (*The Story of Women*) (1988; 110 mins.; Claude Chabrol) Isabelle Huppert portrays an abortionist in Vichy, France; based on true story of the last woman to be guillotined in France.
Petite Voleuse (*Little Thief*) (1989; 100 mins.; Claude Miller)—female teenage delinquent
Thelma and Louise (1991; Ridley Scott)
Au pays des Juliets (1992; 94 mins.; Mehdi Charef) Three women inmates are granted twenty-four hours of freedom.

FILMMAKING

Les Rendez-vous d'Anna (1978; Chantal Akerman)
Journal inachevé (*Unfinished Journal; Unfinished Diary*) (1982–83; Marilú Mallet)
La Femme de l'hôtel (1984; Léa Pool)
Diary for My Loves (1987; Márta Mészaros [Hungarian])
A Man in Love (1987; Diane Kurys)
Zanzibar (1989; 95 mins.; Christine Pascal)
Il y a longtemps que je t'aime (1989; directed by Anne Claire Poirier/Sicotte)
Qui est Alice Guy? Vidéo Femmes—about Alice Guy
Jacquot de Nantes (1991; Agnès Varda)
Les Demoiselles de Rochefort ont eu 24 ans (1993; Agnès Varda)
Les Cent et une nuits (1995; 125 mins.; Agnès Varda)

By men

8½ (1963; 135 mins.; Federico Fellini) This is probably the most important such film; there are dozens.

FRIENDSHIP BETWEEN WOMEN

Les Instants privilégiés (1975 to 1988; Anne Claire Poirier)
L'Une chante, l'autre pas (1976; Agnès Varda)
Entre nous (1983; Diane Kurys)

Pas d'amitié à moitié (1991; Diane Létourneau)
Girlfriends (1978; Claudia Weill)
Adoption (1975; 89 mins.; Márta Mészaros [Hungarian])

By men

The Color Purple (1985; Steven Spielberg)
Steel Magnolias (1989; Herbert Ross)

HOMOSEXUALITY; LESBIANISM; CROSS-DRESSING

Important documentaries on homosexuality in film: (1) *The Celluloid Closet*, assembled by Rob Epstein and Jeffrey Friedman, narration written by Armistead Maupin and read by Lily Tomlin) (2) *The Lavender Lens: 100 Years of Celluloid Queers* (David Johnson)

Lesbianism; by women

Maedchen in uniform (1931; Leontine Sagan [German])
Olivia (*The Pit of Loneliness;* 1951; Jacqueline Audry)
Je tu il elle (1974; Chantal Akerman)
Films of Barbara Hammer—A collection of six films: *Menses; Superdyke, Our Trip,* and so on; *Lesbian Humor* (1975–87; 59 mins.)
Néa (1976; Nelly Kaplan)
Avskedet (*The Farewell*) (1980; Tuija-Maija Niskanen [Finland])
La Femme de l'hôtel (1984; 89 mins.; Léa Pool)
Desert Hearts (1985; Donna Deitch) [See Maio, Kathi. *Feminist in the Dark.*]
The Berlin Affair or *Interno berlinese* (1985–86; 97 min.; Liliana Cavani [Italian])—made in Germany; adapted from the novel *The Buddhist Cross* by Junichiro Tanizaki. (In prewar Germany 1938 Hitler is seducing an entire country, while Mitsuko, the daughter of the Japanese ambassador to Germany, is doing her own seductions!)
Een Vrouw als Eva (*A Woman Like Eve*) (1979; Nouchka van Brakel [Dutch])
Anne Trister (1986; 102 mins.; Léa Pool)
Amorosa (1986; Mai Zetterling)
I've Heard the Mermaids Singing (1987; 92 mins.; Patricia Rozema [Anglo-Canadian]) Shy young woman (who is an amateur photographer) gets job as secretary in an art gallery and becomes fascinated by her dynamic Lesbian "boss"; sly satire of the art scene in Toronto

and a statement about true art are incorporated in this charming comedy. [See Maio, Kathi. *Feminist in the Dark*.]

A Corps perdu (*Straight to the Heart*) (1988; 92 mins.; Léa Pool)

Quest for Truth (aka *Quest for Love*) (1988; Helena Nogueira [South Africa])

She Must Be Seeing Things (1988; Sheila McLaughlin [United States])

Farewell to Africa (1989; Helena Nogueira [South Africa])

A Company of Strangers (1990; Cynthia Scott)—has an interesting lesbian among the group

Seduction: The Cruel Woman (1990; Elfi Mikesch and Monika Treut [German]) A lesbian dominatrix's troupe services customers and stages elaborate S&M performances; gruesome.

Les Amoureuses (1992; Johanne Prégent)

Claire of the Moon (1992; 102 mins.; Nicole Conn) Bookish lesbian therapist and a promiscuous woman novelist find themselves an "odd couple" sharing a cabin retreat at a writers' conference in the Pacific Northwest; exploring each other's differences, they find a path to mutual understanding and an erotic tryst; interesting.

Go Fish (1993; 85 mins.; Rose Troche)

Gazon maudit (*French Twist*) (1994–95; 105 min; Josiane Balasko)

Le Poisson d'Amour (1993–94; Paula Gauthier) short

When Night Is Falling. (1995; 94 mins.; Patricia Rozema [Anglo-Canadian])—overtly concerned with a love relation between a painter and a circus performer. Considered less successful than *I've Heard*. . . . [See Louise-Véronique Sicotte in *Séquences* 179 ([July–August 1995]): 44–45.]

By male directors about lesbianism

Thérèse et Isabelle (1968; 102 mins.; Radley Metzer)

Lianna (1983; John Sayles)

Salmonberries (1992, 94 mins.; Percy Aldon) stars k. d. lang

About male homosexuality; by women

La Triche (1984; Yannick Bellon)—concerns an affair between a young homosexual musician and a married police inspector

Sand and Blood (1987, 101 mins.; Jeanne Labrune)—concerns male friendship if not homosexuality

Salut, Victor! (1988; 85 min.; Anne Claire Poirier)—touching story of two old men in a nursing home who manage to bond despite their disparate backgrounds

Les Sexe des étoiles (1993; Paule Baillargeon)—sex change, not homosexuality

About male homosexuality; by men

This Special Friendship (1964, 99 mins.; Jean Delannoy)
We Were One Man (1980; 90 mins.; Philippe Vallois)
Being at Home with Claude (1991; Jean Beaudin)—a violent film in which the murderer explains that he killed his lover at the peak of joy so that he might never have to come down, so to speak
La Cage aux Folles I, II (1979 and 1981; Edouard Molinarox)
    Remake: *The Birdcage* (1995; directed by Mike Nichols, written by Elaine May; stars Robin Williams, Nathan Lane, and Gene Hackman)
La Cage aux Folles III (1986; George Lautner)
L'Homme blessé (1984; Patrice Chereau)
Le Déclin de l'empire américain (1986, 1 hr. 42 mins.; Denys Arcand)
De l'amour et des restes humains (1993; Denys Arcand)
    (Arcand appears to be critical of homosexuality)
La Saga des Martin (Available from Films for the Humanities, Princeton, New Jersey). In one of the three stories in this film a young man nightly turns into a woman and in the morning again resumes his male identity.

Films about cross-dressing

Officer Henderson (1913; Alice Guy-Blaché); *I Don't Want to Be a Man* (1918; stars Ossi Oswalda); *Morocco* (1930; Josef von Sternberg; stars Marlene Dietrich); *Queen Christina* (1933; Rouben Mumoulian; stars Greta Garbo); *Sylvia Scarlett* (1935; George Cukor; stars Katharine Hepburn); *The Devil Is a Woman* (1935; Josef von Sternberg; stars Marlene Dietrich); *Calamity Jane* (1953; David Butler; stars Doris Day); *Some Like It Hot* (1959; Billy Wilder)
La Garçonne (1957; Jacqueline Audry); *Le (Secret du) Chevalier d'Eon* (1960; Jacqueline Audry); *Outrageous* (1977; Richard Benner); *Victor, Victoria* (1982; directed by Blake Edwards); *Yentl* (1983; Barbra Streisand); *She Must Be Seeing Things* (1988; 85 mins.; Sheila McLaughlin); *Paris Is Burning* (1990; Jennie Livingston); *Dressed to Kill* (1980; Brian De Palma); *Tootsie* (1982; Sydney Pollack); *The Crying Game* (1992; Neil Jordan); *Mrs. Doubtfire* (1993; Chris Columbus); *Farewell My Concubine* (1993; Chen Kaige); *Madame B . . .; The Adventures of Priscilla Queen of the Desert* (1994; Stephan Elliott); *Farinelli* (1994; Gérard Corbiau) [a superb film about an eighteenth-century castrato singer and his

tortured existence] and on and on.
[See: Anthony Slide, *Great Pretenders*.]

HOUSEHOLD DUTIES (THE WEB OF . . . ; DRUDGERY; SERVITUDE; BREAKING AWAY)

La Souriante Madame Beudet (1922–28; Germaine Dulac)
Hustruer (Wives) (1975; Anja Brejen [Norway])
Jeanne Dielman, 23 Quai du Commerce, 1080 Bruxelles (1975; 225 mins.; Chantal Akerman)
Toi Ippon no Michi (The Far Road) (1977; Sachiko Hidari [Japanese woman director])
Melancoly Baby (1979; Clarisse Gabus)
Kobieta samotna (A Woman Alone) (1982; Agnieszka Holland)
Jument Vapeur (1982; Joyce Buñuel)
Fiela se kind (Fiela's Child) (1988; Katinka Heyns [South Africa])
Milk and Honey (1988; 90 mins.; Rebecca Yates and Glen Salzman [Can./Great Britain].)—Jamaican housekeeper goes to Toronto where she experiences many trials. She and and a white Canadian male have an affair. Stars Josette Simon, Lyman Ward, and Richard Mills. Written by Salzman and Trevor Rhone; photography by Guy Dufaux. (See racism; interracial relations also.)

By men

Moderato Cantabile (1959; 90 mins. Peter Brook)—based on novel of Marguerite Duras. (Available from Version Française without subtitles.) Stars Jeanne Moreau and J.-P. Belmondo.
La Noire de . . . (1966; Ousmane Sembène)
Belle de Jour (1967; Luis Buñuel)
Diary of a Chambermaid (1964; 97 mins. Luis Buñuel—in French)—clash of classes; exploitation; rape—stars Jeanne Moreau.
Les Bonnes (by Jean Genet) (Available from Films for the Humanities, Princeton, New Jersey)
Scent of Green Papaya (*L'Odeur de la papaye verte;* 1993; Trân Anh Hùng [French prod.])
Gervaise (1956; René Clément)—from Zola's *l'Assommoir*—stars Maria Schell [There are other films based on this novel.]

INCEST

The Bridegroom, the Comedienne and the Pimp (*Der Bräutgigam, Die Komôddiantem und der Zuhälter*) (1968; Danièle Huillet [Fr./ co-dir.])—prostitution in Munich

Rien qu'un jeu (Just a Game) (1983; Brigitte Sauriol [Québec])
Loyalties (1987; Anne Wheeler[Canadian])

By men

Lolita (1962; Stanley Kubrick)
Insect Woman (1963; Shahei Imamura) (rape, incest, prostitution, exploitation of woman)
Le Souffle au coeur (1971; Louis Malle)
Le Crime quotidien (1994–95; 57 mins.; Nina Toussaint [Belgian])
Dolores Claiborne (1995; Taylor Hackford)

[Sexual Abuse of Children]

The Oldest Profession (1967; 97 min.; Claude Autant-Lara et al. [incl. Jean-Luc Godard)—stars Raquel Welch, Jeanne Moreau, Elsa Martinelli
Pretty Baby (1978; Louis Malle)—about child prostitution (stars Brooke Shields)
Nell (1994; Michael Apted)
The Boys of Saint Vincent's (Canadian made for TV—excellent)

INDOCHINA (FRENCH)—SEE COLONIALISM

Vietnam Triology by Ann Hui [Hong Kong]
Tou Bin Nuhai (The Boat People) (1982; Ann Hui [Hong Kong])
Surname Viet, Given Name Nam (1989; Trinh T Minh-Ha)—addresses Vietnamesse women and women refugees in America

By men

Morte en fraude (1957; 100 mins.; Marcel Camus) A man's life is in jeopardy in Indochina.
Apocalypse Now (1979; Francis Ford Coppola)—stars Martin Sheen and Marlon Brando
The Killing Fields (1984; Roland Joff)—stars Dr. Haing S. Ngor and Sam Waterston
Indochine (1992; Régis Vargnier) (see colonialism and mother-daughter)
Scent of Green Papaya (*L'Odeur de la papaye verte;* 1993; Trân Anh Hùng [French prod.])

MARRIAGE OR RELATIONSHIP GONE BAD (FAMILY)

Le Bonheur (1965; Agnès Varda)

Le Destin de Juliette (1982; Aline Isserman)

L'Eté prochain (1986; 100 mins.; Nadine Trintignant)—shows the ups and downs of married life; several couples involved

Saturday, Sunday and Monday (1990; 115 mins.; Lina Wertmuller) Sophia Loren plays a wife caught in a web of jealousy and love.

The Piano (1993; Jane Campion)

La Femme rompue (story by Simone de Beauvoir)—"modern" woman abandoned by the man. (Available from Films for the Humanities, Princeton, New Jersey)

By men

Et Dieu créa la femme (1956; Roger Vadim)

Le Chat (1975; 88 mins.; color; Pierre Granier-Deferre) A marriage twenty-five years in the making has turned to a hate relationship but the hate serves as a bond for Julien and Clemence. They spend their time in silence and in spying on each other. How the cat figures in this strong film is unforgettable. Stars Jean Gabin and Simone Signoret

Ju Dou (1989; Zhang Yimou)

War of the Roses (1989; 116 mins.; Danny De Vito)

Raise the Red Lantern (1992; Zhang Yimou)

Camille Claudel (1990; 149 mins.; Bruno Nuytten)

Arranged Marriages

Mississippi Mermaid (1969; François Truffaut)

Madame Bovary (1991; Claude Chabrol; 130 min) with Isabelle Huppert

Wide Sargasso Sea (1993; John Duigan; [United States-Australian])

Noces de Papier (1989; 86 mins.; Michel Brault [Québec])

Green Card (1990; Peter Weir [United States-Australian])

Other

La Femme du boulanger (1938; Marcel Pagnol)

Les Amants crucifiés (1954; Chikamatzu Monogatari; Kenji Mizoguchi [Jap.]) The plot has certain elements in common with Ju Dou.

Les Amants (1958; Louis Malle)

Le Miroir à deux faces (1959; André Cayatte)

Une Femme mariée (1964; Jean-Luc Godard)

La Femme infidèle (1969; Claude Chabrol)

MONOLITHS (STUDY OF A WOMAN)

Nana (1934; Dorothy Arzner)—starring Anna Sten (whom Goldwyn hoped to make into a new Garbo)
Sans toit, ni loi (1985; Agnès Varda)

By men

Nana French version(s), for example, by Christian Jacque (1957; 100 mins.); with Charles Boyer and Martine Carol
Gervaise (1957; René Clément)—from *L'Assommoir* by Emile Zola; with Maria Schell
L'Histoire d'Adèle H. (1975; Truffaut)
Kamouraska (1973; Claude Jutra [Québec])
J. A. Martin, Photographe (1976; Jean Beaudin [Québec])
La Vie devant soi (Madame Rosa) (1977; 101 mins. Moshe Mizrahi)
Camille Claudel (1988; Bruno Nuytten)
Dolores Claiborne (1995; Taylor Hackford)

MOTHER-DAUGHTER CONFLICT/RELATIONSHIP

The theme, so well defined in French literature (*Lettres* de Mme Sévigné; *La Princesse de Clèves; Une mort si douce;* etc.), is less prevalent in film, but it certainly does appear, as witnessed below:
La Maternelle (aka *Children of Montmartre*) (1933 black and white; 83 min.; Maria [or Marie] Epstein and Jean Benoît-Levy)
Nathalie Granger (1972; Marguerite Duras)
Daughter Rite (Michelle Citron; 1978 [United States])—mock cinéma-vérité style
Years of Hunger (1979; Jutta Brückner)
Some Interviews on Personal Questions (1979; Lana Gogoberidge [Soviet Union or Georgia])
Deutschland, bleiche Mutter (Germany, Pale Mother) (1979, Helma Sanders-Brahms [Germany])
L'Arrache-coeur (1979; Mireille Dansereau [Québec])
Deux femmes en voyage (Marquise Lepage; projected in *Zoom sur elles* 49; completion date unknown)
Cocktail Molotov (1980; Diane Kurys)—this one in particular, but other films of this director as well
The Ties That Bind (1984; Su Friedrich)
Fluegel und Fesseln (The Future of Emily) (1984; Helma Sanders-Brahms [Germany])

Smooth Talk (1986; Joyce Chopra)
Qui a tiré sur nos histoires d'amour? (1986; Louis Carré)
Anne Trister (1986; Léa Pool)
High Tide (1987; Gillian Armstrong)
Gas Food Lodging (1992; Allison Anders)
This Is My Life (1992; Nora Ephron)
Les Silences du Palais (1994; 116 mins.; Moufida Tlatli)

By men

Two Women or *La Ciociara* (1961; Vittorio De Sicca)
Les Bons Débarras (1980; Francis Mankiewicz [Québec]) One of the
    best presentations of the theme ever filmed.
Terms of Endearment (1983; 130 mins.; James L. Brooks) with Shirley
    McLaine, Debra Winger, and Jack Nicholson—studies a thirty-
    year relationship
Postcards from the Edge (1990: Mike Nichols)
Indochine (1992; Régis Vargnier)
The Lover (1992; Jean-Jacques Annaud)
Heavenly Creatures (1994; Peter Jackson [New Zealand])
Dolores Claiborne (1995; Taylor Hackford)
[See Annette **Kuhn** 242–48 for discussion of "mother-daughter
    films."]

MOTHERHOOD

Maternale (1975; Giovanna Gagliardo)
High Tide (1987; Gilian Armstrong [Australian])
"Qui va chercher Gisèle à 3h45?" (1989; Sylvie Groulx)—a documen-
    tary on problems of motherhood
Dolores Claiborne (1995; Taylor Hackford)

OLDER WOMEN, YOUNGER MEN/BOYS (OR VICE VERSA)

[One might read in conjunction with this theme the memoir by Mar-
    guerite Duras, *Yann Andréa Steiner* (1992). Of course, for the same
    theme in reverse, her memoir *L'Amant* might be read and the film
    The Lover (1992; Jean-Jacques Annaud) be shown as a unit.]
Het Debuut (*The Debut*) (1977; Nouchka van Brakel [Dutch])
Y si platicamos de Agosto (1980; Maryse Systach [Mexico])
Le Petit Amour (1989; Agnès Varda)

By men

Le Diable au corps (1947; 112 mins.; Claude Autant-Lara)
Tea and Sympathy (1956; Vincente Minnelli)
Bonjour Tristesse (1958; Otto Preminger)
Lolita (1962; Stanley Kubrick)
The Graduate (1967; Mike Nichols)
Last Tango in Paris (1973; Bernardo Bertolucci [French-Italian])
Get Out Your Handkerchiefs (*Préparez vos mouchoirs*) (1978; 109
   mins.; Bertrand Blier) Took Oscar for best foreign film of that year.
In Love with an Older Woman (1982; Jack Bender)
La Petite Sirène (1985; 104 mins.; Roger Andrieux)

PORNOGRAPHY

The Story of O (1975; Just Jaeckin) Part 2: 1987

PORNOGRAPHY (STUDY OF)

Love Story—a Film about Pornography (1981; Bonnie Sherr Klein
   [Anglo Québécoise]). A former striptease artist takes us through
   pornographic spots.
Variety (1983; Betty Gordon [United States])
[See Annette Kuhn on pornography]

PREGNANCY (UNWANTED, OTHER)

De mère en fille (*"Mother to Be"*) (1967–68; Anne Claire Poirier)—
   reflections on pregnancy and on maternity
Joyce at 34 (1972; Joyce Chopra)—made with Claudia Weill and documents Chopra's pregnancy.
Adoption (1975; 89 mins.; Márta Mészaros [Hungarian]) Kati wants
   a child, but her married lover refuses, so Anna, her friend, will
   help her have the child.
Sur la terre comme au ciel (*In Heaven as on Earth*) (1992; 80 mins.;
   Marion Haensel).
Angie (1994; 98 min.; Martha Coolidge) Angie is pregnant but refuses
   to marry the father; stars Geena Davis.

By men

Fanny (1931, 120 min.; Marc Allegret)

In Trouble (original title of French version: *Le Viol d'une jeune fille douce;* 1967; 82 mins.; Gilles Carle); the dubbed version from Facets is unfortunate, but the themes of unwanted pregnancy, mother-hood, and alienation of marginal persons (Jews from Morocco, for example) come through clearly.

Wedding in White (1972; William Fruet)—a retelling of Pagnol's Fanny story in a Scottish-Canadian setting

Hyenas (1992; in Wolof; 113 min.; Djibril Diop Mambety [Senegal])

Une Femme mariée (sometimes *La Femme mariée*) (1964; Jean-Luc Godard) A married woman finds herself pregnant by her lover.

Histoire vraie (based on Maupassant; available from Films for the Humanities, Princeton, New Jersey) Young servant girl is seduced, impregnated and abandoned by her master.

L'Enfant (based on Maupassant; available from Films for the Humanit-ies, Princeton, New Jersey)—death during childbirth

PROSTITUTION

La Maternelle (aka *Children of Montmartre*) (1933 black and white; 83 mins.; Maria [or Marie] Epstein and Jean Benoît-Levy)

Nana (1934; Dorothy Arzner)—starring Anna Sten (whom Goldwyn hoped to make into a new Garbo)

The Bridegroom, the Comedienne and the Pimp (*Der Bräutgigam, Die Komöddiantem und der Zuhälter*)(1968; Danièle Huillet [Fr./ co-directed])—prostitution in Munich

Conozco a las tres (*I Am Acquainted with the Three*) (1981; Maryse Systach [Mexico])

La Finacée du pirate (*A Very Curious Girl*) (1969; Nelly Kaplan)

Born in Flames (1983; Lizzie Borden)

Broken Mirrors (*Gebroken Spiegels*) (1985; 110 mins.; Marleen Gorris)—about seven prostitutes and a psychopath who assaults them and holds them hostage, so they ultimately starve to death ("Staunch feminist agenda"—*Video Hound's Golden Movie Retriever.*)

Working Girls (1986; Lizzie Borden)

Marie s'en va-t-en ville (1987; Marquise Lepage [Québec])

The Reincarnation of Golden Lotus (1989; Clara Low)—prostitute/courtesan; exploitation of woman

By men

Nana (1926; Jean Renoir)

La Chienne (1931; Jean Renoir)—stars actress Janie Marèze

Jaguar (1954, completed form 1967; Jean Rouch)—forms of African Gold Coast prostitution.

Nana (1955; 120 mins.; Christian Jacque)—stars Martine Carol

En cas de malheur (1958; Claude Autant-Lara)

Mamma Rosa (1963, 110 mins.; Pier Paolo Pasolini)

The Oldest Profession (1967; 97 mins.; DeBroca/Godard/Autant-Lara)—stars Raquel Welch, Elsa Martinelli, and Jeanne Moreau

Deux ou trois choses que je sais d'elle (1967; Jean-Luc Godard)

Belle de jour (1967; Luis Buñuel)

La Vie, l'amour, la mort (1968; Claude Lelouch)

La Vie devant soi (Madame Rosa) (1977; 101 mins.; Moshe Mizrahi)—stars Simone Signoret

Plusieurs tombent en amour (1980; Guy Simoneau [Québec])

Eréndira (1983; 103 mins.; Ruy Guerra [African-Angolan]) Film situated in Mexico and based on a story by Gabriel García Marquez

Crimes of Passion (1984; Ken Russell)

Une Affaire de femmes (The Story of Women) (1988; Claude Chabrol)

Pretty Woman (1990; Garry Marshall)

Hyenas (1991; 113 mins.; Djibril Diop Mambety [Senegal]; in Wolof)

De l'amour et des restes humains (1993; Denys Arcand [Québec])—*Love and Human Remains* (The film was first made in English.)

Dolores Claiborne (1995; Taylor Hackford)

RACISM; INTERRACIAL RELATIONSHIPS

Hari-Kiri [(*Seppuku*) (1963; Kobayashi)]

Una Pareja de oro (A Mixed Couple) (1986; Mayra Vilasis [Cuba])

Daughters of the Country—four powerful Canadian films about interracial relations. See especially *Ikwe* (1986), produced and directed by Norma Bailey; written by Wendy Lill, edited by Lara Mazur. Art direction: Jane McLeod; director of photography: Ian Elkin. An Indian chief barters with a Scottish trader, using his daughter as tender.

Chocolat (1988; 105 mins.; Claire Denis)

Milk and Honey (1988; 90 mins.; Rebecca Yates and Glen Salzman [Canada/Great Britain.])

Romuald et Juliette (Mama, there's a man in your bed) (1989; 111 mins.; Coline Serreau)

Mississippi Masala (1992; directed by Mira Nair [Afro-Indian]) An Afro-American male and an Afro-Indian-American fall in love.

By men

Hiroshima, Mon amour (1959; 91 mins.; Alain Renais)

Guess Who's Coming to Dinner (1967; Stanley Kramer) "Glossy tale of mixed marriage" (Maltin)

City Lovers, Country Lovers (Two Nadine Gordimer stories)
Interracial relationships and taboo. Set this film against: *Mississippi Masala; Jungle Fever;* other films dealing with this theme. The story of Romeo and Juliet is not that far removed from these.
City Lovers (1982; Barney Simon) A "Cape colored" woman and a German scientist indulge in a dangerous, illicit, and disastrous love affair.
Country Lovers (1982; Marie van Rensburg) A white boy has sexual relations with a black woman whose father works on the boy's father's farm; she becomes pregnant, and the situation deteriorates.

The Lover (1992; 110 mins.; Jean-Jacques Annaud)

RAPE AND BATTERING; OPPRESSIVE CUSTOMS IN PATRIARCHAL SOCIAL STRUCTURES

Baby riazanskie (Peasant woman from Raizan) (1927; Olga Preobraz-henskaia) Married woman is raped by her father-in-law. (See Kuhn 324–35.)

Voldtekt (Rape) (1971; Anja Brejen [Norway])

Amour violé (Rape of Love) (1977; Yannick Bellon)

Chaperons rouges (1979; Hélène Bourgault and Helen Doyle)

Mourir à tue-tête (or *Scream from Silence*) (1979; Anne Claire Poirier)

Loved Honored and Bruised (1980; Gail Singer [Canadian])

Conozco a las tres (I Am Acquainted with the Three) (1981; Maryse Systach [Mexico])

A Question of Silence (1982; 92 mins.; Marleen Gorris)—rape-revenge theme

Broken Mirrors (1985; Marleen Gorris) About seven prostitutes and a psychopath who assaults them and holds them hostage, so they ultimately starve to death.

Rape II (directed by Yoko Ono with John Lennon)

White Room (1991; 90 mins.; Patricia Rozema) The rape is somewhat tangential to the plot.

After the Montreal Massacre (1990; Gerry Rogers; 27 minutes)
J'ai plus sommeil (I Can't Sleep) (1993; Claire Denis)

By men

The Virgin Spring (1959; Ingmar Bergman)
Two Women (1961; 99 mins.; Vittorio De Sica)
Diary of a Chambermaid (1964; 97 mins.; Luis Buñuel)
Ramparts of Clay (1970; Jean-Louis Bertucelli)—oppression;
   patriarchy
Wedding in White (1972; William Fruet [Canadian])
F.V.V.A.: Femmes, villa, voiture, argent (1972; Mustapha Alassane
   [African])—satiric study of African male chauvinism
Rape Culture (1975)—Cambridge Documentary Films
The Color Purple (1985; Steven Spielberg)
The Accused (1988; Jonathan Kaplan)
Finzan (1990; 107 mins.; Cheick Oumar Sissoko [Mali])—oppressive,
   patriarchal traditions
Nell (1994; Michael Apted)

RELIGION AND WOMEN

Les Servantes du Bon Dieu (1978; 90 mins; Diane Létourneau [Qué-
   bec]) Portrait of a community of nuns formed to serve priests; the
   film does not seek to show these women in any ironic light, but
   with honesty and respect.

Critique of religion:

La Fiancée du pirate (1969; 105 mins.; Nelly Kaplan)
The Trouble with Angels (1966; Ida Lupino)
Behind the Veil (1984; Margaret Wescott) Superb! Wescott is Québécoise but anglophone; she also made *Some American Feminists;
   Eve Lambart;* and so on.
Camila (1984; 105 mins.; Maria-Luisa Bemberg [Argentina])—powerful film about an 1847 incident in Argentina, in which a girl of
   good family and a young Jesuit priest go in disguise to a village
   where they live as a married couple until they are discovered. Both
   are executed. Because this film is a statement about personal and
   political freedom, it touches everyone everywhere. In Spanish.
   Stars Susu Pecoraro and Imanol Arias.
Teresa de Jesús (1984; Josefina Molina; Spanish)

Le Moine et la sorcière (*Sorceress*) (1985; 98 mins.; Suzanne Schiffman)

Yo la peor de todas (1989; also by Bemberg) About the life of Sor Juana de la Cruz, "the Sappho of Spanish Literature."

Priest (1995; Antonia Bird)

Women and Spirituality—Three important reference videos under this title are: *Full Circle; Goddess Remembered; Burning Times.* All three directed by Donna Read; original music by Loreena McKennitt; coproduced by National Film Board of Canada and Great Atlantic and Pacific Film Company.

By men

La Merveilleuse Vie de Jeanne d'Arc (directed by Marc de Gastyne)

La Passion de Jeanne d'Arc (1928; 114 mins.; Carl-Theodore Dreyer)— played by René Falconetti; silent film with original organ score by Rosa Rio. [Available on Video Images (Video Yesterday #459).]

La Symphonie pastorale (1946; Jean Delaunoy)

Joan of Arc (1948; Victor Fleming)—starring Ingrid Bergman

Thérèse Desqueyroux (1962; Georges Franju)—also concerns marriage

La Religieuse (aka *Suzanne Simonin, La Religieuse de Diderot;* in English, *The Nun*) (1965–66; 140 mins.; Jacques Rivette)—stars Anna Karina

Act of the Heart (1970; Paul Almond)—stars Geneviève Bujold and Donald Sutherland

Agnes of God (1985; Norman Jewison)

Je vous salue, Marie (1985; Jean-Luc Godard)

Thérèse (1986; 90 mins.; Alain Cavalier)—stars Catherine Mouchet

Jeanne La Pucelle (1994; two parts: 1. *Les Batailles* 160 mins and 2. *Les Prisons* 176 mins; Jacques Rivette)—stars Sandrine Bonnaire

Hildegard (1995?; 45 mins; James Runcie) Original music and poetry by Hildegard von Bingen, medieval nun, poet, musician, physician, theologian, mystic; episodes from her life are portrayed by Patricia Routledge; photography by John Rhodes; edited by Graham Taylor; music by Harvey Brough.

Viridiana (1961; Buñuel)

Sister Act (1992; Emile Ardolino)—comedy (cf. *Nunsense,* made for TV)

SUICIDE (EUTHANASIA)

Sonatine (1983; Micheline Lanctôt [Québec])

La Demoiselle sauvage (1991; Léa Pool [Québec])

A force de mourir (1987; Diane Létourneau)
Fuir (*Flight* ; 1979; Hélène Girard)
[*Hara Kiri* (*Seppuku*) (1963; Kobayashi)]

By men

La Noire de . . . (1967; Ousmane Sembene)
Les Cousins (1959; Claude Chabrol) Two cousins compete for the
same woman.

SURREALISM (WOMEN DIRECTORS OF . . .)

(list supplied in part by Georgiana Colvile)
Alice Guy-Blaché
Germaine Dulac—fantasy and dream sequences; oneiric
Marie Epstein—dream sequences, and so forth
Nicole Védrès—*La Vie commence demain* (1950)
Nelly Kaplan/Belen—*Le Regard Picasso* (1967); also a film on An-
dré Masson
Jeanne Crépeau—*Cartes sur la table* (1994)
Patricia Rozema—*I've Heard the Mermaids Singing* (1987)

WANDERING; IDENTITY (ALSO SEE ALIENATION)

La Vagabonde (1917; Musidora)
Sans toit ni loi (1985; 105 mins.; Agnès Varda)
Le Camion (1977; Marguerite Duras)
Je tu il elle (1974; Chantal Ackerman)
Anne Trister ((1986; Léa Pool)
The Hitch-Hiker (1953; Ida Lupino)
Mima (1991; Philomène Esposito)

By men

Thelma and Louise (1991; Ridley Scott)

WOMEN'S MOVEMENT

Some American Feminists (1977; 56 mins.; Luce Guilbeault, Québec)
L'Une chante, l'autre pas (1977; Varda)

Fatma '75 (1975; Selma Bakkar) History of Tunisian women; film banned by the Tunisian government.

There are many films on the women's movement, including other women's struggles over various issues. To locate these, I suggest consulting Kuhn's *Women's Companion* . . . : articles on Cinema of women; Cinemien; Women Make Movies; Documentary, Studio D, Sydney Women's Film Group, and so forth, and also looking at the discussions of separate countries (e.g., China, Cuba, etc.).

The list of directors given in this book (See: Directors and Their Films) will also provide information on many documentaries and films on these subjects.

WORKING CONDITIONS OF WOMEN

(Two videos from the Québec collective Actions féministes par l'image (Groupe Intervention Vidéo):

Pour qui tourne la roue (1983)

On ne voulait pas des miracles (1985)

Working Mothers (series 1974–75; Kathleen Shannon-NFB-Studio D ([Canada])

Films of Márta Mészáros

OF RELATED INTEREST—WOMEN IN FRENCH AND FRANCOPHONE FILMS

Finzan (1990; 107 mins.; Cheick Oumar Sissoko—Mali)

Yeelen (1987; Soulemayne Cissé)

Manon des sources; Jean de Florette (both 1986; both directed by Claude Berri)

See most films with Simone Signoret, including *Madame Rosa* (*La Vie devant soi*) (1977; 101 mins.; Moshe Mizrahi); *Le Chat; Les Granges brulées; Diabolique,* and so on, where a strong woman is portrayed. Films of hers as Mme le Juge. *La Veuve Couderc,* as well (1971; Pierre Granier-Deferre). However, note that Kahn [166] finds Signoret plays the "strong" heroine in films of co-optation (one type of male directors' reaction to feminism.)

Coup de Grace (1978; Volker Schlondorff)—starring Margarethe von Trotta; film is based on the novel by Marguerite Yourcenar.

Note: For many films on women's issues (both fiction and documen-tary), especially American and Canadian films, consult: Kaye Sullivan, *Films for, by and about Women.*

Glossary

English terms with definitions and, where appropriate, French equivalents.

Accéléré. FAST MOTION. *en accéléré.*

AERIAL SHOT. A long shot, often taken from a helicopter. *Prise de vue aérienne.*

Amorce. LEADER.

Angle (prise de vue). SHOT.

ANTENNA. *Antenne.* Dish antenna. *Antenne parabolique.*

Arret sur image. FREEZE-FRAME.

Artifice cinématographique. TRICK(s) (OF THE CAMERA).

AUTEUR THEORY. A theory of film popularized by the critics of the French journal "Cahiers du cinéma" in the 1950s. The theory emphasizes the director as the major creator of film art. A strong director (an *auteur/ auteure*) stamps the material with his or her personal vision, even when working with an externally imposed script or "genre." *Auteur; auteure; cinéma d'auteur(e).*

Bande-sonore (f.) SOUND TRACK.

BIRD'S EYE VIEW. A shot in which the camera photographs a scene from directly overhead.

BLACK HUMOR. *Humour noir.*

Bobine. REEL.

BOOM. Mechanical moveable arm that holds the camera or microphone. *(Une)Grue.*

Bruitage. SOUND EFFECTS.

Cadre: FRAME. *Cadrage:* FRAMING.

Caméra de plateau.

Chaîne. NETWORK (TV).

Champ-contre champ. FIELD-REVERSE FIELD SHOT. *(hors champ)*

Cinéma d'auteur(e). See auteur theory.

CINEMA VERITE. A method of documentary filming. Such films are made with handheld camera and portable sound equipment. A related technique characteristic of Canadian documentary is called *CINEMA DIRECT.*

159

Clip. FILM CLIP.

CLOSE-UP. A detailed view of a person or object without much context provided. *Gros-plan*.

Commandite. Any film solicited and financed by a federal or provincial ministry, or by any organization, governmental agency, institution, union, pressure group, or private company. (*Dictionnaire . . .*, Houle)

COMPILATION FILM. A film "compiled" from other films and photographs. Often, use is made of archival footage. In such a film, *montage* or editing becomes even more important than usual.

Copie. PRINT.

Contre-plongée. TILT-SHOT (DOWN)

Coupure. CUT.

Court métrage. SHORT.

CRANE SHOT. A shot taken from a special device, called a crane, which resembles a huge mechanical arm. *Grue*.

CROSSCUTTING. The alternating shots from two sequences. *Plans parallèles* or *montage parallèle*.

CUT. *Coupure*

CUTAWAY. *Flash*.

CUTTING. *Découpage*.

DAY FOR NIGHT. Use of filter during daylight to give illusion of night. *Nuit américaine*.

Découpage is used for editing, as well as montage. CUTTING.

DEPTH OF FIELD. *Profondeur de champ*.

DEEP FOCUS. A photographic technique that permits all distance planes to remain clearly in focus, from close-up to infinity. See FOCUS.

(En) direct. LIVE.

DIRECTOR. The one in charge of all aspects of the film. (See auteur.) In French, one usually says *réalisateur/réalisatrice;* only occasionally does one hear *metteur (metteuse)-en-scène*.

DISSOLVE. Disappearance of one scene into another (melting effect). *Fondu-enchaîné*. One may have a "dissolve in" (*ouverture en fondu*) or a "dissolve out" (*fermeture en fondu*).

DOLLY SHOT. Traveling (m). A shot in which the camera is moved, following an actor or some other event. (See tracking.)

DUB. (v. *doubler*). Replacing the original sound track with one in a different language, usually with other actors' voices. (Sometimes used to make the sound track clearer when filming has been done in noisy area.) DUBBING (in French *doublage*) of foreign films is disliked by some; preferred by some to subtitles. Each technique has its drawbacks and its merits.

Doubler. DUB. *doublage*. DUBBING

Eclairage. LIGHTING.

Ecran. SCREEN: *Grand écran*: movie screen; wide screen: *Petit écran*: TV screen.

EDITING. Selecting the shots or sequences of film that are to be kept and placing them in an artistic and meaningful order. *Montage.* (To edit: *monter*; editor: *monteur*.) *Découpage* is also used for editing.

Effets visuels. MONTAGE (Eng.). (Not editing, but the simultaneous superimposing of several images).

Encadrer. To frame. *Image* or *cadre*: frame. *Cadrage*: FRAMING.

ESTABLISHING SHOT. A long shot at the beginning of a scene or sequence that informs viewer of the locus of the action. *Plan général.*

(En) exclusivité. FIRST RUN.

EXPRESSIONISM. A style of filmmaking that distorts time and space as ordinarily perceived in reality. *Expressionisme.*

FADE-IN. Slow introduction of next scene, with last scene melting into new one. *Fondu; ouverture en fondu.*

FADE-OUT. Slow disappearance of a scene, melting into the next one.

FAST MOTION. Natural speed is accelerated. *Accéléré.* In fast motion: *accéléré.*

Fermeture en fondu. DISSOLVE OUT or FADE-OUT.

Feuilleton. MINISERIES.

FIELD-REVERSE FIELD SHOT. *Champ-contre champ.*

(Un) film. A FILM.

Filmer. To make a film. To film (a picture).

TO FILM (a picture). *Tourner un film* or *filmer.* A FILM; *Un film.*

FILM CLIP. Short excerpts. *(Un) Clip.*

FILM NOIR. Genre of American film (ca. 1945–55). In it gangsters or murderers covort; stylistically, there is heavy use of chiaroscuro.

FIRST RUN. First showing, limited showing. *En exclusivité.*

Flash. CUTAWAY; FLASH CUTTING.

FLASHBACK. An editing technique that suggests the interruption of the present by a shot or series of shots representing the past. *Flash de rappel* or *flashback.*

FLASH CUTTING. *Flash.*

Flash de rappel or *flashback.* FLASHBACK.

Flou. OUT OF FOCUS.

(TO) FOCUS. To adjust camera or projector so that visual effect is normal. **Mettre au point.** Focus (noun): *mise au point.* Out of focus: *flou.* In focus: *net (nette).*

Fond sonore.

Fondu au noir or *fermeture en fondu* (See *Fondu-enchaîné*)

Fondu-enchaîné. DISSOLVE. *ouverture en fondu:* Dissolve in or FADE-IN; *fermeture en fondu:* dissolve out or FADE-OUT.

FRAME. A single shot. *Ecran* (m.) or *cadre* (m.) or *image* (f.).

TO FRAME: *encadrer.*

FRAMING. *Cadrage.*

FREEZE-FRAME. A shot composed of a single frame that is reprinted a number of times on the filmstrip. When projected, this gives the illusion of a still photograph. *Arrêt sur image.*

GENRE. A recognizable type of movie, characterized by conventions.

(Une)Grue. BOOM.

HIGH-ANGLE SHOT: A shot in which the subject is photographed from above. (Overhead)

Intrusion ralentie. IN SLOW MOTION.

JUMP CUT. A cut in the film that speeds up the action and gives a jerky effect to the scene. *Saute.*

LEADER. Edge of frame; starting film. *Amorce* (f.)

LENS. *Objectif* (m.)

LIGHTING. *Eclairage* (m.)

LIVE. *En direct.*

Long métrage. Full-length movie.

LONG SHOT. *Plan éloigné.*

LONG TAKE.

MEDIA. *Média* (m. pl. noun).

MELODRAMA. *Un mélodrame* or *un mélo.*

Métrage. Denotes length of film: *court métrage, moyen métrage; long métrage.*

Metteur en scéne. Occasionally used for *réalisateur* (director).

Mettre au point. (TO) FOCUS.

MINISERIES. *Feuilleton.*

Mise au point. Focus (noun): Out of focus: *flou.* In focus: *net (nette).*

MISE-EN-SCENE. The arrangement of visual weights and movements within a given space.

MONITOR (TV). *Un téléviseur.*

MONTAGE. In English, not editing, but the simultaneous superimposing of several images. *Effets visuels.*

Montage américain: cursive; elliptical; rarely repetitive.

Montage parallèle. CROSSCUTTING.

MOTIF: Any unobtrusive technique, object, or thematic idea that is systematically repeated throughout a film. *Motif.*

NEOREALISM. An Italian film movement that produced its best works between 1945 and 1955. *Néorealisme.*

NETWORK (TV). *Chaîne.*

NEWSREEL. *Ciné-actualités* (m.) or *film (m.) d'actualités.*

NEW WAVE. A group of young French directors who came to prominence during the late 1950s: François Truffaut, Jean-Luc Godard, Alain Resnais, Claude Chabrol, Eric Rohmer, Jacques Rivette (and Marguerite Duras?). They held to the *auteur* theory (for which see **Boggs** 240). New Wave or *Nouvelle Vague* had its roots in the critical writings of young film enthusiasts (Bazin, Valcroze). The first great commercial success of the New Wave film was *Et Dieu créa la femme* (or *And God Created Woman*) (directed by Roger Vadim). Others followed. Examples: Truffaut's *Les 400 Coups* (*400 Blows*), Godard's *A Bout de souffle,* or *Breathless.* **Katz** claims that the movement had spent itself by the end of the 70s. While the style is admired by many, it is detested by some lovers and critics of cinema (e.g., Jacques Lourcelles).

Nouvelle Vague. New Wave.

Nuit américaine. DAY FOR NIGHT

Objectif. LENS.

Objectif grand-angle. WIDE-ANGLE LENS.

Onéfien, onéfienne. This is an adjective formed on the initials ONF (Office National du Film; or National Film Board [of Canada]).

Ouverture en fondu. Dissolve in.

Panoramique. PAN, PANNING SHOT.

PAN, PANNING SHOT. A revolving horizontal movement of the camera from left to right or vice versa. *Panoramique.*

Piste sonore. SOUND TRACK.

Plan. SHOT.
    Plan américain.—see montage
    Plan éloigné—LONG SHOT
    Plan général—ESTABLISHING SHOT
    Plan large
    Plan moyen
    Plan normal fixe
    Plans parallèles—CROSS CUTTING.
    Plan rapproché
    Plan d'ensemble
    Gros Plan—CLOSE-UP

Plateau. SET.

Plongée. TILT SHOT (UP).
    Contre-plongée. TILT SHOT (DOWN)
    filmer en plongée.

Point de vue. POINT-OF-VIEW.

POINT-OF-VIEW: Any shot that is taken from the vantage point of a character in the film; what he or she sees. *Point de vue*.

POSTMODERN. Mobility of interpretation. Culture of incoherent fragmentary sensations. Media barrage or pounding.

Prise de son. Sound (Act of capturing sound).

Prise de vue aérienne. AERIAL SHOT.

PRINT. A copy of the film. *Copie* (f.).

Profondeur de champ. DEPTH OF FIELD.

Raccord. SPLICE.

Raccorder. TO SPLICE.

(Le) ralenti. SLOW MOTION.

Réalisateur/réalisatrice. DIRECTOR.

REEL. Spool upon which film is wound. *Bobine* (f.).

Reprise. RERUN.

RERUN. Any showing but the first. *Reprise* (f.).

Saute. JUMP CUT.

Scénario. SCREENPLAY (SCRIPT).

SCENE. Not a frame, but a series of frames making up a meaningful whole as regards both time and space. *Scène*.

SCREEN. Movie screen. Wide screen: *Grand écran*. TV screen: *Petit écran*.

SCREENPLAY (SCRIPT). Sometimes, but not always, a mere outline with rudimentary dialogue, from which the director works. *Scénario*.

SEQUENCE. A series of scenes or shots linked together in a meaningful whole with respect to the story. *Séquence*.

SET. In a movie, the background, place, or room against which a shot or series of shots is taken. *Plateau*.

SHORT. *Court métrage* (as opposed to a full-length movie, *long métrage*).

SHOT. *Point de vue; plan*.

(Un) téléviseur. MONITOR (TV).

TO SHOOT (a film). *Tourner un film*.

SLAPSTICK (or SCREWBALL COMEDY). *Farce* (or *comédie lufoque*).

SLOW MOTION. Camera trick that causes motion on the screen to appear at much slower speed than in reality. *Le ralenti*.

Son. SOUND

SOUND. *Son*. Sound, in the sense of recording sound: *prise de son*.

SOUND EFFECTS. *Bruitage* (m.).

SOUND TRACK. *Bande sonore; piste sonore; voie sonore*. (all fem.)

SPECIAL EFFECTS (TRICKS). *Trucages* or *truquages* (m.).

SPLICE. Joining together of two pieces of film. *Raccord.* TO SPLICE: *raccorder.*

STILL. A photograph made from a shot in a movie. *Arrêt (m.) sur image* or just *photographie (f.).*

SUBTITLES. Brief translations of dialogue usually running at the bottom of the screen (*Sous-titres* [m.]). TO SUBTITLE: *Sous-titrer.* SUBTITLED (*Sous-titré*): Said of a film shown in the original version (*version originale*), but equipped with subtitles.

Sujet libre. In film milieus, this term designates films that, although financed by public funds, answer to no demand expressly formulated by the administration. (*Dictionniare . . . ,* Houle).

SURREALISM. An avant-garde movement in the arts stressing Freudian and Marxist ideas, unconscious elements, irrationalism, and the symbolic association of ideas. For example, See Germaine Dulac. (*Le Surréalisme; surréaliste.*)

SYMBOL: A figurative device in which an object, an event, or cinematic technique has significance beyond its literal meaning.

TELEPHOTO LENS. Camera lens that can make something far off seem close up. *Objectif téléphoto.*

(Un) téléviseur. TV Monitor.

TILT SHOT (UP). *Plongée.*

TILT SHOT (DOWN). *Contre-plongée.*

Tourner un film or *filmer.* TO FILM (a picture).

TRACKING SHOT. A shot made with the camera moving on a dolly. Also called a dolly shot. *Un travelling.*

Travelling (m). DOLLY SHOT; TRACKING SHOT; TRAVELING SHOT.

TRAVELLING SHOT. (Tracking shot.) *Un travelling.*

TRICKS (OF THE CAMERA). *Trucage;* or *truquage.* (*artifice cinématographique*).

Trucage; or *truquage* (*artifice cinématographique*). TRICK(S) (OF THE CAMERA); SPECIAL EFFECT(S).

VOICE-OVER. A nonsynchronous spoken commentary in a movie, often used to convey a character's thoughts or memories. The person speaking is not shown by the camera. (*En*) *voix-off* or *voice-off.*

(En) voix-off or *voice-off.* VOICE-OFF

Voie sonore. SOUND TRACK.

Volet. WIPE.

(Un) Western. WESTERN.

WESTERN. A film genre, with action set in the American West. *Un Western.*

WIDE-ANGLE LENS. *Objectif grand-angle.*

WIDE SCREEN (See screen).

WIPE. Special effect relating to appearance or disappearance of the picture. *Volet (m.).*

ZOOM. *Zoom.* Zoom-back: *Zoom arrière.* Zoom in (or up): *Zoom avant.*

Types of Comedy

(A breakdown of different kinds of tragedy and drama into a separate section has not seemed necessary; forms such as melodrama (mélodrame) are found in the main glossary.)

BLACK HUMOR (*humour noir*). Comedy that draws laughter from something serious or macabre.

BURLESQUE. (From Italian, "burla"—Jest.) An artistic composition that, for the sake of laughter, vulgarizes lofty material or treats ordinary material with mock dignity. (*burlesque*)

CARICATURE. (From Italian "caricare"—to distort.) A picture, a description exaggerating the peculiarities or defects of persons or things. (*caricature*)

COMEDY. A play, movie, and so forth, of humorous and light character with a happy and cheerful ending. *Comédie. Farce* (slapstick); *comédie loufoque* (screwball comedy).

COMEDY OF MANNERS. A comedy satirizing the manners and customs of a social class, especially dealing with the amorous intrigues of a fashionable society. (*comédie de moeurs*)

COMMEDIA DELL'ARTE. Italian popular comedy—developed during the sixteenth to eighteenth century. In it, masked entertainers improvise from a plot outline, based on themes associated with stock characters and situation. Some of the stock characters were Arlecchino (Harlequin), Pulcinello (Punch), and Colombina.

FARCE/farce. (From the Italian, "Farsa"). A light, humorous play in which the plot depends on a skillfully exploited situation rather than on the development of character. Slapstick. (*farce*)

GROTESQUE. (From Italian, "Grotta"—cave.) Odd or unnatural in shape, appearance, or character; fantastically odd and absurd. (*grotesque*)

PARODY. A humorous or satirical imitation of a serious piece of literature, musical composition, person, event, and so forth. Its purpose is to ridicule or satirize. (*parodie*)

SATIRE. A work in which human folly, vice, and so on, are held up to scorn, derision, or ridicule. Satire emphasizes the weakness more than the weak person and usually implies moral judgment and corrective purpose. (*satire*)

SCREWBALL COMEDY. (*comédie loufoque*)

ZANY. (From Italian "Zanni," corruption Gianni [John].) Ludicrously or whimsically comical, clownishly crazy. (*zan[n]i; bouffon*)

Questions for Film Analysis

GENERAL

1. What is the film's primary concern or focus: plot, emotional effect, character, style or texture . . . or idea?
2. If you think the film makes a significant statement, why and in what way is it significant?
3. What makes the story believable? Pick out specific scenes to illustrate what kind of truth is stressed by the film.
4. What major symbols appear in the film and what do they represent? Are the major symbols related to the theme?
5. What methods of characterization are employed? What about each character's motivation? Point out bits of dialogue, images, or a scene that you consider effective in revealing character.
6. What, if anything, marks the film as made by a woman?

CONFLICT

1. Identify the major conflict.
2. Is the conflict internal (woman against herself), external, or a combination of both? Is it primarily a physical or a psychological conflict?
3. Express the major conflict in general terms.
4. How is the major conflict related to the theme?
5. Which of the core concepts is involved in this conflict? (There may be more than one.)
6. What is the resolution of the conflict, if any? Is that resolution satisfactory?

SETTING

1. Which of the four environmental factors (temporal factors, geographical factors, social structures and economic factors, and fac-

tors involving customs, moral attitudes, and codes of behavior) play(s) a significant role in the film?
2. Why did the director choose this particular location for filming this story?
3. How does the film's setting contribute to the overall emotional atmosphere?
4. What kind(s) of important interrelationships exist(s) between settings and the characters, or between setting and plot?
5. Is the setting symbolic in any way? Does it function as a microcosm?

IRONY

1. What examples of irony can be found in the film?
2. Do any particular examples of irony achieve comic and tragic effects at the same time?
3. Where in the film is suspense or humor achieved through dramatic irony?
4. How do the ironies contribute to the film?

SIGNIFICANCE OF THE TITLE

1. Why is the title appropriate?
2. How many different levels of meaning(s) can you find in the title?
3. Is the title ironic? What opposite meanings or contrasts does it suggest?

CINEMATIC QUALITIES

1. To what degree is the film cinematic (i.e., made up of images; moving pictures)? Cite specific examples.
2. Does the cinematography create clear, powerful, and effective images in a natural way?
3. Which technical methods does the director use to draw our attention to the object of greatest significance?
4. Rhythm. Does the rhythm of a (this) woman's film differ from that of a man's? Chantal Akerman claims no generalization about this can be made (see Doane, ed. Re-vision . . . : essay by Mayne: 59). Do you agree?

CINEMATIC VIEWPOINT

1. Based on your reaction to the film as a whole, do you feel that you were primarily an objective, impersonal observer of the action, or did you have the sense of being a participant? Or of being manipulated? (Was the film "exploitative"?)
2. In what scenes were you aware that the director was employing visual techniques to comment on or interpret the action, forcing you to see the action in a special way?
3. Make a mental (or written) note of those pictorial effects that struck you as especially effective, ineffective, or unique.
4. What was the director's aim in creating these images, and what camera tools or techniques were employed?
5. Were there "stereotypes" of women in the film(s) viewed? Why would women directors prolong these?
6. Are images of women in women's film (this one and others) more "real" than those in men's films you have seen? (Obviously, we tend to have problems with the words real and reality; this too provokes discussion.)

SOUND EFFECTS AND DIALOGUE

1. Where in the film are off-screen or invisible sounds effectively employed to enlarge the boundaries of the visual frame, or to create mood or atmosphere.
2. Where is sound employed to represent subjective states of mind and how effective is it?
3. Is sound used to provide important transitions in the film?
4. If voice-over soundtracks are used for narration or internal monologues, can you justify their use?
5. Is dialogue used unnecessarily? too profusely? not enough?
6. Where in the film is silence employed as a sound effect to intensify suspense, or to create special dramatic effects?
7. Was the music effective? Too obtrusive? Explain.

ACTING

1. Which actors did you feel were correctly cast in their part?
2. If a performance was unconvincing, explain why.
3. In which scenes are the actor's facial expressions used? (Use of [close-up] reaction shots.)

TIME; PACING

1. Allowing for a difference of pacing between American and European/Canadian films, how is time handled in the film?
2. If the pacing seems too slow, what scene(s) would you have edited?
3. If the pacing seems too fast, where would you slow the action; what would you explore more fully?

QUESTIONS REGARDING FILM STUDIES AND THE ROLE OF WOMEN IN FILM STUDIES (PREPARED BY PROFESSOR HARRIET MARGOLIS OF VICTORIA UNIVERSITY, WELLINGTON, NEW ZEALAND)

1. What has the feminist contribution to the discipline of film studies been?
2. How might it be characterized?
3. How have women influenced the discipline's research, teaching, and practices?
4. What is the status of women in the discipline?
5. Have women been more successful integrating themselves into this discipline than into others?
6. Why might the discipline of film studies be different?
7. Can it serve as a pattern for women in other disciplines?
8. What has been the effect on women in the discipline as both jobs and interest in women's issues have decreased?
9. Have there been generational conflicts in the discipline?
10. Between women and women? Between women and men?

Annotated Bibliography

GENERAL

Acker, Ally. *Reel Women: Pioneers of the Cinema: 1896 to the Present*. New York: Continuum, 1991. [No Balt. Call: 791.43/A]. Many errors and inaccuracies, but some useful information. Reviewed by Janis L. Pallister in *Journal of Popular Film & Television* 20, no. 2 (summer 1992): 38–39.

Barthes, Roland. "On the Face of Garbo." In *A Barthes Reader,* edited by Susan Sontag, 82–84. New York: Hill and Wang, 1982.

Bazin, André. *What Is Cinema?* Edited and translated by Hugh Gray. Vol. 1. Berkeley: University of California Press, 1987.

———. *Le Cinéma de la cruauté*. Paris: Flammarion, 1987.

Bergan, Ronald and Robyn Karney. *The Holt Foreign Film Guide*. New York: Henry Holt and Company. 1988. Credits and brief *scénario*.

Bluestone, George. *Novels into Films: The Metamorphosis of Fiction into Cinema*. Berkeley: University of California Press, 1957.

Boggs, Joseph M. *The Art of Watching Film*. 2d ed. Mountain View, Calif.: Mayfield Publishing Company, 1985.

Bordwell, David. *Making Meaning: Inference and Rhetoric in the Interpretation of Cinema*. Harvard Film Studies, Harvard University Press, 1989. Canada not included.

———. *Narration in the Fiction Film*. Madison: University of Wisconsin Press, 1985.

Boyum, Joy Gould. *Double Exposure: Fiction into Film*. New York: Universe Books, 1985.

Brûlé, Michel. *Vers une politique du cinéma au Québec, document de travail*. Québec: Direction générale du cinéma et de l'audiovisuel, ministère des Communications, 1978.

Brunette, Peter and David Wills. *Screen/Play: Derrida and Film Theory*. Princeton, N.J.: Princeton University Press, 1989.

Brunsdon, Charlotte, ed. *Films for Women*. London: British Film Institute, 1986. Feminist studies of films by and for women and issues of concern; for example, pornography.

Cixous, Hélène, and Catherine Clement. *The Newly Born Woman*. Minneapolis: University of Minnesota Press, 1986.

Cole, Janis, and Holly Dale. *Calling the Shots: Profiles of Women Filmmakers*. Ontario: Quarry Press, 1993.

Conley, Tom. *Film Hieroglyphs*. Minneapolis: University of Minnesota Press, copyright 1991.

Cristall, Ferne, and Barbara Emanuel. *Images in Action: A Guide to Using Women's*

Film and Video. Toronto: Between the Lines, 1986. Some foreign references. See directory of distributors for foreign films. Detailed practical guide to designing film programs and organizing small-group and public showings. Includes a chapter on feminist filmmaking and signals landmarks of women in film history.

De Lauretis, Teresa. *Alice Doesn't (Feminism, Semiotics, Cinema).* Bloomington: Indiana University Press, 1984.

Doane, Mary Ann. *The Desire to Desire.* Bloomington: Indiana University Press, 1987. Concerned with American films of the 40s; see, however, passages on voyeurism; fetishism; sexuality.

Doane, Mary Ann, Patricia Mellencamp, and Linda Williams, eds. *Re-Vision: Essays in Feminist Film Criticism.* Frederick, Md.: University Publications of America, Inc. (The American Film Institute Monograph Series), 1984. A very important, if now somewhat dated, collection of essays by Judith Mayne, Mary Ann Doane, Teresa de Lauretis, et al. Useful bibliographical information, but no general index and no general bibliography, so one must scout in this book. (see *Re-Vision . . .* infra.)

Donaldson, Laura E. *Decolonizing Feminisms: Race, Gender & Empire Building.* Chapel Hill: University of North Carolina Press, 1992.

Dwoskin, Stephen. *Film Is the International Free Cinema.* Woodstock, New York: The Overlook Press, 1985.

Erens, Patricia, ed. *Issues in Feminist Criticism.* Bloomington: Indiana University Press, 1980.

———. *Sexual Stratagems: The World of Women in Film.* New York: Horizon Press, 1979. Two-part work divided between Male-Dominated Cinema and Women's Cinema. Treatment and filmographies of, among others: Audry, Blaché, Dulac, Kaplan, Akerman, Yannick Bellon, Mireille Dansereau, Duras, Anne-Claire (sic) Poirier.

Flitterman-Lewis, Sandy. *To Desire Differently: Feminism and the French Cinema.* Champaign, Ill.: University of Illinois Press, 1990. Study of Germaine Dulac (representing First Avant-Garde of the 1920s); Marie Epstein (redefining Poetic Realism of the 30s); and Agnès Varda (initiating New Wave of early 60s). Author uses biographical, historical, and textual analyses to portray an alternative feminist cinematic tradition.

Ford, Charles. *Femme cinéastes, ou le triomphe de la volonté.* Paris: Editions Denoël-Gonthier, 1972. Dated, but good information here, especially on early Varda films.

Foreman, Alexa L. *Women in Motion.* Bowling Green, Ohio: Bowling Green University Popular Press, 1983. "Women in motion is concerned with the women who have been active within the motion picture industry as well as independent filmmakers." (Intro.)

Foster, Gwendolyn Audrey. *Women Film Directors: An International Bio-Critical Dictionary.* Westport Conn.: Greenwood Press, 1995.

Frauen/Film: New Approaches to teaching film. Edited by Linda Kraus Wroley, University of Kentucky. Place of publication and publisher unspecified. Published in 1989.
Contains sample syllabi; pedagogical tools; film sources and bibliography. Compare California Newsreel catalog(s) for pedagogical tools (questions) and definitions of film terms.

Gentile, Mary. *Film Feminisms: Theory and Practice.* Westport, Conn.: Greenwood Press [Series: Contributions in Women's Studies], 1985.

Grant, Barry Keith, ed. *Film Study in the Undergraduate Curriculum*. New York: MLA, 1983. ISBN PAPER 305-9 [J250P]. Six essays discussing original approaches to film study . . . are followed by detailed descriptions of eleven other programs. Contributors discuss a wide range of questions and issues.

Haskell, Molly. *From Reverence to Rape: The Treatment of Women in the Movies*. New York: Henry Holt and Company, 1974. Claims the movie industry has, for the most part, reinforced "the big lie . . . of women's inferiority" (1–2). Parts are devoted to European film.

Heck-Rabi, Louise. *Women Filmmakers: A Critical Reception*. Metuchen, N.J.: The Scarecrow Press, 1984. Generous chapters on Blaché, Dulac, and Varda.

Heller, Scott. "Once-theoretical Scholarship on Film. . . ." *Chronicle of Higher Education* (21 March 1990): A6–8; A–12.

Issues in Feminist Criticism. Edited by Patricia Erens. Bloomington: Indiana University Press, 1980?

Johnson, Lincoln F. *Film: Space, Time, Light and Sound*. New York: Holt, Rinehart and Winston, 1974. Important analysis of Varda's *Le Bonheur*.

Johnston, Claire. "Women's Cinema as Counter-Cinema." In *Movies and Methods*, edited by Bill Nichols, I, 208–17. Berkeley: University of California Press, 1976.

Kaplan, E. Ann. *Women & Film: Both Sides of the Camera*. New York: Methuen, 1983. Feminist film criticism; analyses of specific films; contains a glossary, a bibliography, and sample syllabi.

———. *Women in Film Noir*. Revised edition. London: British Film Institute, 1980.

Katz, Ephraim. *The Film Encyclopedia*. New York: Harper-[Perennial]-Collins, 1994.

International Index to Film Periodicals. An annual annotated guide to writings on film and films.

Kowalski, Rosemary Ribich. *Women and Film: A Bibliography*. Metuchen, N.J.: Scarecrow Press, 1976. More than two thousand entries; now dated, of course, but still useful.

Kuhn, Annette. *Women's Pictures: Feminism and Cinema*. London: Routledge and Kegan Paul, 1982. 2d ed. London: Verson, 1994. Passages on Akerman; feminism, and cinema (3–18); Nelly Kaplan's *Néa*, 122–23; and many other issues, such as the spectator, voyeurism, pornography, mother-daughter films, repression and suppression of female, and so on.

Kuhn, Annette, ed. *The Women's Companion to International Film*. Berkely: University of California Press, 1994.

Kuhn, Annette, and Susannah Radstone, eds. *Women in Film: An International Guide*. New York: Fawcett Columbine, 1990.

Lejeune, Paule. *Le Cinéma des femmes (1895–1987)*. Paris: Atlas Lherminier, 1989. One hundred five French and francophone women directors with filmographies and biographies.

(Flitterman-)Lewis, Sandy. *To Desire Differently: Feminism and the French Cinema*. Urbana: University of Illinois Press, 1990. Extensive studies of Germaine Dulac; Marie Epstein; Agnès Varda.

Lloyd. (See Robinson.)

Luhr, William. *World Cinema since 1945*. See Handling (Piers) in Québec section of this bibliography.

Magill's Survey of Cinema (Foreign Language Films). English-speaking reader's reference for all important foreign films. See also *Magill's Cinema Annual*.

Macinnis, Craig. *Private Novels, Public Films*. Athens: University of Georgia Press, 1989.

Maio, Kathi. *Feminist in the Dark*. Freedom, Calif.: The Crossing Press, 1988. (See for *I've Heard the Mermaids Singing* and *Desert Storm* [core concepts]: lesbianism.)

Maio, Kathi. *Popcorn and Sexual Politics*. Freedom, Calif.: The Crossing Press, 1991.

Maltin, Leonard. *TV Movies and Video Guide*. New York: (Penguin Books) Signet, 1989; 1990; 1991; 1994.

Mast, Gerald, et al., eds., *Film Theory and Criticism*. New York: Oxford University Press, 1992. "Extremely comprehensive and well organized—a stunning array of cutting-edge commentary. Enjoyable and informative."—Christopher Little, Old Dominion University.

Mayne, Judith. "Feminist Film Theory and Women at the Movies." *Profession 87* (1987): 14–19. Main subject is voyeurism and female spectatorship in the Hollywood cinema. (Mayne has a similar article in *Signs* 11: 1 [1985].)

Mayne, Judith. *The Woman at the Keyhole: Feminism and Women's Cinema*. Bloomington: Indiana University Press, 1990. Study of the relationship between subject and object, inside and outside, and other oppositions in Laleen Jayamanne's *A Song of Ceylon*, Patricia Rozema's *I've Heard the Mermaids Singing*, Agnès Varda's *Cleo from 5 to 7*, and other films by women directors. Passing reference to Pool, Dulac, Varda, Akerman, et al. Treatment of homosexuality in film.

Metz, Christian. *Film Language: a Semiotics of the Cinema*. Translated from French by Michael Taylor. New York: Oxford University Press, 1974.

Miller, Lynn Fieldman, ed. *The Hand that Holds the Camera*. New York: Garland, 1980.

Morrissette, Bruce. *Novel and Film*. Chicago: University of Chicago Press, 1985.

Paris, James Reid. *The Great French Films*. Secaucus, N.J.: Citadel Press, 1983.

Penley, Constance. *Feminism and Film Theory*. New York: Routledge, 1988.

Oshana, Maryann. *Women of Color: A Filmography of Minority and Third World Women*. New York: Garland, 1985. Principally devoted to American movies; nine hundred entries. Deals with film from 1930 to 1982.

———. *The Future of an Illusion: Film, Feminism and Psychoanalysis*. Minneapolis: (Media and Society) University of Minnesota Press, 1989.

Quart, Barbara Koenig. *Women Directors*. New York: Praeger, 1988. Considerable reference to Varda and Diane Kurys. Some passing reference to other French women directors, for example, Bellon, Dulac, or Trintignant, and to Third World women directors, for example, Maldoror, or Palcy.

Rabinovitz, Lauren. *Points of Resistance: Women, Power, and Politics in the New York Avant-Garde Cinema, 1943–71*. Champaign: University of Illinois Press, 1991. Though recent feminists have sought a nonpatriarchal, resistant cinema, Rabinovitz claims this has been the practice since the 1940s, in the case of Maya Deren, Shirley Clarke, and Joyce Wieland. Useful for possible relationship to similar practices historically and presently in francophone women directors.

Re-vision: Essays in Feminist Film Criticism. Edited by Mary Ann Doane, Patricia Mellencamp, and Linda Williams. Los Angeles: American Film Institute Monograph Series, 1984. Essays by Judith Mayne, Mary Ann Doane, Linda Williams, Teresa de Lauretis, et al. Mayne's essay deals with (among others) Dulac, Akerman, Duras.

Rice, Susan. "Some Women's Films." *Take One* 34 (November–December, 1971): 19–31.

Robinson, David and Ann Lloyd, eds. *The Illustrated History of the Cinema.* New York: Macmillan, 1986. Section on Canadian Film.

Rollyson, Jr., Carl E. *Marilyn Monroe. A Life of the Actress.* Ann Arbor, Mich.: UMI Research Press, 1986.

Roof, Judith. *A Lure of Knowledge: Lesbian Sexuality and Theory.* 1993. "Challenging the heterosexism of film theory and feminist theory, this book analyzes the rhetorical use of lesbian sexuality in a range of discourses, from the works of such authors as Anaïs Nin . . . Julia Kristeva . . . Luce Irigaray . . . to films such as *Emmanuelle, Desert Hearts, Entre Nous,* and *I've Heard the Mermaids Singing.*"

Rosenberg, Jan. *Women's Reflections: The Feminist Film Movement.* Ann Arbor, Mich.: UMI Research Press, 1983.

Sadoul, Georges. *Dictionary of Films.* Translated, edited, and updated by Peter Morris. Berkeley: University of California Press, 1972.

Sadoul, Georges, and Emile Breton. *Dictionnaire (microcosme) des cinéastes.* (4e ed. mise à jour, octobre 1989.) Paris: Collection de Poche, 1989.

——*Dictionnaire (microcosme) des films.* (4e ed. mise à jour, mai 1989.) Paris: Collection de Poche, 1989.

Scheuer, Steven H., ed. *Movies on TV, 1986–87.* New York: Bantam Books, copyright 1985.

Sinyard, Neil. *Silent Movies.* New York: Gallery Books, W. H. Smith Publishers, 1990.

Slide, Anthony. *Early Women Directors.* New York: A. S. Barnes, 1977; and New York: DaCapo, 1984.

Slide, Anthony. *Great Pretenders.* Lombard, Ill.: Wallace-Homestead Book Company, 1986. A history of male and female impersonation in the performing arts.

Sloan, Kay. *The Loud Silents: Origins of the Social Problem Film.* Champaign: University of Illinois Press, 1988. [192 pp.; illus.] "An important volume documenting early silent films from the teens and earlier which dealt with such social issues as women's rights, labor and politics." (*Classic Images.*)

Smith, Sharon. *Women Who Make Movies.* New York: Hopkinson and Blake, 1975. Though now dated, contains good chapter on Alice Guy Blaché, including an interview with Blaché's daughter Simone.

Solomon, Charles. *The History of Animation: Enchanted Drawings.* New York: Alfred A. Knopf, 1989.

Stam, Robert. *Subversive Pleasures: Bakhtin, Cultural Criticism and Film.* Baltimore, Md: Johns Hopkins University Press, 1989.

Studlar, Gaylyn. "Masochism and the Perverse Pleasures of the Cinema." In *Movies and Methods,* edited by Bill Nichols, vol 2: 602–21. Berkeley: University of California Press, 1985.

Sullivan, Kaye. *Films for by and about Women.* Metuchen, N.J.: Scarecrow Press, 1980; series 2, 1985.

Sultanik, Aaron. *Film: A Modern Art.* Cornwall Books, 1986.

Trinh T. Minh-Ha. *Woman, Native, Other.* Bloomington: Indiana University Press, 1989.

Vincendeau, Ginette, and Bérénice Reynaud, eds. *20 ans de théories féministes sur le cinéma. CinémAction* no 67. Corlet-Télérama, 1993. See review by Marie-Noëlle Little, *French Review* 68, no. 6 (May 1995): 1111–12.

Walsh, Andrea S. *Women's Films and Female Experience: 1940–1950.* New York: Praeger, 1984. Social history, film plot descriptions, and thematic analyses.

Warren, Denise. "Beauvoir on Bardot: The Ambiguity Syndrome." *Simone de Beauvoir et les féminismes contemporains* 13 (fall–winter 1987): 39–50.

Williams, Alan. *Republic of Images: A History of French Filmmaking.* Cambridge, Mass.: Harvard University Press, 1992. [ISBN 0.674.7628.1.] Views Alice Guy Blaché's work as a development of the aesthetic side of early filmmaking; Varda as on the periphery of New Wave cinema!

Women and Film (published in Santa Monica)

Women Make Movies Film and Video Catalogue. (New York: Women Make Movies, Inc. (1992–94), 16; 40.

Women's Art Journal. ISBN 8357–1400–4. Issue #22, 154 pp., 1983 (on cinema).

The Women's Companion to International Film: see Kuhn.

AFRICA

Anon. (*Aljadid* staff.) "Tunisian Director Tlatli Speaks on Making Films 'On Women by a Woman.'" *Aljadid* 5 (March 1996): 3–4; 20. Complete coverage of *The Silences of the Palace.*

Beck, Lois, and Nikki Keddie, eds. *Women in the Muslim World.* Cambridge: Harvard University Press, 1978. (Obviously very out of date.)

Boughedir, Férid. *Le Cinéma africain de A à Z.* Brussels: Editions OCIC, 1987. Part 3 lists more than two hundred filmmakers and their works with brief summaries.

Cham, Mbye, and Claire Andrade-Watkins, eds. *Black Frames: Critical Perspectives on Black Independent Cinema.* Cambridge: MIT Press, 1988.

Dejeux, Jean. *Assia Djebar: romancière algérienne, cinéaste arabe.* Sherbrooke, Qué.: Editions Naaman, 1984.

Demy, Catherine. "L'Afrique et la Caribe au rendez-vous sur la croisette." *Amina* 315 (July 1996): 20–21; 34.

Diawara, Manthia. *African Cinema: Politics and Culture.* Bloomington: Indiana University Press, 1992.

Gabriel, Teshome H. *Third Cinema in the Third World. The Aesthetics of Liberation.* Ann Arbor: UMI Research Press, 1979; 1982.

André Gardies and Pierre Haffner. *Regards sur le cinéma négro-africain.* Brussels: Editions OCIC, 1987.

Hennebelle, Guy, and Catherine Ruelle, eds. *Cinéastes d'Afrique noire. CinemAction* (special ed.) #49 (1979).

Hoberman, J. "Inside Senegal." *Village Voice* (6 February, 1978): 42, 48. (Safi Faye.)

Larouche, Michel, ed. *Films d'Afrique.* Montréal: Guérnica, 1991. Article on women in African films (but no woman editor) and an article on Maldoror. This book is flawed by superficial articles, lack of index, and repeated instances of pages out of order.

Malkmus, Lisbeth, and Roy Aimes. *Arab and African Film Making.* Zed Books, 1991. Has filmographies and extensive bibliography.

Martin, Angela. "Four Filmmakers from West Africa." *Framework* 11 (1979): 16–21. Interview with Safi Faye.

"Ousmane Sembène: Africa's Premier Cinéaste." *Africa Report* 35, no. 5 (1990). Here Ousmane is interviewed by Margaret A. Novicki & Daphne Topouzis. [Knowledge of the role of women in Sembene's writings and film is important to appreciation of same elsewhere.]

Pallister, Janis, L. Ousmane's *Black Girl [la Noire de . . .]* compared with *Milk and Honey*. *Modern Language Journal* 22, no. 4 (fall 1992): 76–87.

Pfaff, Françoise. *Twenty-five Black African Filmmakers.* Westport, Conn.: Greenwood Press, 1988. Consult for Safi Faye and Sarah Maldoror. However, besides these two and Sita Bella, Pfaff notes that "Black African cinema remains a male-dominated sphere" (118).

———. *The Cinema of Ousmane Sembene.* Westport, Conn.: Greenwood Press, 1984.

"Rethinking Visual Anthropology: The Images of Africa." *Society for Visual Anthropology Review,* 6, no. 1 (spring 1990). Contains articles by Manthia Diawara, Françoise Pfaff, and Keyan Tomaselli.

Salmane, Hala. *Algerian Cinema.* London: BFI, 1976. Very out of date.

Schissel, Howard. "Africa on Film: The First Feminist View." *Guardian* (9 July 1980): 7. On Safi Faye.

Schmidt, Nancy J. *Sub-Saharan African Films and Filmmakers: An Annotated Bibliography.* (Hans Zell, 1988; 402 pp.). ISBN 0–905450–32–9. Comprehensive bibliography on more than seventy books and 3,500 articles that review films made in Africa by African filmmakers. Schmidt also has work entitled "Publications on African Film: Focus on Burkina Faso and Nigeria," in *African Book Publishing Record* 26, no. 3 (1990). Schmidt compiles lists of recent films by sub-Saharan African filmmakers and has contributed at least four such lists to the A(frican) L(iterature) A(ssociation) Bulletin. (e.g., vol. 17, no. 1 [winter, 1991] has a quite recent list on pp. 7-11). See also winter 1995 and vol. 22, no. 1 (winter 1996).

Shiri, Keith. *Directory of African Film-Makers and Films.* Westport, Conn.: Greenwood, 1992. Review by N. Frank Ukadike in *Research in African Literatures* (fall 1995: 207) states that the work "fails to acknowledge women practitioners." Why are we not surprised?

Stoller, Paul. *The Cinematic Griot: The Ethnography of Jean Rouch.* Chicago; University of Chicago Press, 1992. Review: Janis L. Pallister. *Journal of Popular Film and Television* 22, no. 3 (fall 1994): 137.

Taylor, Clyde. "Light from Darkness," in *Arete* 2, no. 5 (March–April 1990).

Taylor, Clyde. First Chapter in *World Cinema since 1945*, edited by William Luhr, 1–21. New York: Ungar, 1987.

Ukadike, N. Frank. "Reclaiming Images of Women in Films from Africa and the Black Diaspora." *Frontiers* vol. 15, no. 1 (1994). Indispensable article that shows how both men and women filmmakers are engaged in a thoroughgoing cinematic decolonization of women. The discussion of Safi Faye and her *Selbe: One Among Many* is most relevant.

Vieyra, Paulin Soumanou. *Le Cinéma africain des origines à 1973.* Paris: Présence Africaine, 1975. (Little information on women cinéastes, but chapter on Maldoror.)

———. *Sembène Ousmane, cinéaste.* Paris: Présence Africaine, 1972.

Waldman, Peter. "'Burning Bed' meets 'Thelma and Louise' in Egyptian Movies." *Wall Street Journal,* Thursday, 19 March 1992, section A1. Here one may read about "Lady Killer," made by Inas el-Degheidy, "Egypt's most successful woman filmmaker."

BELGIUM

Le Court en dit long. Brussels: Communauté française de Belgique, 1987–88; 1989–90; 1992–93; 1993–94; 1994–95; 1995–96.

De Long en large. Brussels: Communauté française de Belgique, two issues s.d. [Contact: Marie-Hélène Massin, Bd. Léopold II, 44; B-1080 Brussels. Tel. 32.2 413 22 71 or fax 32.3 413 20 68.]

Encyclopédie des cinémas de Belgique. Edited by Guy Jungblut; Patrick Leboutte; Dominique Païni. Paris: Musée d'Art Moderne de la Ville de Paris (Editions Yellow Now, 1990). Although there are excellent entries on Chantal Akerman and Mary Jimenez, few other women cinéastes are cited by entry in this entire work.

Head, Anne. *A True Love for Cinema: Jacques Ledoux*. The Hague (The Netherlands): University Press Rotterdam, 1988.

Mendes da Costa, Yolande and Anne Morelli, eds. *Femmes, Libertés, Laïcité*. Brussells: Editions de l'Université de Bruxelles, 1989. Nothing on film, but an excellent background to women's films and films about women, as it portrays the status of women in Belgium historically and sociologically.

Revue belge du cinéma.

[On Chantal Akerman:]
Hommage à Chantal Akerman. Ed., Roger Dehaybe. Brussels: Communauté française de Belgique, 1995. [At: Avenue Louise 65, Boîte 9, B-1050 Bruxelles.]

Pastor, A., and D. Turco. "Conversazione con Chantal Akerman." *Filmcritica* 42 [n 417/418] (September–October 1991): 422–25.

Kwietniowski, R. "Separations." *Movie* [England] 34–35 Winter, 1990): 108–18.

CARIBBEAN

Boukman, Daniel. "Antilles." *CinémAction/Tricontinental*. Numéro Spécial: "Le Tiers Monde en Film" (1982): 95–97.

Cham, Mbye. *Ex–ile, Essays on Caribbean Cinema*. African World Press, 1992. A group of essays and interviews on some well-known filmmakers [Elsie Haas, Euzhan Palcy, Daniel Boukman, Felix de Rooy et al.] and some less well known. Short but interesting essay by Maryse Condé. Good bibliography to be found in footnotes.

Pick, Zuzana. "Chilean Cinema in Exile." *Framework* 34 (1987): 39–57. On Marilú Mallet.

Ruelle, Catherine. "Le Contexte et l'Histoire du Cinéma Antillais." *Racines Noires 1985*. Black Arts and Culture Festival brochure 38–41. Paris: Association pour la Promotion des Cultures du Monde Noir, 1985.

For articles on Palcy see Foster's Selected Bibliography, 299.

FRANCE

Abel, Richard. *French Cinema: The First Wave, 1915–1929*. Princeton: Princeton University Press, 1984.

Armes, Roy. *French Cinema*. Secker and Warburg. New York: Oxford University Press, 1985. Extensive bibliography of books in French and in English.

Armes, Roy. *French Film since 1946*. In vol. 2: *The Personal Style*. New York: A.S. Barnes & Co., 1976.

Bachy, Victor. *Alice Guy-Blaché (1873–1968): La Première Femme cinéaste du monde*. Paris [or Perpignan]: Institut Jean Vigo, 1993. Exhaustive and definite biofilmography of Blaché, based on rare documents, interviews, personal papers, film catalogs, press stories of the period. (See Mario Cloutier review, *Séquences* [May–June 1994]: 59.)

Benjamin, Sonia. "Love after Love: L'amour dans les années 1990." *Journal Français d'Amérique* (1–14 April 1994): 17. Re Diany Kurys's *Après l'amour*.

Buss, Robin. *The French through Their Films*. New York: Ungar, 1988.

Cazals, Patrick. *Musidora: la Dixième Muse*. Paris: Editions Henry Veyrier, 1978.

Colvile, Georgiana M. M. "Mais qu'est-ce qu'elles voient? Regards de Françaises à la caméra." *The French Review* 67, no. 1 (October 1993): 73–81.

DalMolin, Eliane. "Fantasmes de maternité dans les films de Jacques Demy, Coline Serreau et François Truffaut." *The French Review* 69, no. 4 (March 1996): 616–25.

Dictionnaire Larousse du Cinéma français, 1987.

Doty, David. "Insider's France: Anne Fontaine." *France Insider's News* (November–December 1995; January 1996): 16. (This is a quarterly supplement to the *France Discovery Guide*.)

Duras, Marguerite. *Green Eyes (Les Yeux verts)*. Translated by Carol Barko. New York: Columbia University Press, 1990.

Ehrlich, Evelyn. *Cinema of Paradox: French Filmmaking under the German Occupation*. New York: Columbia University Press, 1985. (240 pp.; illus.)

Gants, Emily. *Creative Encounters with French Films*. Lewiston, Ma: Mellen Research University Press, 1993. Manual and guide for a more complete understanding of auteur films and of New Wave cinema. Covers twenty-one "major films."

Garrity, Henry. *Film in the French Classroom*. Cambridge, Mass.: Polyglot Productions, 1987. Some tips on teaching film; no woman director's film is treated; gender and sexuality are not singled out as issues. Glossary has been utilized in this guide.

Gillain, Anne. "L'Imaginaire féminin au cinéma." *French Review* 70; 2 (December, 1996): 259–70.

Glassman, Deborah N. *Marguerite Duras: Fascinating Vision and Narrative Cure*. Cranbury, N.J.: Fairleigh Dickinson University Press [Associated University Presses], 1991. Review by Janis L. Pallister in *Journal of Popular Film and Television* 20, no. 2 (summer 1992): 38–39.

Grand-Chavin, Stéphane. "La Mémoire percée d'Agnès Varda." *France-Amérique* (30 March–5 April 1996): 13.

Hayward, Susan, and Ginette Vincendeau, eds. *French Film: Texts and Contexts*. London, Routledge, 1990.

Hayward, Susan. *French National Cinema*. London: Routledge (National Cinema Series), 1993. Review by Tom Conley (*French Review* [December 1995]: 361–63) finds the tone scolding and "schoolmarmish." "French cinema is redressed for moral and ethical shortcomings, sexism, sanitized visions of the French bourgeoisie and prurience."

Hughes, Philippe de, and Dominique Muller, eds. *Gaumont: 90 ans de cinéma*. Paris: Ramsaye, 1986.

Johnston, Claire, ed. "Nelly Kaplan, An Introduction." In *Notes on Women's Cinema*. London: British Film Institute, 1973.

Mandolini, Carlo. "*Augustin.*" *Séquences* 183 (March–April 1996): 41–42.

Porter, Melinda Camber. *Through Parisian Eyes: Reflections on Contemporary French Arts and Culture*. New York: Oxford University Press, 1986. (244 pp.; photos). Interviews, including Marguerite Duras; Delphine Seyrig; Monique Wittig; Françoise Giroud (on the status of women).

Prédal, René. *Le Cinéma français depuis 1945*. Paris: Nathan-Université, 1992. Review by Jean Decock (*French Review* [February 1994]: 545–46) finds book sometimes marked by personal taste; that is, Diane Kurys seems to be severely judged.

Slide, Anthony, ed. *The Memoirs of Alice Guy-Blaché*. Translated by Roberta and Simone Blaché. Metuchen, N.J.: Scarecrow Press, 1986–88.

Tranchant, Marie-Noëlle. "Jeanne Moreau: 'Je me ressemble.'" *France-Amérique*. (14–20 January 1995): 12. J. M. as a figure of the New Wave (cf. Agnès Varda). Lists new discs (readings) and reissues (*Jeanne Moreau . . . toujours,* chez Jacques Canetti: Musidisc) and gives bibliography for works on Jeanne Moreau:
Jeanne Moreau. By Jean-Claude Moireau. Chez Ramsay.
Jeanne Moreau portrait d'une femme. By Michaël Delmar. Editions Norma.

Varda, Agnès. *Varda par Agnès*. Paris: Editions de l'Etoile, *Cahiers du Cinéma*, 1994.

Willis, Sharon. *Marguerite Duras: Writing on the Body*. Champaign, Ill.: University of Illinois Press, 1987. 204 pp. Treats Duras's literary and cinematic production together.

Québec

Abel, Marie-Christine; André Giguère; and Luc Perrault. *Le Cinéma québécois à l'heure internationale*. Montréal: Les éditions internationales Stanké, 1990.

Annuaire du cinéma québécois 1989. Montréal: Cinémathèque Québécoise, 1990.
——— *1990* (published in 1991).
These directories contain virtually all information on films one could desire, including complete film credits.

Aujourd'hui le cinéma québécois: (Dossier). Edited by Louise Carrière; preface by Dominique Noguez. Paris: Cerf: Office Franco-Québécois pour la jeunesse, 1986. Extremely useful publication.

Baby, François. "La Lanterne magique." *Découvrir Québec: Guide culturel*. Sainte-Foye: Les Publications Québec Français, 1987: 79–82. This 1987 issue asks whether the recent intense activity in *québécois* cinema will continue, and whether the industry will be able to continue its commercial turn without sacrificing quality or becoming complacent.

Bachand, Denis. "La Réception des films québécois en France." *Québec Studies* 9 (fall 1989–winter 1990): 69–78.

[Bailey, Cameron. "*I've Heard the Mermaids Singing.*" *Cinema Canada* (November 1987): 25.]

Beaulieu, Janick. "Les Chemins de Léa Pool." Interview with Léa Pool. *Séquences* 170 (March 1994): 12–16.

Bersianik, Louky. "L'Empire du statu quo." *Le Devoir* (9 August 1986): C1; C6. Feminist analysis claims *Le Déclin . . .* reproduces "clichés de la politique sexuelle" from beginning to end. [Le Devoir received many letters objecting to what was considered too limited a view as presented in this article.]

Boileau, Josée. "Images récentes dans les films à succès." In Femmes et Cinéma Québécois, edited by Louise Carrière, 113–29. Montréal: Boréal Express, 1983.

Bonneville, Léo. "A la recherche du Sexe des étoiles." Séquences 163 (March 1993): 10–12.

——. Le Cinéma québécois par ceux qui le font. Montréal: Ed. Paulines, 1978. Treats, among others, Denys Arcand; Jean Beaudin; Michel Brault; Gilles Carle; Mireille Dansereau; Jacques Godbout; Claude Jutra; Jean-Claude Labrecque; Arthur Lamothe; Jean-Pierre Lefebvre; Jean-Claude Lord; Francis Mankiewicz; Pierre Perrault; Anne Claire Poirier.

—— Dossiers de cinéma. Montréal et Ottawa: Fides, 1968.

——. "Joan Pennefather." Séquences 150 (January 1991): 76–80.

Bor, Aaron. "An Interview with Léa Pool." Québec Studies 9 (fall 1989): 63–68.

Bottin professionnel du cinéma. Montréal: Conseil Québécois pour la Diffusion du Cinéma, 1972.

Burnett, Ron. Explorations in Film Theory. 22 Essays from Ciné-Tracts, edited by Burnett. Bloomington: Indiana University Press, 1991.
    Review by Janis L. Pallister, Journal of Popular Culture 26, no. 2 (fall 1992): 168–69.

Carrière, Louise. "A propos des films faits par des femmes au Québec." CopieZéro 11 (1981): 44–51.

——. See also CinemAction, infra; and Femmes et cinéma . . . , infra.

Chabot, Claude, Michel Larouche, Denise Pérusse, and Pierre Véronneau, eds. Le Cinéma québécois des années 80. Montréal: Cinémathèque québécoise/Musée du cinéma, 1989.
    Reviewed by Jean-Claude Jaubert, The French Review (December 1990): 374–75.

La Châtelaine. Special Issue on Women's Films (April 1990).

Cinéma au féminin. Montréal: (Cinéma Libre) Bibliothèque nationale du Québec, 1990.

(Le) Cinéma aujourd'hui: Films, théories, nouvelles approches. Edited by Michel Larouche. Montréal: Guernica, 1988. (See Larouche, infra.)

(CinémAction:) Aujourd'hui le cinéma québécois. Edited by Louise Carrière, preface by Dominique Noguez. Paris: Cerf-OFQJ, 1986. [CinémAction is under the general editorship of Guy Hennebelle.] See also under Aujourd'hui, supra.

"Cinéma québécois, nouveaux courants, nouvelles critiques." Dérives 2 (Montréal 1986).

Cinémas canadiens et québécois. Montréal: Collège Ahuntsic (August 1977). A history from the silent film to 1977; chiefly a list of titles and dates.

(Les) 50 ans de l'ONF. Montréal: Editions Saint-Martin, 1989. Articles on documentaries (39–50); fictional films (51–64); animation (65–78); English production (79–92); Women at the ONF, esp. Anne Claire Poirier (93–108); technical services (109–24); distribution (125–38); chronology of the ONF (163–66).

Clanfield, David. Canadian Film. Toronto: Oxford University Press, 1987. Excellent quick reference with many brief appreciations included.

Claude, Renée. "Claude Renée rencontre Léa Pool." Montréal, ce mois-ci. (June 1986): 12–14. An interview, in which L.P. reveals her concept of physical beauty.

Cloutier, Mario. "*Deux Actrices* " (Micheline Lanctôt). *Séquences* 168 (January 1994): 41–42.

CopieZéro. Annuaire (1985). "Improvisation sur un thème connu." Josée Beaudet speaks about her first solo directing with her *Film d'Ariane:* 8–9.

———. Special issue on the Documentary. 30 (December 1986). Remarks on: *Quel numéro?* (*What number?*); *Journal inachevé; Au rhythme de mon coeur; Le futur intérieur; Albedo.*

———. Special issue on Anne Claire Poirier. 23 (February 1985).

Coulombe, Michel, and Marcel Jean. *Le Dictionnaire du cinéma québécois.* 2d ed. Montréal: Boréal, 1991.

Dandurand, Anne. "Léa Pool et le cinéma du dedans." *La Châtelaine* (February 1986): 40–43.

Dansereau, Mireille. "*Le Sourd dans la ville.*" *Lumière* 2, no. 7 (May–June 1987): 8.

Daudelin, Robert. "The Encounter between Fiction and the Direct Cinema." In *Self-Portraits,* edited by Pierre Véronneau and Piers Handling, 94ff. Ottawa: Canadian Film Institute, 1980.

———. *Vingt ans de cinéma au Canada français.* Québec: Ministère des Affaires culturelles, 1967.

Denault, Jocelyne. "Le Cinéma féminin au Québec." *CopieZéro* 11 (1981): 36–43.

Deslandes, Jeanne. "*La Demoiselle Sauvage.*" *Séquences* 155 (November 1991): 56–57.

Dictionnaire du cinéma québécois. Compiled by Michel Houle and Alain Julien. Montréal: Fides, 1978.

Dictionnaire du cinéma québécois, Le. See Coulombe, supra.

Documents in Canadian Film. Edited by Douglas Fetherling. Peterborough, Canada: Broadview Press, Ltd., 1988.
      Review: Janis L. Pallister, *Journal of Popular Film and Television* 17, no. 4 (winter 1990): 173.

Donohoe, Joseph I., Jr., ed. *Essays on Quebec Cinema.* East Lansing: (Can. Series #2) Michigan State University Press, 1991. (see *Essays,* infra.)

———. "*Sonatine* in Context: A Neglected Film of Micheline Lanctôt." In *Essays on Quebec Cinema,* edited by Joseph I. Donohoe, Jr., 157–67. East Lansing: (Can. Series #2) Michigan State University Press, 1991.

Elia, Maurice. "Hotel Chronicles." *Séquences* 150 (January 1991): 97–98.

Essays on Quebec Cinema. Edited by Joseph I. Donohoe, Jr. East Lansing: Michigan State University Press, 1991.

Euvrard, Michel. "Le Rôle d'acteur, malheureusement." *Cinéma/Québec* (March–April 1973): 11–14. Interview between Euvrard and Geneviève Bujold just prior to release of *Kamouraska.*

Evans, Gary. *In the National Interest: A Chronicle of National Film Board from 1949–1989.* Toronto: University of Toronto Press, 1991. Insufficient reflection of the French minority in the NFB (ONF). Many portraits, analyses of films.

Faucher, Carol. *La Production française à l'ONF. 25 ans en perspective.* Montréal: (Les Dossiers de la Cinémathèque 14) Cinémathèque québécoise, 1984.

Feldman, Seth, ed. *Take Two: A Tribute to Film in Canada.* Toronto: Irwin Publishing, 1984. Synopses. See Brenda Longfellow's pedantic piece dealing with Mireille Dansereau's *La Vie rêvée* and Paule Baillargeon's "brechtian" *Cuisine rouge.*

Feldman, Seth, and Joyce Nelson. *Canadian Film Reader.* Toronto: (Take One Film

Series) Peter Martin, 1977. Contains interview with Mireille Dansereau on *La Vie rêvée* (250–57).

Femmes et cinéma québécois. Edited by Louise Carrière. Montréal: Boréal Express, 1983. Contributions by Louise Beaudet, Sophie Bissonnette, Danielle Blais, Josée Boileau, Louise Carrière, Monique Caverni, Nicole Hubert (w/Diane Poitras), Pascale Laverrière, Marquise Lepage, Jacqueline Levitin, Marilú Mallet, Christiane Tremblay-Daviault.

Film Canadiana. Montréal: National Film Board, 1980–82; 1983 and 1985. History of the Canadian film.

Fournier-Renaud, Madeleine, and Pierre Véronneau. *Ecrits sur le cinéma (bibliographie québécoise 1911–1981)*. Montréal: La Cinémathèque québécoise, 1982.

Gaudreault, André, et al. "Au pays des ennemis du cinéma: Pour une nouvelle histoire des débuts du cinéma au Québec." Québec: QC: Nuit Blanche Editeur, 1996.

Gaulin, Suzanne. "Pool's Splash." *Cinema Canada* (October 1984): 8. Interview with the Québécoise filmmaker, Léa Pool.

Gauthier, Jean-Louis. "Louise Forestier, sans compromis." *Châtelaine* 35, no. 9 (September 1994): 22–23; 26; 28. Aperçu of Louise Forestier's accomplishments: *Les Ordres; X–13;* theater, *Vingt personnages en quête d'une chanteuse.* (L.F. née Louise Belhumeur.)

Gay, Richard. "Canada's Young and Diversified Film Industry." *Canada Today/ Canada Aujourdhui* 20, no. 1 (1989). [Washington: D.C.: Canadian Embassy, 1989]: 19–20.

Girard Martin. "Geneviève Rioux." *Séquences* 150 (January 1991): 29–34.

Godfrey, Stephen. "A ride on a feminist rollercoaster." *Toronto Globe and Mail.* (15 June 1990): C8.

Green, Mary Jean. "Léa Pool's *La Femme de l'hôtel* and Women's Film in Quebec." *Québec Studies* 9 (fall 1989): 49–62.

Guenette, Jean T. *National Film, Television and Sound Archives*. Public Archives of Canada: Minister of Supply and Services, 1983. Archives, acc. to subject areas.

——— and Jacques Gagné. *Inventory of the Collections of the National Film, Television and Sound Archives*. Public Archives of Canada: Minister of Supply and Services, 1983. Especially useful are stills.

Haim, Monica. "Le Lecteur fait le film." *CopieZero* (22 July 1987): 6–7. *Le Déclin's* real subject is history or the historical experiences the sexes have in common.

Hamelin, Lucien, and Lise Walser *(Petit Guide du) Cinéma québécois*. Montréal: Conseil Québécois pour la Diffusion du Cinéma, 1973.

Handling, Piers. *Canadian Feature Films: 1913–1969*. Ottawa: (Canadian Filmography Series No. 10) Canadian Film Institute, 1975.

———. Chapter entitled "Canada." In *World Cinema since 1945*, edited by William Luhr, 86–115. New York: Ungar, 1987. A panoramic view of Canadian cinema, with scattered critical insights. Finds major theme to be study of "victim figures" (103).

Hébert, Pierre. "Cinéma québécois—cinéma d'animation québécois?" In *Cinémas du Québec,* edited by Patrick Leboutte, 73–4. Crisnée [Liège]: Editions Yellow Now, 1986. Brief history, stressing effects of establishment of NFB in Montréal ("in 1954") on Québec animation; theory that Québec animation shows same tendencies as other types of cinema from Québec, but may have more connection with animation cinema on an international scale than with *québécois* cinematography.

Houle, Michel, and Alain Julien. *Dictionnaire du cinéma québécois.* Montréal: Fides, 1978.

Jaffe, Chapelle, ed. *Who's Who in Canadian Film and Television.* Toronto: Academy of Canadian Cinema and Television, 1986.

Lafrance, André A. & Gilles Marsolais. *Cinéma d'ici.* Montréal; Ottawa: Leméac, 1975.

Lamartine, Thérèse. *Elles cinéastes ad lib 1895–1981.* Montréal: Ed. du Remue-ménage, 1985.

Lamy, Suzanne. Commentary on *Anne Trister. Spirales* (summer 1987): 8.

Larouche, Michel, ed. *Le Cinéma aujourd'hui—Films, théories, nouvelles approches.* Montréal: Les éditions Guérnica, 1988. Valuable chapter on the "mise en espace-temps" of women in Québec cinema, with Poirier's *Mourir à tue-tête* as focal (see Pérusse).

Leboutte, Patrick, ed. *Cinémas du Québec au fil du direct.* Crisnée [Liège]: Editions Yellow Now, 1986. Interview with Léa Pool (54–56). (Other articles by Jacques Kermabon (53), Louise Carrière [on animation], 67–70 et al.) See also *CopieZéro* 32, no. 6 (1987).

Lefebure Du Bus, Olivier. "Bilan: le cinéma québécois en France." *Séquences* 151 (March 1991): 55. Reception of Québecois films in France.

Lemieux, Louis-Guy. "Filmer la vie en trompe-l'oeil: l'art de Léa Pool." (Entretien avec Léa Pool). *Le Soleil* (8 March 1986): s.p.

Lever, Yves. *Cinéma et Sociéte Québécoise.* Montréal: Editions du Jour, 1972. Contains critiques of *Valérie; Chambre blanche; Q-Bec, my love; Red; Deux Femmes . . . en or?; Acte du coeur; Un Pays sans bon sens;* and others.

———. *Histoire du cinéma au Québec.* Montréal: Boréal, 1988. Indispensable and monumental history.

———. *Histoire générale du cinéma au Québec.* Montréal: Boréal, 1995. 640 pages. Reworking of above; monumental, impeccable, authoritative. Thesis is that the keys to a national cinema are to be found among the persons who preserved the warmth and vitality of it through films unique in their genre . . . Good reading. (*Séquences* 177 [March/April 1995]: 59.)

Longfellow, Brenda. "From Didactics to Desire." *Canadian Forum* (February 1985): 28–32. On women's films, esp. those of Léa Pool.

Major, Ginette. *Le Cinéma québécois à la recherche d'un public. Bilan d'une décennie: 1970–1980.* Montréal: Presses de l'Université de Montréal, 1982. Gives plots and themes.

Martin-(Thériault), Agathe. "*Le Temps d'avant* (Anne Claire Poirier)." *Cinéma/ Québec* 42; 5: 2 (1975): 32 ff. Discusses this early work on abortion.

Martin-(Thériault), Agathe. "Jeunes femmes en proie aux images." *Cinéma/Québec* 2, no. 3 (November 1972): 30–31. A review of Mireille Dansereau's *La Vie rêvée.*

Millot, Pascale. "Léa Pool, femme du monde." *Châtelaine* 37; 12 (December 1996); 16; 18.

Morris, Peter. *Canadian Feature Films: 1913–63,* part 2. 1941–63. Ottawa: (Canadian Filmography Series, No. 7) Canadian Film Institute, s.d. [after 1969].

———. *Embattled Shadows: A History of the Canadian Cinema, 1895–1939.* Montréal: McGill-Queen's University Press, 1978; reprinted 1992.
    Review by Janis L. Pallister in *Journal of Popular Film & Television* 20, no. 3 (fall 1992): 83.

————. *The National Film Board of Canada: The War Years*. Ottawa: (Canadian Filmography Series, No. 3) Canadian Film Institute, 1965; repr. 1972.

National Film, Television and Sound Archives. See Guénette.

National Film Board of Canada, International Film and Video Resource Guide (U.S. edition). New York: National Film Board of Canada, 1987.

Noguez, Dominique. *Essais sur le cinéma québécois*. Montréal: Editions du Jour, 1971. Chapter on the teaching of the film.

Nunes, Julia. "Researching the ratings." *(Comment faire l'amour.) The Toronto Globe and Mail* (15 June, 1990): A12N.

Office national du film: Répertoire (Vidéo). Textes by Louise Dugas; Révision by Jacqueline Généreux. Montréal: Office national du film du Canada, 1988; 1989. Catalogue of most films in French available from the ONF.

Page, James E. *Seeing Ourselves: Films for Canadian Studies*. Montréal: National Film Board of Canada, 1979–80. Designed as a guide to the use of film as a teaching tool. Mostly shorts. Arranged by themes.

Pallister, Janis L. *The Cinema of Québec: Masters in Their Own House*. Cranbury, N.J.: Fairleigh Dickinson University Press (Associated University Presses), 1995. Historical and aesthetic study of Québec major films. Chapter on women directors.

———— "Léa Pool's Gynefilms." In *Essays on Quebec Cinema*, edited by Joseph I. Donohoe, Jr., 111–34. East Lansing: Michigan State University Press, 1991.

Perreault, Luc. "*Anne Trister*: L'artiste et sa quête." *La Presse* (8 February 1986): E19.

————. "Le cinéma selon Léa Pool: Une exigence intérieure." *La Presse* (8 February 1986): E1 & E16. (An interview.)

Pérusse, Denise. *Micheline Lanctôt: La Vie d'une héroïne*. Montréal: L' Hexagone, 1995. Interviews granted to Pérusse are the basis of this study of the vicissitudes in the career of Lanctôt, directress and actress. Reviewed by Maurice Elia in *Séquences* 181 (November–December 1995): 57–58.

————. "*Mourir à tue-tête*." In *Le Cinéma aujourd'hui*. Edited by Michel Larouche. Montréal: Les éditions Guérnica, 1988: 81–96.

Pratley, Gerald. Canadian section in *International Film Guide*. London: Tantivy Press, 1987.

————. *Torn Sprockets: The Uncertain Projection of the Canadian Film*. Newark: University of Delaware Press; Toronto (Associated University Presses), 1987. One of the best references in English to pan-Canadian film. Many stills. Review by Janis L. Pallister: *Journal of Popular Film and Television* 13, no. 3 (fall 1988): 134–35.

Prat[ley], [Gerald]. "*Laura Laur*." *Variety* 335–37 (31 May–7 June 1989): 34. "The pace is slow, the camerawork unimaginative, the acting uneven."

Québec Studies 9. (fall 1989–winter 1990). Special issue on the cinema of the province. Articles separately listed in the present bibliography by authors.

Reid, Alison. *Canadian Women Film Makers, an Interim Filmography*. Ottawa: Canadian Film Institute, 1972.

Répertoire Vidéo. Textes, Louise Dugas. Montréal: Office National du Film du Canada, 1988.

Richler, Mordecai. *Home Sweet Home*. Markham, Ontario, Canada: Penguin Books Canada, Ltd., 1985: 142–55. (Section on the October crisis.)

Rist, Peter. "*Primal Fear*." In *Magill's Survey of Cinema (Foreign Language Films)*,

V, 2461–66. Englewood Cliffs, N.J.: Salem Press, 1985. *Primal Fear* is the alternate English title of *Mourir à tue-tête.*

Self-Portraits: Essays on the Canadian and Quebec Cinemas. Edited by Pierre Véronneau and Piers Handling. Ottawa: Canadian Film Institute, 1980. Useful reference, with short histories and some criticism; but only goes to 1980.

Sicotte, Louise-Véronique. Review of *Le Jardin oublié: La vie et l'oeuvre d'Alice Guy-Blaché. Séquences* 181 (November–December 1995): 44–45.

Silence elles tournent. Festival occurs in Montréal. Catalog. See *Sequences* (May–June 1994): 8–9 for Johanne Larue's account of the eighth edition.

Smith, Martin. "Léa Pool: les belles images d'un voyage intérieur." *Le Journal de Montréal* (15 February 1986): 15. An interview.

Tadros, Jean-Pierre. "*Grand Remue-ménage* pour une fondamentale remise en question." *Cinéma/Québec* 58; 6–8 (September–October 1978): 15–17. Article on the film by Sylvie Groulx/Francine Allaire.

———. "Luce Guilbeault, Cinéaste et Ménagère." *Cinéma/Québec* 57; 6:7 (July–August 1978): 14–16; 54. Interview in which Guilbeault explains that she has chosen to do a film on housewives because of a "hereditary" problem, her own and that of all Québécoises, who are plagued with a double task: the need to make everything in the house Spic and Span; to run the house and do one's job. She prefers to make films about women, because "it is less frightening." Guilbeault also speaks of her transformation from housewife (*ménagère*) to actress to director.

———. "Paule Baillargeon, au rouge." *Cinéma/Québec* 57; 6:7 (July August 1978): 12–16; 54. Deals with the ONF program committee's decision not to finance projects that are submitted by filmmakers "de l'extérieur"—that is, *cinéastes-pigistes.* Baillargeon's *La Cuisine rouge* fell victim to this policy after much of the work was already in place, so she had to launch a subscription campaign. (See also Feldman.)

Tad[ro]s, J[ean].-P[ierre]. "*La Vie rêvée.*" *Variety* 13 s.p. (16 October 1972). New York: Garland Publishers, 1983.

Tremblay-Daviault, Christine. *Structures mentales et sociales du cinéma québécois (1942–1953): Un cinéma orphelin.* Montréal: Québec/Amérique, 1981.

Turner, D. J[ohn]. *Canadian Feature Film Index* or *Index des films canadiens de long métrage: 1913–1985.* Canada [Ottawa]: National Film TV and Sound Archives [Archives publiques], 1987–88. Feature-length films from *Evangeline* (Nova Scotia and Québec, 1913) to *Le Million tout-puissant* (1985). Indexes of films (by title), of actors, of technicians—with filmographies under each name. Index of coproductions with foreign countries.

Véronneau, Pierre. *L'Histoire du Cinéma au Québec, I et II.* In *Les Dossiers de la Cinémathèque,* vol. 3 (*Le Succès est au film parlant français*); vol. 5 (*L'Office National du Film, l'enfant martyr,* 1979); and vol. 7 (*Cinéma de l'époque duplessiste*). Montreal: Le Musée du Cinéma, 1979.

———. *L'Histoire du cinéma au Québec, III. Résistance et affirmation: la production francophone à l'ONF—1939–1964.* Montréal: Cinémathèque Québécoise, 1987.

———. *L'Histoire du cinéma au Québec.* 3 vols. Montréal: Cinémathèque québécoise, 1969–88.

———, ed. *Montréal, Ville de Cinéma.* Montréal: Cinémathèque Québécoise, 1992. Heavily illustrated (black and white).

———. "Repères bibliographiques sur le Cinéma québécois des années 80." *Québec Studies* 9 (fall 1989): 79–84. Updated bibliography.

————, and Piers Handling, eds. *Self-Portrait: Essays on the Canadian and Quebec Cinemas*. Ottawa: Canadian Film Institute, 1980. Essays include "The First Wave of Quebec Feature Films: 1944–1953," by Pierre Véronneau" [54 ff.]; "Direct Cinema by Michel Euvrard and Pierre Véronneau [77 ff.] "Animation," by Louise Beaudet [107 ff.] "Some Ideological and Thematic Aspects of the Quebec Cinema: 1963–1977," by Michel Houle [159 ff]; and lists of 75 filmmakers and 125 films. Many stills.

Walser, Lise. *Répertoire des longs métrages produits au Québec 1960–1970*. Montréal: CQDC, 1971.

Warren, Paul. "Les Québécois et le cinéma: un mode spécifique d'exhibition." In *Dialogue*, edited by Pierre Véronneau et al., 109–20. Montréal: Médiatexte: Cinémathèque Québécoise, 1987. Even features like *La Quarantaine* and *Laure Gaudreault* by their documentary configuration follow in Pierre Perrault's trajectory (116–19).

————. "Le refus du jeu." *Revue d'histoire littéraire du Québec et du Canada Français* 11 (1986): 123–28. "The Québec cinema has an undeniable documentary approach. The analysis of two films—*La Quarantaine* of Anne Poirier and *Rencontre avec une femme remarquable, Laure Gaudreault* of Iolande Cadrin-Rossignol—illustrates this approach to cinema."

Weinmann, Heinz. *Cinéma de l'imaginaire québécois, de La petite Aurore à Jésus de Montréal*. Saint-Laurent, Québec: l'Hexagone, 1990. Strong biases in theses of Québec as orphaned by France, martyred by English; and of Québec as a closed society. Serious errors regarding Catholicism.
    Review: Janick Beaulieu. *Séquences* 147 (September 1990): 17.
    Review: Janis L. Pallister. *Québec Studies* 12 (spring–summer 1991): 187–88.

Zoom sur elles. Montréal: Office National du Film du Canada (winter), 1990. Information on women directors, actresses, and so on.

Zucker, Carole. "Les oeuvres récentes d'Anne Claire Poirier et Paule Baillargeon." *CopieZéro* 11 (Special feature on *Vues sur le cinéma québécois*, 1982): 52–54.

*There is an enormous amount of information regarding women's films and women in films—including recent bibliography—on the Internet. Consult for supplementary data.

Films and Films about Films

Women Who Made Movies (directed and written by Gwendolyn Foster-Dixon).

Pioneers of the French Film.

Cinéma d'ici (1972; 11 parts; Radio Canada). A documentary history of Québec cinema, including interviews and excerpts.

Dreamland: A History of Early Canadian Movies, 1895–1939. (1974; Donald Brittain, NFB). A Documentary with extracts from films of the period.

Fantasmagorie (1974; Glover/Patenaude, NFB). History of animation at the ONF, since 1941; in English called *The Light Fantastick*.

Has Anyone Here Seen Canada? A History of Canadian Movies. 1939–53 (Kramer, NFB, 1978). A documentary with clips from films of the period.

Three Women Directors. PBS. (1987).

Film Sources

California Newsreel (*Africa*)
149 Ninth Street
San Francisco, CA 94103
Tel.: 415-621-6196
Fax: 415-621-6522
(Their catalog gives a long list of resource centers.)

African Films and Videos
DSR, Inc.
9111 Guilford Rd. #100
Columbia, MD 21046
Tel.: 1-303-490-3500 or 1-800-875-0037
Fax: 1-303-490-4146
This company is very expensive and limited in what materials can be
  shown in the United States.

African film resource list (directory)
Julie Sisskind tel. 215-898-744
e-mail SISKIND@MAIL.SAS.UPENN.EDU

Canadian Film Center
Center for the Study of Canada
SUNY Plattsburgh
Plattsburgh, NY 12901

Cinévidéo
360 Place Royale
Montréal (Québec) H2Y 2V1

Evergreen Video
228 West Houston
New York, NY 10014
In NY: 212-691-7362
Elsewhere: 800-225-7783

Facets Multimedia, Inc.
1517 West Fullerton Ave.
Chicago, IL 60614
Tel.: 1-800-331-6197

Films Incorporated
5547 Ravenswood Ave
Chicago, IL 60640
Tel.: 312-878-2600, ext 211
800-323-4222, ext. 211
or Mary Gremley
Senior Sales Programmer
733 Green Bay Rd.
Wilmette, IL 60091
Tel.: 312-256-6600
or 800-323-4222

Foreign Images
1213 Maple
Evanston, IL 60202
Tel.: 312-869-0543

Glenn Video Vistas
6924 Canby Avenue Suite 103
Reseda, CA 91335

Her Own Words (Women's History, Literature, and Art)
P.O. Box 5264
Madison, WI 53705
Tel.: 608-271-70083

National Film Board (see Office National du Film du Canada)

National Women's History Project
7738 Bell Road
Windsor, CA 95492-8518
Tel.: 707-838-6000
Fax: 707-838-0478

New Day Films
853 Broadway, Suite 1210
New York, NY 10003
Tel.: 212-477-4604

New Line Cinema (no 16mm film)
575 Eighth Avenue
New York, NY 10018
Tel.: 212-239-88 ????
(rents *Kamouraska*)

New Yorker Films
16 West Sixty-first St.
New York, NY 10023
Tel.: 212-247-6110

Office National du Film
3155 Chemin de la Côte de Liesse
C.P. 6100 Succ. A
Montréal (Québec)
H3C 3H5T
Tel.: 514-283-9285
Fax: 514-496-1646

Polyglot Productions
P.O. Box 668
Cambridge, MA 02238-0668
Tel.: 617-491-3541

Reel Women Videos (Ally Acker)
c/o Stanlite Corporation
16 East Thirty-eight Street
New York, NY 10016
Tel.: 914-424-33083

Version Française
4822 St. Elmo Avenue
Bethesda, MD 20814
Fax: 1 301 229 0621
Rent: (3050 films in French)
Tel.: 1-301-654-2224
Many of the women directors' films listed in my directory will be
found at this store; however, most have no subtitles.

Vidéo Femmes
56 rue St-Pierre, Bureau 203
Québec (Québec) G1K 4A1
Tel.: 418-692-3090

WAVE (Women's Audiovisuals in English: A Guide to Nonprint
   Resources in Women's Studies)
University of Wisconsin System
Memorial Library Room 430
728 State St.
Madison, WI 53706
Tel.: 608-263-5754

Wolfe Video
P.O. Box 64
New Almaden, CA 95042
Tel.: 800-643-5247

Women Make Movies
462 Broadway, Suite 501
New York, NY 10013
Tel.: 212-925-2052

Sample Syllabi

Professor Georgiana Colvile
Department of French and Italian—French/
  Film Studies 4600, Fall, 1991
University of Colorado at Boulder

Aug. 29	Agnès Varda	*One Sings, The Other Doesn't* (1976) [*L'Une chante, l'autre pas*]
Sept. 5	Germaine Dulac	*The Smiling Madame Beudet* (1922) [*La Souriante Madame Beudet*] and *The Seashell and the Clergyman* (1928) [*La Coquille et le clergyman*]
Sept. 12	Marie Epstein	*La Maternelle* (1933)
Sept. 19	Agnès Varda	*Cleo from 5:00 to 7:00* (1961) [*Cléo de 5:00 à 7:00*]
Sept. 26	Agnès Varda	*Vagabond* (1985) [*Sans toit ni loi*]
Oct. 3	Marguerite Duras	*Nathalie Granger* (1973)
Oct. 10	Coline Serreau	*What Do Women Want?* (1975–78) [*Mais qu'est-ce qu'elles veulent?*]
Oct. 17	Nelly Kaplan	*Néa* (1976)

Oct. 24	Chantal Akerman	*Les Rendez-vous d'Anna* (1978)
Oct. 31	Yannick Bellon	*The Rape of Love* (1978) [*L'Amour violé*]
Nov. 7	Diane Kurys	*Peppermint Soda* (1977) [*Diabolo menthe*]
Nov. 14	Diane Kurys	*Entre nous* (*Coup de foudre*) (1983)
Nov. 21	Diane Kurys	*A Man in Love* (1986–87) [*Un Homme amoureux*]
Dec. 5	Coline Serreau	*Mama, There's a Man in Your Bed* (1990) [*Romauld et Juliette*]

Professor Josette Déléas
Women and Film
Mount Saint Vincent University
Halifax, Nova Scotia
1995–96: First semester

Book Required: *Issues in Feminist Film Criticism*, edited by Patricia Erens, Indiana University Press.

Books Recommended:

Women and Film, A. Kaplan, Routledge.

Women Pictures, A. Kuhn, Verso.

Films for Women, edited by C. Brunsdon

To Desire Differently, S. Flitterman-Lewis, University of Illinois Press.

Ways of Seeing, J. Berger, Penguin Books.

Women and Film: A Sight and Sound Reader, edited by Pam Cook, Philip Dodd, Temple University Press.

Films to be Studied:

1. In Class

Clothelines (1982) (32'), Roberta Cantow (Screening dates: September 12 or 15), September 19–21.

Bowl of Bone (1992) (112'), Jan Marie Martell (Screening dates: September 19 or 22), September 26.

The Acadian Connection (Screening at Wormwood on September 27) or Seven Beauties (1976) (115'), Lina Wertmuller (Screening in the library or at home), September 28.

High Tide (1987) (102'), Gillian Armstrong (Screening dates: September 26 or 29), October 3–5.

La Femme de l'hôtel (1990) (105'), Léa Pool (Screening dates: October 3 or October 6), October 10–17.

Feathertale (1992) (5' 30s), Michèle Cournoyer (Class screening), October 19; Not a Love Story (1981) (69'), Bonnie Klein (Screening dates: October 13 or 17), October 19.

I've Heard the Mermaids Singing, (1987) (81'), Patricia Rozema (Screening dates: October 20 or 23), October 24.

Forbidden Love (1992) (85'), Aerlyn Weissman, Lynne Fernie (Screening in the library or at home), October 26.

A Question of Silence (1982) (96'), Marleen Gorris (Screening dates: October 24 or October 27), October 31–November 9.

Vagabond (1986) (105'), Agnès Varda (Screening dates: October 31 or November 3), November 9–16.

The Ties That Bind (1984) (55'), Su Friedrich (November 14 or 17), November 21.

The Company of Strangers (1991) (101'), Cynthia Scott. (Screening dates: November 21 or 24), November 28–30.

2. At Home

Nathalie Granger (1972) (85'), Marguerite Duras (Screening in library or at home).

Any film directed by a woman and scheduled to be screened in one of the local theaters.

Course Description: A course on women filmmakers. Their contribution to a creative reorientation of cinema will be considered. The course will seek to define the characteristics of feminist cinema. It will, therefore, include a broad consideration of male-directed cinema and its criticism from the feminist perspective.

Course Objective: To study the representation of women in cinema. The emphasis will be placed on the works of women directors who challenge and deconstruct stereotypical images of women in their films.

Women and Film—WOM 332A
Correct use of language is one of the criteria included in the evaluation of all written assignments.

WOMEN AND FILM—WORK SCHEDULE

Class Discussions: Students will lead the discussions by sharing with the class, comments, questions, reactions, on the following films:

Bowl of Bone, September 26

The Acadian Connection or Seven Beauties, September 28.

I've Heard the Mermaids Singing, October 24.

Forbidden Love, October 26.

The Ties That Bind, November 21.

NOTE: If more time is needed to discuss films studied in class, the above films will not be reviewed in class and comments will be given in writing along with the comments related to assigned readings. Also a film screened in one of Halifax theaters could be added to the list.

Essay: The students select their own topic or one can be suggested to them.

Students can work on one of the films studied in class or on a film of their choice as long as they have the approval of the instructor. It is important that they take time to write their essay since their grade will depend greatly on the quality of their written expression. So PLAN AHEAD.

Deadline: November 23.

Oral Assignment: It should be recorded on a tape that will be re-turned to the student with the mark. A tape can be obtained from the language lab supervisor, but in this case, it will not be returned to the student.

Students can do their assignment either on one of the films studied in class or on a film of their choice as long as they have the approval of the instructor.

Deadline: The oral assignment should be handed in on or before October 26.

NOTE: Students can write an essay if they do not wish to do an oral assignment.

N.B. Students are allowed to work on the same film for their essay and oral presentation as long as one assignment is not a replica of the other.

Essay Topics Chosen by Previous Students

A new look at elderly women in The Company of Strangers.

The Vagabonds, how clothes make the characters in High Tide, Smithereens, I've Heard the Mermaids Singing, Vagabond.

Nathalie Granger and postmodern feminism.

One Sings, The Other Doesn't and the third one simply isn't, a comparison of Vagabond and One Sings, the Other Doesn't.

Working Girls Work.

The lesbians live in I've Heard the Mermaids Singing.

Redefining or rethinking motherhood in High Tide.

Smithereens and Seven Beauties, two of a kind.

The social implications of the Romantic/Victorian resurgence in mainstream films.

Water images in Daughters of the Dust.

Language, laughter and silence in Vagabond, Nathalie Granger and A Question of Silence.

Brechtian Drama and Feminist film in Marlene Gorris' A Question of Silence.

Looking at the idea of the spectator . . . at The Company of Strangers . . . at a different way of thinking about LOOKING.

Gypsies and Grandmothers: Female sexuality in High Tide.

Cinema as spirit quest: Jan-Marie Martell's Bowl of Bone.

Lina Wertmüller's Seven Beauties: Revolutionary genius or misogynist drivel?

You can choose one of the following films to work on your oral presentation or write your essay:

Critic's Choice: Entre nous; An Angel at My Table; Sweetie; Any of Chantal Akerman's or of Wertmüller's films; Waiting; The Summer House; Muriel's Wedding; Daughters of the Dust (first African American feature shot by a woman).

MSVU: The Piano; Sugar Cane Alley.

LECTURES AND SUGGESTED READINGS

NOTE: You should also consult the bibliography that has been placed on reserve in the library.

Finally, the following films are available at MSVU: *The Blot* (Lois Weber); *The Piano* (Jane Campion); *Sugar Cane Alley* (Euzhan Palcy—Martinique), 1984 (107')

* * *

September 8–14
Introduction to Women's Filmmaking:

1. The focus of the course.

2. Is the gaze male?
   *Required Reading: *Women and Film* (A. Kaplan), pp. 23–36.

3. Passionate detachment:
   *Required reading: "Visual pleasure and narrative cinema" (L. Mulvey), in *Issues in Feminist Film Criticism* (ed., P. Erens), pp. 28–40.
   —Supplementary reading: Chapter 1, *Women's Pictures* (A. Kuhn), pp. 3–18.

4. Historical background:
   *Required readings:
   Women and the Cinema (K. Kay; G. Peary): pp. 9–26; pp. 139–79; pp. 213–31; pp. 246–62; pp. 337–41. "As Canadian as possible: The female spectator and the Canadian context," Rhona Berenstein, *Camera obscura*, 20/21, pp. 40–53.
   Recommended readings: *Women Directors* (B. Koenig Quart); *Reel Women* (A. Ally).
   Supplementary reading: *To Desire Differently*, S. Flitterman-Lewis, on Dulac, pp. 47–98.

Note: Hand in your comments in regards to the readings assigned for this week.

* * *

September 19–21
Women's Documentary Filmmaking.

*Required reading: "The political aesthetics of the feminist documentary film," *Issues in Feminist Film Criticism* (Erens), pp. 222–38.
Recommended reading: "Bakhtin, Language and Women's documentary filmmaking," *Multiple Voices in Feminist Film Criticism* (D. Carson, L. Dittmar, J. Welsh).

Supplementary readings: "Real women," *Women's Pictures* (Kuhn): 131–56; "Fascinating Fascism" (on Leni Riefenstahl), S. Sontag, in *Women and the Cinema* (Kay, Peary): 352–77. "Leni Riefenstahl: the Body Beautiful, Art, Cinema and Fascist Aesthetics," T. Elsaesser, in *Women and Film, A Sight and Sound Reader* (ed., P. Cook; P. Dodd): 186–98.

Note: Hand in your comments on the readings assigned for this week.

* * *

September 26–28:

Bowl of Bone, Jan Marie Martell.
Topic: Women's spirituality

Seven Beauties, Lina Wertmuller.
Topic: History vs Herstory.

*Required readings: "Swept away", "Interview with Lina Wertmuller," "Is Lina Wertmuller just one of the boys?," "Are women directors different?" in *Women and the Cinema* (Kay, Peary): 56–61; 324–33; 377–84; 429–36; and *Women Directors* (Koenig-Quart): 9, 29, 30, 40, 42.

Note: Hand in your comments on the readings assigned for this week.

* * *

October 3–October 5

High Tide, Gillian Armstrong.
Topic: Motherhood.

*Required readings: "The case of the missing mother," A. Kaplan; "Something else besides a mother," L. Williams, *Issues in Feminist Film Criticism* (Erens): 126–63. Film reviews: *Newsweek* (1988), David Ansen; *Vogue* (1988); *Ms* (1988); Molly Haskell; *New Yorker* (1988), Pauline Kael; *World Press Review* (1988), Rosemary Neill; *Time* (1988), Richard Schichel.

*Recommended readings: *Psychoanalysis and Cinema*, Ann Kaplan, 1990, p. 128; *The Desire to Desire*, Mary-Ann Doane, 1987, p. 70.

Note: Hand in your comments on the readings assigned for this week.

* * *

October 10–17

La Femme de L'Hotel, Léa Pool.
Topic: To desire differently.

* * *

October 19

Feathertale, Michèle Cournoyer.

*Required reading: "Working against the Grain: Women in Animation," I. Kotlarz, *Women and Film, A Sight and Sound Reader* (Cook, Dodd): 101–05.

Not a Love Story, B. Klein.
Topic: Pornography.

*Required reading: "Anti-porn: Soft Issue, Hard World," R. Rich in *Issues in Feminist Film Criticism* (Erens): 405–18.

Note: Hand in your comments on the readings assigned for this week.

* * *

October 24

I've Heard the Mermaids Singing, Patricia Rozema.
Topic: Cinema in question.

*Required readings: "The Woman at the Keyhole," Judith Mayne, p. 49: Screen Tests; "I've heard the mermaids singing," Cameron Bailey, *Cinema Canada* (Nov: 1987): 25; "Reclaiming the subject," George Goodwin, *Cinema Canada* (May 1988): 23; "Scaling the heights," Bruce McDonald, *Cinema Canada* (May 1987): 14.

Recommended readings: "Textual politics", chapter 8, *Women's Pictures* (Kuhn): 156–78; "Introduction", *Women and Film* (Kaplan): 1–21; 36–49.

October 26

Forbidden Love, A. Weissman, L. Fernie.
Topic: Lesbians's voices.

*Required readings: *Women Directors* (Koenig-Quart): 78; 80–82; 84; 100; 147. "Female misbehaviour: the Cinema of Monika Treut," J. Knight, *Women and Film, A Sight and Sound Reader* (Cook, Dodd): 180–86. "Lianna and the Lesbians of Art Cinema," *Films for Women,* C. Brunsdon: 166–79. "Thelma and Louise and the Cultural Genera-tion of the New Butch-Femme," C. Griggers, in *Film Theory Goes to the Movies,* J. Collins, H. Radner, A. Preacher Collins: 129–42. "A Queer Feeling When I Look at You: Hollywood Stars and Lesbian Spectatorship in the 1930s," A. Weiss. "The Hypothetical Lesbian Heroine in Narrative Feature Film," C. Straayer, *Multiple Voices in Feminist Film Criticism* (Carson, Dittmar, Welsh): 330–58.

Note: Hand in your comments on the readings assigned for this week.

*   *   *

October 31–November 9
A Question of Silence, Marleen Gorris.
Topic: Women's silence and laughter as resistance.

*Required readings: *Film Feminisms,* Gentile: 153. "A Jury of Their Peers: Questions of Silence, Speech and Judgment in Marleen Gorris's A Question of Silence," L. Williams, in *Multiple Voices in Feminist Film Criticism* (Carson, Dittmar, Welsch): 432–43. "Feminist or Ten-dentious? Marleen Gorris's A Question of Silence," M. Gentile, in *Issues in Feminist Film Criticism* (Erens): 395–405. "A Question of Silence," J. Murphy. "Distributing A Question of Silence, A Caution-ary Tale," J. Root, *Films for Women* (Brunsdon): 99–109; 213–25.

Note: Hand in your comments on the readings assigned for this film.

*   *   *

November 9–16

Vagabond, Agnès Varda.
Topic: "The impossible portrait of femininity".

*Required readings: Chapter 11, *To Desire Differently,* Flitterman-Lewis: 285–316. *Women Directors,* Koenig-Quart: 61; 136; 138–39; 143–44.

Recommended readings: Chapter 8–10, *To Desire Differently,* Flit-terman-Lewis: 215–84.

Note: Hand in your comments on the readings assigned for this film.

*   *   *

November 21

The Ties That Bind, Su Friedrich.
Topic: Women and History.

*Required readings: "Su Friedrich: Reappropriations," Scott MacDon-
ald, in *Film Quarterly*: 34–48. "Serious Fun" and other texts attached;
"An Interview with Su Friedrich," *Afterimage*: 6–10.

Note: Hand in your comments on the readings assigned for this film.

*   *   *

November 23

Nathalie Granger, Marguerite Duras.
Topic: Language in question.

*Required reading: "Silence as Female Resistance in Marguerite Du-
ras's *Nathalie Granger*," *Women and Film* (Kaplan): 91–104.

Note: Hand in your comments on the readings assigned for this film.

*   *   *

November 28–30

The Company of Strangers, Cynthia Scott.
Topic: Old age revisited.

*Required reading: "In the Company of Strangers," Mary Meigs.

Note: Hand in your comments on the readings assigned for this film.

BIBLIOGRAPHY

Abel, Marie-Christine. *Le Cinéma québécois à l'heure internationale.* Montréal: Stanke, 1990.

Acker, Ally. *Reel Women.* New York: Continuum, 1991.

Adelman, Shonagh. "Representations of Violence against Women in Mainstream Film." *Resources for Feminist Research* 18, no. 2 (June 1989): 21–26.

Anderson, Lisa. J., Lisa L. Kershaw, Ian McCallum, Ingrid Pregel. *A Statistical Profile of Women in the Canadian Film and Television Industry.* Toronto: Toronto Women in Film and Video, 1990.

Armatage, Kay. "Women in Film." *Take One* 6, no. 8 (July 1978): 36–38.

———. "Women in Film. Why not Hollywood?" *Take One* 6, no. 2 (January 1978): 38–39.

———. "Women in Film." *Take One* 6, no. 4 (March 1978): 43.

———. "Here we go again." *Canadian Forum* 61 (December 1981–January 1982): 46–47.

———. "Canadian Women's Cinema." *Canadian Forum* 61 (February 1982): 24–25.

———. "La Vie rêvée." *Take One* 7 (September–October 1971): 34–35.

———. "Women in Film." *To* 3 (May–June 1972): 45–48.

———. "Fashions in Feminist Film Theory." *Descant* 19, no. 2 (summer 1988): 90–115.

———. "The Silent Screen And My Talking Heart." *Canadian Journal of Political and Social Theory* 14(1/3) (1990): 204–14.

———. "Women in Film: Dialectical Blisters." *Take One* 5, no. 12 (1977): 34.

Armatage, Kay, and Barbara Martineau. "Women in Film." *To* 3 (November–December 1971): 35–38.

Arroyo, José, and Jamis Gaetz. "Locked Out of the Women's Room: Montreal International Festival of Women's Films and Videos." *Cinema Canada* 155 (September 1988): 29–30.

Atkins, Thomas. *Sexuality in the Movies.* Bloomington: Indiana University Press, 1975.

ATTWOOD, Lynne, et al. *Red Women on the Silver Screen: Soviet Women and Cinema from the Beginning to the End of the Communist Era.* London: Pandora, 1993.

Aude, Françoise. *Ciné-modèles. Cinéma d'elles.* Lausanne: L'Age d'homme, 1981.

Auchterlonie, Bill. "Joyce Wieland: Filmmaker." *Art Magazine* (December–January 1975–76): 6–11.

Backburn, M. "Comment le cinéma vient aux femmes de mon âge." *CopieZéro* 6 (1980): 19–20.

Bailey, Cameron. "Film review: I've heard the Mermaids Singing." *Cinema Canada* (November 1987): 25.

Banning, Kass. "Surfacing: Canadian women's cinema: Festival of Festivals Surveys Seventy Years of Herstory." *Cinema Canada* 167 (October 1989): 12–16.

Basinger, Jeanine. *A Woman's View: How Hollywood Spoke to Women, 1930–1960.* New York: Knopf, 1993.

Bauer, Dale. M. *Feminism, Bakhtin and the Dialogic.* Albany: State University of New York Press, 1991.

Becker et al. "Lesbians and Film: Introduction to Special Section." *Jump Cut* 24–25 (March 1981): 17–21.

BELL, Elizabeth, ed. *From Mouse to Mermaid: The Politics of Film, Gender, and Culture.* Bloomington: Indiana University Press, 1995.

Bell-Metereau, Rebecca. *Hollywood Androgyny.* New York: Columbia University Press, 1993.

Berenstein, Rhona J. *Attack on the Leading Ladies: Gender, Sexuality and Spectatorship in Classic Horror Cinema.* New York: Columbia University Press, 1996.

Bergstrom, Janet. "Enunciation and Sexual Difference (part 1)." *Camera Obscura* 3–4 (1979): 32–69.

Betts, C. "Women and the NFB." *Cinema Canada* 18 (March–April 1975): 13.

Bonneville, Leo. "Entretien avec Anne Claire Poirier." *Séquences* 81 (Juillet 1975): 4–12.

Bonneville, Leo. "Entretien avec Mireille Dansereau." *Séquences* 93 (Juillet 1978): 4–10.

Bovenschen, Sylvia. "Is There a Feminine Aesthetic." *New German Critique* 10 (winter 1977): 111–37.

Britton, Andrew. *Katharine Hepburn: Star As Feminist.* New York: Continuum, 1995.

Bruno, G. and M. Nadotti, eds. *Off Screen. Women and Film in Italy.* London. New York: Routledge, 1988.

Brunsdon, Charlotte. *Films for Women.* London: British Film Institute, 1986.

Burgwinkle, William. *Significant Others: Gender and Culture in Film and Literature.* New York: Garland, 1993.

Burnett, M. A. "Des cinéastes québécoises anglophones." *CopieZéro* 6 (1980): 32–34.

Butler, Rick. "Caroline Leaf: An Interview." *Canadian Review* 4, no. 9 (February 1977): 50–51.

Byars, Jackie. *All That Hollywood Allows: Rereading Gender in the 1950s Melodrama.* Chapel Hill: University of North Carolina Press, 1991.

Cameron, A. "Fireweed Anne vs the Feminists (Feminist Film and Video Festival)." *Cinema Canada* 51 (November–December 1978): 24–27.

Carlsson, Susanne Chauvel. *Charles and Elsa Chauvel, Movie Pioneers.* Queensland, Australia: University of Queensland Press, 1989.

Carriere, Louise. *Femmes et cinéma québécois.* Montréal: Boréal Express, 1983.

———. "A propos des films faits par des femmes au Québec." *CopieZéro* 11 (1981): 44–51.

Carson, Diane. *Multiple Voices in Feminist Film Criticism.* Minneapolis: University of Minnesota Press, 1994.

Casetti, Francesco. *Les yeux dans les yeux.* (Communications 38) Seuil, Paris, 1983.

Champagne, M., et al. "Attention . . . cinéastes au travail!" *CopieZéro* 6 (1980): 7–17.

Changing Focus: the Future for Women in the Canadian Film and Video Industry. Toronto: Toronto Women in Film and Television, 1991.

Chisholm, E., and P. Thorvaldson. "Women in Documentary: The Early Years." *Motion* 4, no. 5 (1975): 14–19.

Cixous, Hélène. "Le Rire de la Méduse." *l'Arc* 61 (1981).

Clancey, Brian. "Of Black Pudding and Pink Ladies." *Cinema Canada* 25 (February 1976): 38–39.

Cohen, Paula Marantz. *Alfred Hitchcock: The Legacy of Victorianism*. Lexington: Kentucky University Press, 1995.

Cole, Janis. *Calling the Shots: Profiles of Women Filmmakers*. Kingston, Ontario: Quarry Press, 1993.

Collison, Robert. "Châtelaine's Woman of the Year: Sandy Wilson." *Châtelaine* 60, no. 1 (January 1987): 54–55.

Corber, Robert. J. *In the Name of National Security: Hitchcock, Homophobia and the Political Construction of Gender in Postwar America*. Durham: Duke University Press, 1993.

Cook, Pam, ed. *Women and Film: A Sight and Sound Reader*. Philadelphia: Temple University Press, 1993.

Crean, Susan. "Moving Pictures: Women Who Are Everywhere Yet Belong Nowhere (Visible Colours, an International Film and Video Festival). *Canadian Art* 7, no. 1 (spring 1990): 21–22.

Creed, Barbara. *The Monstrous Feminine: Film, Feminism, Psychoanalysis*. London. New York: Routledge, 1993.

Cristall, Ferne. *Images in Action: A Guide to Using Women's Film and Video*. Toronto: Between the Lines, 1986.

———, et al. "Images in Action: A Guide to Using Women's Film and Video." *Cinema Canada* 142 (June 1987): 30–31; *Canadian Materials* 15, no. 5 (September 1987): 211.

Dascher, Helge. "Other Visions: Turning the World Upside Down at the Festival of Films and Videos by Women." *Montréal Magazine* 19, no. 5 (June 1990): 17–18.

Dash, Julie. *Daughters of the Dust: The Making of an African American Woman's Film*. New York: New Press, 1991.

Dawson, B. "Women and International Festival '73 in Toronto." *FLQ* 6, no. 4 (1973): 36–38.

Delaney, Marshall. "Wielandism: A Personal Style in Full Bloom." *Saturday Night* 9 no. 1/3 (May 1976): 76–77.

De Lauretis, Teresa. *Alice Doesn't*. Bloomington: Indiana University Press, 1984.

De Lauretis, Teresa. *Technologies of Gender. Essays on Theory, Film and Fiction*. Bloomington: Indiana University Press, 1987.

Déléas, Josette. "Le Cinéma de Léa Pool ou le regard interpellé." In *Paroles rebelles*. Edited by Marguerite Andersen and Christine Klein Lataud, 263–77. Montréal: Les Editions du Remue Ménage, 1992.

———. "Anne Trister, cet obscur sujet du désir." *Actes du Congrès Mondial de Casablanca*, 217–25. Conseil International d'Etudes Francophones, 1995.

———. "La Traversée du miroir en compagnie de deux cinéastes: Marleen Gorris et Patricia Rozema." *Journal of the Canadian Society for the Comparative Study of Civilizations* 5 (1990): 37–47.

———. "'Détruire' disent-elles: Une étude du refus dans les films *Nathalie Granger* de Marguerite Duras et *Sans toit ni loi* d'Agnès Varda." *Bulletin de la Société des Professeurs de français en Amérique*, 189–97. New York, 1989.

———. "L'Espace du non-dit dans les écritures de France Daigle et d'Agnès Varda." *Journal of the Canadian Society for the Comparative Study of Civilizations* 4 (1988): 43–54.

Demers, Pierre. "Luce Guilbeault, réalisatrice." *Cinéma Québec* 6, no. 7 (1975): 16–17.

———. "Denyse Benoît comédienne." *Cinéma Québec* 1 (1976): 37–38.

Denault, J., et al. "Le Cinéma féminin au Québec." *Copie Zéro* 11 (1981): 36–44.

Des Femmes de Musidora, ed. *Paroles elles tournent*. Paris: Editions des femmes, 1976.

Diggins, Flo. "Women Hold Film Festival." *That's Showbusiness* 2, no. 14 (27 June 1973): 1.

Doane, Mary-Ann. "Misrecognition and Identity." *Ciné-Tracts* 11 (fall 1980): 25–32.

Doane, Mary-Ann. *The Desire to Desire: The Woman's Film of the 1940s*. Bloomington: Indiana University Press, 1987.

Doane, Mary Ann. *Femmes fatales: Feminism, Film Theory, Psychoanalysis*. New York: Routledge, 1991.

Drew, W. *Speaking of Silents: First Ladies of the Screen*. New York: Vestal Press, 1989.

Dyer, Richard. *Now You See It: Studies on Lesbian and Gay Film*. London. New York: Routledge: 1990.

Edwards, N. "Women and Film Festival." *Cinema Canada* 9 (August–September 1973): 14–18.

Erens, Patricia. *Issues in Feminist Film Criticism*. Bloomington: Indiana University Press, 1990.

Euvard, M. "Femmes en lutte." *Cinéma Québec* 6, no. 5 (1978): 31–33.

Evanchuk, P. M. "Conversation with Arla Saare." *Motion* (March–April 1973): 28–30.

Felman, Shoshana. "Rereading Femininity." *Yale French Studies* 62 (1981): 19–44.

Ferlita, E. J. R. May. *The Parables of Lina Wertmüller*. New York: Paulist Press, 1977.

Fetherling, Doug. "Films/Wieland's Vision." *Canadian Forum* 56 (May 1976): 40–41.

———. "Joyce Wieland in Movieland." *The Canadian* 24 (January 1976): 10–12.

Fieldman Miller, Lynn. *The Hand that Holds the Camera: Interviews with Women Film and Video Directors*. New York: Garland, 1987.

Film Review Annual, 1985:
  Linda Gross, 934.
  J. Hoberman, 935–36.
  Sheila Johnson, 934–35.
  William Johnson, 931–33.
  Alex Keneas, 935.
  Barbara Quart, 938–51.
  Ruby Rich, 936–40.
  Amy Taubin, 936.

Film Reviews 1988
  David, Ansen, *Newsweek*
  Molly, Haskell, *Ms; Vogue*
  Kael, Pauline, *New Yorker*
  Rosemary Neill, *World Press Review*
  Richard, Schichel, *Time*

Flitterman-Lewis, Sandy. *To Desire Differently: Feminism and French Cinema*. Urbana: Illinois University Press, 1990.

Forsyth, Louise. "Women's Cinema Reality." *Broadside a Feminist Review* 9, no. 8 (June 1988): 8–9.

Foster, Gwendolyn Audrey. *Women Film Directors: An International Bio-critical Dictionary.* Wesport: Greenwood Press, 1995.

Frieden, Sandra. *Gender and German Cinema.* Providence: Berg, 1993.

Gaffney, Maureen, "Beverly Shaffer, Documentary Filmmaker." *A Newsletter Called Fred* 6, no. 7 (March 1978): 131–35.

Gaines, Jane. "Women and Representation. Can we enjoy alternative pleasure?" In *Issues in Feminist Film Criticism.* Edited by Patricia Erens. Bloomington: Indiana University Press, 1990.

Galerstein, Carolyn. *Working Women on the Hollywood Screen.* New York: Garland, 1989.

Gallop, Jane. *Reading Lacan.* Ithaca: Cornell University Press, 1985.

Garson, B. "The Wertmuller Ethic." *Ms* (May 1976): 71–75, 128.

Gauthier, G. "La Femme dans le cinéma québécois." *Image et Son* 126 (January 1973): 10–17. *Revue Cinema* 267 (January 1973): 10–17.

Gentile, Mary. "Feminist or Tendentious? Marleen Gorris' "A Question of Silence." In *Film Feminisms: Theory and Practice.* London: Greenwood, 1985.

Gever, Martha, ed. *Queer Looks: Perspectives on Lesbian and Gay Film and Video.* Toronto: Between the Lines, 1993.

Gill, Alexandra. "The Violin Lady (Women in Film)." *Cinema Canada* 156 (October 1988): 18–19.

Gledhill, Christine. *Stardom: Industry of Desire.* New York: Routledge, 1990.

Goodwin, George. "Reclaiming the Subject." *Cinema Canada* (May 1988): 23.

Green, Ronald. "On Mary Gentile's Film Feminisms Theory and Practise." *The Womens Studies Review* (Ohio State University) 8, no. 4 J1 A (1986): 4–6.

Green, Shelley. *Radical Juxtaposition: The Films of Yvonne Rainer.* Metuchen, N.J.: Scarecrow Press, 1994.

Greenbaum, C. "Musidora: The Organization of the First Women's Film Festival in Paris." *Women and Film* 2, no. 7 (Summer 1975): 4–9.

Guilbeault, Luce. "Luce Guilbeault au festival de Berlin." *Cinema Quebec* 10 (1977): 18–21.

Hadleigh, Boze. *Hollywood Lesbians: Conversations with: Sandy Dennis, Barbara Stanwick, Marjorie Main, Nancy Kulp, Patsy Kelly, Agnes Moorehead, Edith Head, Dorothy Arzner, Capucine, Judith Anderson.* New York: Barricade Books, 1994.

———. *The Lavender Screen: The Gay and Lesbian Films: Their Stars, Makers, Characters, and Critics.* New York: Carol Publishing Group, 1993.

Hart, Lynda. *Fatal Women: Lesbian Sexuality and the Mark of Aggression.* Princeton, N.J.: Princeton University Press, 1994.

Hartt, L. "Kathleen Shanon; Working Mothers Series." *Cinema Canada* 2, no. 15 (August–September 1974): 55.

———. "Anne Claire Poirier, en tant que femmes." *Cinema Canada* 2, no. 15 (August–September 1974): 52–54.

Haskell, Molly. "Mommie Merest." *Vogue* J1 (1988): 80.

———. *From Reverence to Rape.* New York: Holt, Rinehart, Winston, 1974.

Heath, Stephen. "Difference." *Screen* 19, no. 3 (autumn 1978): 50–112.

———. *Questions of Cinema.* Bloomington: Indiana University Press, 1981.

Hinton, David. *The Films of Leni Riefenstahl.* Metuchen, N.J.: Scarecrow Press, 1978.

Holub, Robert. C. *Crossing Borders: Reception Theory, Poststructuralism, Deconstruction*. Madison: University of Wisconsin Press, 1992.

Ibranyi-Kiss, A. "Women in Canadian Films." *Cinema Canada* 5 (December–January 1972–73): 26–27.

———. "Mireille Dansereau: La Vie rêvée." *Cinema Canada* 5 (December–January 1972–73): 28–31.

———. "Women in Canadian Films." *Cinema Canada* 5 (December–January 1972): 26–31.

———. "At 99—A Portrait of Louise Tandy Murch." *Cinema Canada* 17 (December–January 1974–75): 4–12.

———. "Fantasy, Film and Feminism or an Affirmation of Male Paranoia." *Cinema Canada* 19 (May–June 1975): 54–55.

———. "Bonnie Kreps: Feminist Filmmaker." *Cinema Canada* 14 (June–July 1974): 16–17.

———. "Carol on Camera." *Cinema Canada* 16 (October–November 1974): 42–44.

Jacobs, Lea. *The Wages of Sin: Censorship and the Fallen Woman Film 1928–1942*. Madison: University of Wisconsin Press, 1991.

Johnson, Terry. "The Ladies of the Prairies: An Edmonton Film (*Prairie Women*) Portrays the History of the Farm Women's Movement." *Western Report* 2, no. 23 (29 June 1987): 49–50.

Jorgesen, Lynne. "Extraordinary Women on Film ("Doctor, Lawyer, Indian Chief.") *Kathou* 5, no. 5 (July 1987): 9.

Kaplan, E. Ann, ed. *Psychoanalysis and Cinema*. New York. London: Routledge, 1990.

———. *Women and Film: Both Sides of the Camera*. New York and London: Methuen, 1983.

Kael, Pauline. "The Current Cinema : The Lady from the Sea" *The New Yorker* F22 (1988): 84–85.

Kay, K. G. Peary, eds. *Women and the Cinema: A Critical Anthology*. New York: Dutton, 1977.

Kay, K. "You can get a man with a gun or the true story of Annie Oakley." *Velvet Light Trap* 8 (1973): 11–13.

Keal, Pauline. "Seven Fatties." *The New Yorker* 51 (16 February 1976): 1, 15.

Kirkham, Pat. *You Tarzan: Masculinity, Movies and Men*. New York: St. Martin's Press, 1993.

———, ed. *Me Jane: Masculinity, Movies and Women*. New York: St. Martin's Press, 1995.

Koller, Georg Csaba. "The True Nature of . . . Micheline Lanctot." *Cinema Canada* 10 (October 1973): 26–27; 11 (January 1974): 73–74.

Kristeva, Julia. *Ellipse sur la frayeur et la séduction spéculaire*. (Communications 23) Paris (1975).

Kuhn, Annette. *Cinema, Censorship and Sexuality, 1909–1925*. New York: Routledge, 1988.

———. *Women's Pictures. Feminism and Cinema*. London: Routledge, 1982.

———. *The Power of the Image: Essays on Representation and Sexuality*. London. Boston: Routledge, 1985.

———. *The Women's Companion to International Film*. London: Virago, 1990.

————, ed., *Women in Film: An International Guide*. New York: Fawcett Columbine, 1991.

————, ed., *Queen of the 'B's: Ida Lupino behind the Camera*. Westport: Greenwood Press, 1995. London: Flicks Books, 1995.

Lamartine, Thérèse. "Du cinéma et, de-ci de-là, des femmes." *Copie Zéro* 6 (1980): 30–32.

————. *Elles cinéastes ad lib*. Montréal: Les Editions du Remue-Ménage, 1985.

Lant, Antonia. *Blackout: Reinventing Women for Wartime British Cinema*. Princeton: Princeton University Press, 1991.

Lawrence, Amy. *Echo and Narcissus: Women's Voices in Classical Hollywood Cinema*. Berkeley: University of California Press, 1991.

Lenskyj, Helen. "Seeing Is Believing—New Films on Women." *Broadside A Feminist Review* 9, no. 6 (April 1988): 6–7.

Lesage, Julia. "The Human Subject—You, He or Me? (Or the Case of the Missing Penis)." *Screen* 16, no. 2 (summer 1975): 83–90.

Leyda, Jay. *Films Beget Films*. New York: Hill and Wang, 1964. (Includes chapter on Russian Esther Schub).

Lipzin, D. C. "Talking with Joyce Wieland." *Cinemanews* 5 (September–October 1978): 1, 25.

Longfellow, Brenda. "Women in Gear." *Cinema Canada* 85 (June 1982): 20–21.

MacDonald, Judy. "Of Mice and Batmen (or Woman as Wimp)." *This Magazine* 23, no. 4 (November 1989): 32–34.

Mackinnon, Kenneth. *Misogyny in the Movies: The De Palma Question*. Newark: University of Delaware Press; Cranbury: Associated University Presses, 1990.

Macleod, Catherine. "Great Grandmother." *Pot Pourri* (spring 1977): 39.

Maio, Kathia. *Popcorn and Sexual Politics: Movie Reviews*. Freedom: Crossing Press, 1991.

Marchessault, Janine. "Is the Dead Author a Woman? Some Thoughts on Feminist Authorship/L'auteur mort est-ce une femme? Reflexions sur la pratique féministe." *Parallèlogramme* 15, no. 4 (spring 1990): 20–24.

Marshy, Leila. "Through Her Eyes (the Troisième festival international de films et vidéos de femmes)." *Cinema Canada* 144 (September 1987): 32–33.

Martin-Theriault, A. "*La Vie rêvée*. Jeunes Femmes en proie aux images." *Cinéma Québec* 11, no. 3 (1972): 30–31.

Martineau, Barbara. H., et al. "Paris/Chicago: Womens Film Festivals 1974." *Women and Film* 2, no. 7 (1975): 10–27.

————. "Women vs. Cannes." *Cinema Canada* 9 (August–September 1973): 50–52.

————. "The New York Women's Film Festival: a Contextual Fragmentation." *Cinema Canada* 5 (December–January 1972–73): 34–36.

————. "Notes for a Study of Women's History in the Media." *Cinema Canada* 51 (November–December 1978): 30–34.

————. "Canadian Women Filmmakers." *Cinema Canada* 71 (1981): 33.

————. "Leading Ladies Behind the Camera." *Cinema Canada* 71 (1981): 17–32.

Masavisut, Nitaya. *Gender and Culture in Literature and Film: East and West Issues of Perception and Interpretation: Selected Conference Paper*. Honolulu: College of Languages, Linguistics, and Literature, University of Hawaï Press, 1994.

Mason, Joyce. "Feminist Film: What Do Women Want?" *Broadside: a Feminist Review* 10, no. 5 (August–September 1989): 16–17.

Matlock, Jann. *Scenes of Seduction: Prostitution, Hysteria and Reading Difference.* New York: Columbia University Press, 1994.

Maurice, Elia. "Caroline Leaf." *Séquences* 91 (January 1978): 105–18.

Mayne, Judith. *Directed by Dorothy Arzner.* Bloomington: Indiana University Press, 1994.

———. *The Woman at the Keyhole.* Bloomington. Indiana University Press, 1990.

McCallum, Mark. "*Loyalties* Wins in Europe (Creteil Women's Film Festival)." *Windspeaker* 5, no. 12 (29 May 1987): 1.

McClary, Susan. *Feminine Endings: Music, Gender and Sexuality.* Minneapolis: University of Minnesota Press, 1991.

McCreadie, Marsha. *The Casting Couch and Other Front Row Seats.* New York. Westport. Conn: Praeger, 1990.

———. *Women on Film: The Critical Eye.* New York: Praeger, 1983.

McDonald, Bruce. "Scaling the Heights." *Cinema Canada* (May 1987): 14.

McIlveen, Lynne. "Women in Film." *Pulse* 1, no. 9 (June 1975): 14–15.

Meigs, Mary. *In the Company of Strangers.* Vancouver: Talonbooks, 1991.

Mellen, Joan. *Women and Their Sexuality in the New Film.* London: Davis-Poynter, 1973.

Mellencamp, Patricia. *Indiscretions: Avant-Garde Film, Video and Feminism.* Bloomington: Indiana University Press, 1990.

———. *A Fine Romance . . . Five Ages of Film Feminism.* Philadelphia: Temple University Press, 1995.

Merck, Mandy. *The Sexual Subject: Screen Reader in Sexuality.* New York: Routledge, 1992.

Metcalfe, Robin. "Women and Video Exploration: A Premiere Screening. National Film Board." *Arts Atlantic* 7, no. 4 (spring 1987): 8–9.

Metz, Christian. *Le Signifiant Imaginaire.* (Communications 23) Paris: Seuil, 1975.

Mieville, Anne-Marie. *Jean-Luc Godard's Hail Mary: Women and the Sacred in Film.* Carbondale: Southern Illinois University Press, 1993.

Mitchell, Mickie. *Interview with Donna King.* Ottawa: National Film Television and Sound Archives, 1982.

Modleski, Tania. *The Women Who Knew Too Much: Hitchcock and Feminist Theory.* New York: Routledge, Chapman and Hall, 1987.

———. *Feminism without Women: Culture and Criticism in a "Postfeminist Age."* New York: Routledge, 1991.

Montgomery, Michael V. *Carnivals and Commonplaces: Bakhtin's Chronotope, Cultural Studies.* New York: Peter Lang, 1993.

Moore, L. "Cultural Crosscurrents: Ten Women's Experience." *Cinema Canada* 74 (May 1981): 57.

Moore, Susan. *Looking for Trouble: On Shopping, Gender and the Cinema.* London: Serpent's Tail, 1991.

Mootoo, Shani. "Visible Difference: In Visible Colors, International Film and Video Symposium, Vancouver, B.C., November 15–19, 1989." *Fuse Magazine* 13, no. 4 (spring 1990): 31–32.

Mueller, Roswitha. *Valie Export: Fragments of the Imagination (Women Artists in Film)*. Bloomington: Indiana University Press, 1994.

Mulvey, Laura. "Visual Pleasure and Narrative Cinema." *Screen* 16, no. 3 (autumn 1975): 6–18.

Mulvey, Laura. *Visual and Other Pleasures*. Bloomington: Indiana University Press, 1989.

Murray, Raymond. *Images in the Dark: An Encyclopedia of Gay and Lesbian Film and Video*. Philadelphia: TLA Publishing, 1995.

National Film Board of Canada. Beyond the Image: A Guide to Films about Women and Change. Montreal: National Film Board of Canada, 1982.

Neill, Rosemary. "Her Brilliant Career (cont'd)." *World Press Review. Stanley Foundation* 35, no. 1:60.

Nelson, Martha. "Punk Fantasy." *Ms* 11 (February 1983): 103.

Newton, Judith. *Starting Over: Feminism and the Politics of Cultural Critique*. Ann Arbor: University of Michigan Press, 1994.

Notar, Clea. "Cinéma femmes/5th Festival International de Films et Vidéos Montréal." *Cinema Canada* 167 (October 1989): 8–9.

Olivier, Christiane. *Les Enfants de Jocaste*. Paris: Denoël-Gonthier, 1980.

Ott, Günter. "NFB Series for Women." *That's Showbusiness* 4, nos. 5–6 (26 March 1975): 11.

Parish, James Robert. *Gays and Lesbians in Mainstream Cinema: Plots, Critiques, Casts and Credits for 272 Theatrical and Made-for-Television Hollywood Releases*. Jefferson, N.C.: McFarland & Co., 1993.

———. *Prostitution in Hollywood Films: Plots, Critiques, Casts and Credits for 389 Theatrical and Made-for-Television Releases*. Jefferson, N.C.: McFarland & Co., 1992.

Parmar, Pratibha. *Queer Looks: Perspectives on Lesbian and Gay Film and Video*. Toronto: Between the Lines, 1993.

Pelletier, Johanne. "Cinema femme: film frenzy." *Broadside: a Feminist Review* 9, no. 9 (July 1988): 8–9.

Penley, Constance, ed. *Feminism and Film theory*. New York: Routledge, 1988.

——— et al., ed. *Close Encounters: Film, Feminism and Science Fiction*. Minneapolis: University of Minnesota Press, 1990.

———. *The Future of an Illusion: Film, Feminism and Psychoanalysis*. Minneapolis: University of Minnesota Press, 1989.

Perlmutter, Ruth. "Feminine Absence: A Political Aesthetic in Chantal Akerman's *Jeanne Dielman* . . ." *Quarterly Review of Film Studies* 4, no. 1 (1979): 125–33.

Petro, Partice. *Joyless Streets: Women and Melodramatic Representation in Weimar Germany*. Princeton: Princeton University Press, 1989.

Petty, Sheila. "Women's Societal Roles and Their Depiction in Black African Film." *Resources for Feminist Research* 17, no. 2 (June 1988): 27–29.

———. "Women and Language in Francophone West African film." *Parachute* 52 (September–November 1988): 45–47.

Poirier, Anne Claire. "Je suis née femme, je suis devenue cinéaste." *Copie Zéro* 6 (1980): 18–19.

Portuges, Catherine. *Screen Memories: The Hungarian Cinema of Márta Mészaros*. Bloomington: Indiana University Press, 1993.

Pribram, Deidre, ed. *Female Spectators: Looking at Film and Television*. London: Verso, 1988.

Quart-Koenig, Barbara. *Women Directors: The Emergence of a New Cinema*. New York: Praeger, 1988.

Rainer, Yvonne. *The Films of Yvonne Rainer*. Bloomington: Indiana University Press, 1989.

Rabinovitz, Lauren. *Points of Resistance : Women, Power and Politics in the New York Avant-garde Cinema, 1943–71*. Urbana: University of Illinois Press, 1991.

Red Crow, Jackie. "Tantoo to Speak at (Pincher Creek) Native Film Festival." *Windspeaker* 5, no. 15 (19 June 1987): 2.

Reid, Alison. *Canadian Women Filmmakers*. Ottawa: Canadian Film Institute, 1972.

Riefenstahl, Leni. *Leni Riefenstahl: A Memoir*. New York: St. Martin's Press, 1993.

Rodowick, David. *The Difficulty of Difference: Psychoanalysis, Sexual Difference and Film Theory*. New York: Routledge, 1990.

Rosen, Marjorie. *Popcorn Venus: Women, Movies and the American Dream*. New York: Coward, McCann & Geoghegan, 1973.

Rosenberg, Jan. *Women's Reflections: The Feminist Film Movement*. Ann Arbor, Mich.: UMI Research Press, 1983.

Rowe, Kathleen. *The Unruly Woman: Gender and the Genres of Laughter*. Austin: University of Texas Press, 1995.

Russell, Catherine. "Room for a View (Women's Cinema)." *Cinema Canada* 160 (February–March 1989): 20.

Saint-Jean, Armande. *Pour en finir avec le patriarcat*. Montréal: Primeur, 1983: 181–303.

Scherbarth, Chris. "Canada's Studio D: A Woman's Room with an International Reputation." *Canadian Women's Studies* 8, no. 1 (spring 1987): 24–27.

———. "Who not D? an Historical Look at the NFB's Woman's Studio." *Cinema Canada* 139 (March 1987): 9–13.

Schlesinger, Philip, et al. *Women Viewing Violence*. London: BFI, 1992.

Schreiber, Dorothy. "Doctor, Lawyer, Indian Chief: Film Pays Tribute to Women." *Windspeaker* 6, no. 2 (18 March 1988): 13.

The Sexual Subject: A Screen Reader in Sexuality. (No Author) London: Routledge, 1992.

Secteur, P. "Jeunes cinéastes, au féminin: Candide au Québec: 'Mais comment le dire?'" *C Practiq* 127 (November–December 1973): 229–31.

Segrave, Kerry. *The Post-Feminist Hollywood Actress: Biographies and Filmographies of Stars Born After 1939*. Jefferson, N.C.: McFarland & Co, 1990.

Selous, Trista. *The Other Woman: Feminism and Femininity in the Work of Marguerite Duras*. New Haven: Yale University Press, 1988.

Shannon, Kathleen. "Women at NFB." *Access* 12 (summer 1973): 31.

———. "Alanis Obomsawin." *Pot Pourri* (spring 1977): 22–24.

Silverman, Kaja. *The Subject of Semiotics*. New York: Oxford University Press, 1983.

———. *The Acoustic Mirror: The Female Voice in Psychoanalysis and Cinema*. Bloomington: Indiana University Press, 1988.

Smith, J. "Nell Shipman: Girl Wonder from God's Country." *Cinema Canada* 51 (November–December 1978): 35–38.

Stacey, Jackie. *Stargazing: Hollywood Cinema and Female Spectatorship*. London. New York: Routledge, 1994.

Staiger, Janet. *Bad Women: Regulating Sexuality in Early American Cinema*. Minneapolis: University of Minnesota Press, 1995.

Steel, Dawn. *They Can Kill You but They Can't Eat You: Lessons from the Front*. New York: Pocket Books, 1993.

Stefanoni, L. "Claudia Weill: 'Girlfriends.'" *Canadian Forum* 190 (December 1979): 774–83.

Sternberg, Barbara. "On (Experimental) Film (Feminist Film Theory and Avant-garde Film)." *Cinema Canada* 161 (March–April 1989): 28.

"Studio D: the Jewel in the Crown Corporation." *Cinema Canada* 139 (March 1987): 9–13.

Stimpson, Catherine R. *Where the Meanings Are*. New York: Methuen, 1988.

Studlar, Gaylin. *In the Realm of Pleasure*. Urbana: University of Illinois Press, 1988.

Tadros, Connie. "Spotlight on Prudence Emery." *Cinema Canada* 42 (November 1977): 8–11.

———. "Linda Beath Distribution Dynamo." *Cinema Canada* 44 (February 1978): 10–11.

Tajibnapis, Marjah. "Foregrounding Women: An Annotated Index to 52 Canadian Women Filmmakers." *Resources for Feminist Research* 8, no. 4 (1979): 4–46.

Take One 3, no. 2 (1972). Special issue on Women in Film includes an interview with Joyce Wieland.

Tanner, Laura E. *Intimate Violence: Reading Rape and Torture in Twentieth-Century Fiction*. Bloomington: Indiana University Press, 1994.

Thomadaki, Katerina. *Film Portraits of Women by Women*. Toronto: The Funnel, 1986.

Thumim, Janet. *Celluloid Sisters: Women and Popular Cinema*. New York: St. Martin's Press, 1992.

Trapunski, Edward. "Murmurs of the Heart." *Macleans* 100, no. 28 S (1987): 48.

Trauble, Elizabeth. *Dreaming Identities: Class, Gender and Generation in 1980s Hollywood Movies*. Boulder: Westview, 1992.

Trelles, Plazaola, Luis. *Cine y Mujer en America Latina: Directoras de largo metrajes*. Rio Pedras, P.R.: Editorial de la Universidad de Puerto Rico, 1991.

Trinh, Thi Minh-Ha. *Framer Framed*. New York: Routledge, 1992. (Feminist film-maker of Vietnamese background; politics of the documentary).

———. *When the Moon Waxes Red: Representation, Gender & Cultural Politics*. New York: Routledge, 1991.

Tulloch, Elspeth. "Women's Film Series Gives Birth to Workshops for Women Film-makers in the Atlantic Provinces." *Cinema Canada* 165 (July–August 1989): 16.

———. "Directing Films from the Female Perspective." *Atlantic Advocate* 80, no. 9 (May 1990): 50–52.

Varda, Agnès. "Agnès Varda: notes sur Toronto." *Image et Son* 283 (April 1974): 63–66.

Wayne, Valerie. *Translations/Transformations: Gender and Culture in Film and Literature*. Honolulu: College of Languages, Linguistics, and Literature, University of Hawaii Press, 1993.

Weinberger, Gabriele. *Nazi Germany and Its Aftermath in Women Directors' Auto-

biographical Films of the Late 1970's in the Murderers' House. San Francisco: Mellen Research University Press, 1992.

Weiss, Andrea. *Vampires and Violets: Lesbians in Film.* London: Cape, 1992; New York: Penguin Books, 1993.

Wexman, Virginia Wright. *Creating the Couple: Love, Marriage and Hollywood Performance.* Princeton: Princeton University Press, 1993.

Wittgens, Claudia. "The Champagne of Script Assistants." *Motion* (January–February 1974): 28–29.

———. "Monique Champagne." *Motion* (May–June 1974): 13.

Young, Lola. *Fear of the Dark: Race, Gender and Sexuality in the Cinema.* London: Routledge, 1996.

Zucker, C., et al. "Les Oeuvres récentes d'Anne Claire Poirier et Paule Baillargeon." *Copie Zéro* 11 (1981): 52–55.

Professor Ruth Hottell
(La Production Féminine)
University of Toledo (OH)
Fall 1994

French 486
La Production Féminine
UH 4290
3:45–5:25 MW

Course Content:

The French contribution to theory and intellectual life is evident in various fields. One finds, to cite only a few, Jacques Lacan in psychoanalysis; Christian Metz in semiotics and film theory; Jacques Derrida, Michel Foucault, and Jean-Paul Sartre in philosophy; and André Bazin in film theory. The significant contributions are not restricted to male production, for numerous women are foremost among the major artistic giants. This course deals with examples of feminine production which have influenced French culture, mainly in the areas of film, literary criticism, literature, philosophy, psycho-analysis, and semiotics. Furthermore, the feminine artists concerned have been recognized internationally for ground-breaking work in various domains. Consequently, students will observe the met-onymic, intertextual relationship between French Feminine/Femi-nist thought and French/International philosophy.

Works by the following women will be studied: Evelyne Accad, Simone de Beauvoir, Marie Cardinal, Hélène Cixous, Claire Denis, Germaine Dulac, Marguerite Duras, Luce Irigaray, Julia Kristeva, Diane Kurys, Euzhan Palcy, Coline Serreau, Agnès Varda, and Monique Wittig.

The underlying questions under consideration with regard to read-ings and viewings are the following:

—Does *écriture féminine* exist, as separate from masculine modes of discourse? If so, how is it represented and articulated?

—Do women and men react to (read and view) texts differently in ways that can be delineated along gender lines?

Course Goals and Objectives:

Through readings, class discussions, and film viewings, students will gain an understanding of women's contributions to the evolution of French thought.

Theories of feminine writing styles will be considered and manifestations sought in the texts read and viewed.

Theories of feminine reading and spectatorship strategies will be studied and discussed, especially in conjunction with course readings and viewings.

Requirements:

1) Active participation in class discussions. **All discussion will be in French.**

2) Exposé. Students will present an oral *exposé*. (10–15 minutes). Topics will be chosen (in consultation with the instructor) from a list of suggested topics dealing with works (theory, film, or novel) covered in the scope of the course meetings. They may also choose a work outside the class syllabus.

3) Short reaction papers. Students will write two short papers (3–5 pages) in which they interact with feminine theory and fiction.

4) Final paper (8–10 pages). Students will synthesize theories studied, refute the validity of those theories, or explore the manifestation of feminine modes of discourse in filmic or literary works. At least 8 outside sources are required for the bibliography.

Evaluation:

Daily Discussion	15%
Exposé	25%
Reaction papers (2)	30%
Final paper	30%

Additional Comments:

Students will confer with instructor at mid-term to show understanding of readings and to discuss exposé topics.

Course Outline:

LA THÉORIE

26 septembre	Introduction; Film: *La Souriante Mme Beudet* (Germaine Dulac)
28 septembre	Cixous, "Le Rire de la Méduse."
3 octobre	Irigaray, *Ce Sexe qui n'en est pas un* (excerpts)
5 octobre	Irigaray, *Ce sexe qui n'en est pas un* (excerpts)
10 octobre	Irigaray, *Ce sexe* (excerpts)
12 octobre	Irigaray, *Speculum*
17 octobre	Kristeva, *Histoires d'amour*
19 octobre	Kristeva, *Histoires d'amour*
24 octobre	Kristeva, *Histoires d'amour*

LE ROMAN ET LE CINEMA

26 octobre	Kurys, *Coup de foudre* (1983) 110 min.
31 octobre	Cardinal, *Au pays de mes racines*
2 novembre	Varda, *Sans toit ni loi*
4 novembre	**Paper 1 due (la théorie)**
7 novembre	Accad, *Les Blessures des mots*
9 novembre	Palcy, *La Rue Cases-Nègres* (1983) 103 min.
14 novembre	Chédid, *La Maison sans racines*
16 novembre	Kurys, *Cocktail Molotov* (1980) 97 min.
18 novembre	**Paper 2 due (roman ou film)**
21 novembre	Groult, *Les Vaisseaux du coeur*
23 novembre	THANKSGIVING
28 novembre	Wittig, *Les Guérillères*
30 novembre	Devers, *Chimère* (1988) 94 min.
5 décembre	Boucetta, *Anissa Captive*
7 décembre	Garcia, *Un weekend sur deux* (1990) 100 min.
12–14 décembre	**Final Paper due**

Professor Ruth Hottell
(Le Cinéma Français)

Français 485
Univ. of Toledo (OHIO)
Le Cinéma Français
5210D
MW 4:10–7:10
Carlson Library B16

Texts: Alan Williams. *A History of French Filmmaking.*
Hayward, Susan. *French National Cinema.*

Objectives:

Students will learn the basic concepts of film aesthetics necessary to an appreciation of cinema, along with a critical vocabulary in French for analyzing and discussing films.

Students will acquire a general knowledge of the history of French cinema and its place in world cinema, with particular emphasis on a limited number of key directors.

Presentation:

Films will be screened in the Audio-visual section of Carlson Library. Classroom activities will be of the lecture/discussion format, with emphasis placed on the latter. All classes will be conducted in French.

As outlined below, students are responsible for two short papers (reaction or analysis), a mid-term exam, a final paper (of the researched variety), and an oral presentation.

Oral Presentation: Topic will be selected in consultation with professor. Reports will begin May 4. Topics must be chosen by April 20. Possible topics: another film by a director whom we have studied; a director not covered in class; American or French re-makes. Note: The report may be a condensed version of the final paper. Time: 10–15 minutes. Points will be deducted if time limits are not respected.

Short papers. An analysis of a film (or scenes from a film) screened in class, or an analysis of a film viewed outside class. First paper due April 13. Second paper due May 11.

Final paper: Topic must be chosen by May 9—Due June 6. NOTE: Ten points will be deducted from the grade if student fails to cite works consulted (AND in an accepted bibliographic form. I recommend the MLA Handbook, available at any bookstore and Carlson Library). Similarly, ten points will be deducted from the grade if work consists solely of a plot summary.

ALL WORK MUST BE TYPED. ABSOLUTELY NO LATE WORK WILL BE ACCEPTED (UNLESS ACCOMPANIED BY A MEMO FROM YOUR PHYSICIAN).

Requirements and Evaluation:

Mid-term exam—May 2	20%
Reaction papers (3–5 pages)	30%
Final paper (researched—8–10 pages)	20%
Oral Presentation (10–15 minutes)	15%
Discussion and Participation	15%

Outline of Course:

28 mars	Introduction—courts métrages. (Lumière, Méliès et Renoir).
30 mars	*Un Chien Andalou* (Buñuel, 1929, 17 min.) Avant-garde program (*La Symphonie diagonale, Entr'acte, Ballet mécanique, L'Etoile de mer*). *La Souriante Madame Beudet* (Germaine Dulac, 1922) *Lecture:* Williams, Chs. 1,2,3.
4 avril	*La Passion de Jeanne d'Arc* (Dreyer, 1928, 6720 ft.) *Lecture:* Williams, Chs. 4,5,6
6 avril	*L'Atalante* (Vigo, 1934, 89 min.) Williams, Ch. 7.
11 avril	*La Bête Humaine* (Renoir, 1938, 90 min.) Williams, Ch. 8
13 avril	*Pépé le Moko*

	(Duvivier, 1937) Williams, Ch. 9
18 avril	*Le Salaire de la Peur* (Clouzot, 1953) Williams, Ch. 10
20 avril	*Les Diaboliques* (Clouzot, 1955) Williams, Ch. 11
25 avril	*Les Quatre Cents Coups* (Truffaut, 1958) Williams, Ch. 12
27 avril	*Hiroshima mon amour* (Resnais, 1958) Williams, Ch. 13
2 mai	examen partiel
4 mai	*Cléo de 5 à 7* (Varda, 1961) Williams, Ch. 14
9 mai	*L'Une chante, l'autre pas* (Varda, 1977) Flitterman-Lewis, Ch. 10
11 mai	*La Bataille d'Alger* (Pontecorvo, 1966) Williams, Ch. 15
16 mai	*Les Remparts d'argile* (Bertucelli, 1970) Prédal, 349-62.
18 mai	*Outremer* (Rouan, 1990) Prédal 478–84; Hayward 206–21.
23 mai	*Chocolat* (Denis, 1989) Prédal 519–27; Hayward 221–50.
25 mai	*La Rue Cases-Nègres* (Palcy, 1985) Hayward 250–74.
1 juin	*Camille Claudel* (Nuyten, 1988) Prédal 528–40; Hayward 274–96
6 juin	Exposés, Résumé de classe

Professor Janis L. Pallister
(International Women Film Directors)

Fall 1988. A&S 200 International Women Film Directors (A&S 200, College of Arts and Sciences. 2 cr.; Tues. evenings 6–9; Gish Film Theater, Bowling Green State University, Bowling Green, OH 43403.

***One final paper required; class discussion an absolute requirement.

1. **Alice Guy-Blaché** (French-American) 5 shorts (1911–20). *Canned Harmony; Burstup Homes' Murder Case; Officer Henderson; His Double; A House Divided* [1913]; *The Girl in the Arm-Chair.* and **Germaine Dulac** (French) Two shorts: *La Souriante Mme Beudet* and *La Coquille et le Clergyman.* (1922–25; 55 min. b/w silent).

2. **Lois Weber** (American) *The Blot* (1921) and **Leontine Sagan** (German) *Maedchen in Uniform.* (1931; 87 min. b/w).

3. **Dorothy Arzner** (American) *Craig's Wife.* (1936). With Katharine Hepburn.

4. **Agnès Varda** (French) *Le Bonheur.* (1965; 85 min. Public Performance Rights). Free and open to the public.

5. **Márta Mészáros** (Hungarian) *The Girl* (1968).

6. **Margarethe Von Trotta** (It./German) *The Lost Honor of Katharina Blum* (1975). Directed with her husband Volker Schlondorff.

7. **Lina Wertmuller** (Italian) *Seven Beauties.* (1976; 118 min.).

8. **Nelly Kaplan** (French-Swiss) *Néa.* (1978).

9. **Lee Grant** (USA) *Tell Me a Riddle.* (1980).

10. **Maria-Luia Bemberg** *Camila.* (1984; dubbed from Spanish).

11. **Liliana Cavani.** *Berlin Affair.* (1985; 110 min.).

12. **Doris Dorrie** (German) *Men.* (1985; 94 min.).

13. **Caroline Huppert** (French) *Signé Charlotte.* (1986). Plus Documentary: *Three Women Directors.*

14. **Léa Pool** (Québécoise) *Anne Trister.* (1985). Plus: Animation short by Caroline Leaf: *The Street.*

15. **Suzana Amaral** (Brazil) *Hour of the Star.* (1985).

16. **Patricia Rozema** (Canadian) *I've Heard the Mermaids Singing.* (1987). Plus American Documentary: We Are Not Sugar and Spice . . ."

WOMEN DIRECTORS OF THE WORLD   Pallister (Film Series)

Gish Film Theater Film Series (BGSU)
Tues. evenings—fall (1996) 14–15 weeks

Week 1 *Canned Harmony; Burstup Homes' Murder Case; Officer Henderson; His Double; A House Divided, The Girl in the Arm-Chair* (all ca. 1913), d. Alice-Guy Blaché (French), great director of the silent period. Shorts with English intertitles.

Week—*The Smiling Madame Beudet* (1923?) and *The Seashell and the Clergyman* (1927?), d. Germaine Dulac (French). Madame Beudet, resenting her oppressive husband, contemplates suicide. (French intertitles). The Clergyman has many (sexual) fantasies, depicted in surrealist style. No intertitles.

Week—*Blot* (1921), d. Lois Weber (American). Classic of the silent era. Social values under pressure in small-town America. A teacher's wife steals a chicken for her child.

Week—*Christopher Strong* (1933; 77 mins.), d. Dorothy Arzner (American). A woman flyer (Katharine Hepburn) falls in love with a married man (Colin Clive), who does not want to divorce his devoted wife (Billie Burke).

Week—*A Lotte Reiniger Sampler.* Early animation (via paper silhouettes or ombres chinoises) by this consummate German-Canadian artist (1899–1981). Plus documentary (in English) about her.

Week—*A Very Curious Girl* (aka *Dirty Mary;* or—in French—*La Fiancée du pirate*) (1969; 105 mins.), d. Nelly Kaplan (Argentina-France). A "revenge" film that puts the Dutch film *A Question of Silence* (Marlene Gorris) to shame. In French with English subtitles.

Week—*Seven Beauties* (1976; 115 mins.), d. Lina Wertmuller (Italian). Black comedy relating the story of Pasqualino, a gangster, who will sacrifice anything for the sake of his own survival. In Italian with English subtitles.

Week—*Je tu il elle* (1974; 90 mins.), d. Chantal Akerman (Belgium). A young woman eats raw sugar and rearranges furniture, then goes on the road, accepting a ride with a truck driver and winding up in the home of her woman lover. Lengthy "uneroticized" lovemaking ensues. Themes of estrangement, alienation, lesbianism. In French with English subtitles.

Week—*Adoption* (1975; 89 minutes), d. Márta Mészáros (Hungarian). Kati wants child but her married lover refuses. So Anna, her friend, has the child for her. In Hungarian with English subtitles.

Week—*Scream from Silence (Mourir à tue-tête)* (1979), d. Anne Claire Poirier (French Canadian). Graphic and troubling work on the subject of rape, here de-eroticized and universalized. Film oscillates between documentary and fiction. Not like any other work on rape.

Week—*Camila* (1984; 105 mins.), d. Maria-Luisa Bemberg (Buenos Aires). A young woman runs away with a Jesuit priest. Happy at first in a small village, they are discovered and condemned to death without trial. A strong statement about personal and political freedom.

Week—*The Reincarnation of Golden Lotus* (1989; 99 mins.), d. Clara Law. Stars Joi Wong. A contemporary woman relives the legend of a famous courtesan of ancient China. In Mandarin with English subtitles.

Week—*Song of the Exile* (1990; 100 mins.) d. Ann Hui (Taiwan). A young woman from Hong Kong comes to America to join her "fiancé." The conflicts arising (of both a personal and cultural nature) make for a remarkable drama. Chinese with English subtitles.

Week—*Angel at My Table* (1990; 158 mins.), d. Jane Campion (New Zealand). Stunning, biting autobiography of Janet Frame (played by Kerry Fox), a roly-poly repressed little girl who became New Zealand's most famous novelist/poet.

Week—(1) *These Hands* (1992; 45 mins.), d. Flora M'Mbugu-Schelling (Tanzania)—A profound meditation on human labor. (2) *Women with Open Eyes* (1994; 52 mins.), d. Anne-Laure Folly (Togo)—Portraits of contemporary Africans show why Africa's development is linked to the social and economic progress of its women. (3) *Monday's Girls* (1993; 50 mins.), d. Ngozi Onwurah (Nigeria)—Initiation ceremony. Virgins must show their breasts in public, and be confined for several weeks in "fattening rooms," after which they are considered to be adults.

Week—*Vagabond (Sans toit ni loi),* d. Agnès Varda (Belgian-French). Mona goes on the lam, and meets up with Father Death. An unsentimental portrayal of a person on the "outside," a marginal and exiled figure. In French with English subtitles.

[Alternate for any week (in any emergency): *Strangers in Good Company* (1991), d. Cynthia Scott (anglophone Canadian). A group of women, stranded in the woods, tell each other their deepest secrets and longings.]

Index